WE
ARE
DRIVEN

WE ARE DRIVEN

THE COMPULSIVE BEHAVIORS AMERICA APPLAUDS

Dr. Robert Hemfelt
Dr. Frank Minirth
Dr. Paul Meier

Publishers Since 1798

THOMAS NELSON PUBLISHERS
NASHVILLE

❖ *A Janet Thoma Book* ❖

For information on the Minirth-Meier Clinic nearest you, call
1-800-545-1819.

Copyright © 1991 by Dr. Robert Hemfelt, Dr. Frank Minirth,
Dr. Paul Meier

The accounts presented in this book are composites of true
stories. Names, genders, and identifying details, and family
constellations have been changed to protect the identities of the
individual patients.

All rights reserved. Written permission must be secured from the
publisher to use or reproduce any part of this book, except for
brief quotations in critical reviews or articles.

Published in Nashville, Tennessee, by Thomas Nelson, Inc., and
distributed in Canada by Lawson Falle, Ltd., Cambridge, Ontario.

Scripture quotations are from the NEW KING JAMES VERSION
of the Bible.
Copyright © 1979, 1980, 1982, Thomas Nelson, Inc.,
Publishers.

Scripture quotations noted TLB are from *The Living Bible*
(Wheaton, Illinois: Tyndale House Publishers, 1971) and are
used by permission.

Library of Congress Cataloging-in-Publication Data

Hemfelt, Robert.
We are driven : the compulsive behaviors America applauds /
Robert Hemfelt, Frank Minirth, Paul Meier.
p.   cm.
Includes bibliographical references.
ISBN 0-8407-7071-5
1. Compulsive behavior—Popular works. I. Minirth, Frank B.
II. Meier, Paul D. III. Title.
RC533.H46   1991
616.85'227—dc20   90-19963
CIP

Printed in the United States of America
1 2 3 4 5 6 7 – 96 95 94 93 92 91

ACKNOWLEDGMENTS

The authors are grateful to the friends, family members, and working companions whose contributions and assistance have made the publication of *We Are Driven* possible. As always, we are especially thankful for Susan Hemfelt, Mary Alice Minirth, and Jan Meier, whose patience and graciousness have eased the work. Many thanks also to Holly Miller whose skill with words transformed hours of notes and ideas into a manuscript; to Janet Thoma for her encouragement and editorial wisdom; and to Jennifer Farrar and the in-house staff of Thomas Nelson for their diligence in producing the finished book.

CONTENTS

PART ONE

Unmasking the

Compulsions

America Applauds

Chapter One

Are We Really Having Fun?

"We failed our homework assignment," said Virginia Potter, her lower lip protruding in an exaggerated pout.

"It was Ginny's fault," explained Michael, her husband, hardly able to contain a smile. "We were doing fine—following your directions to the letter, Doctor—but then Ginny started to giggle and gave it all away." He paused. "Come to think of it, we *did* look pretty ridiculous."

As their story unfolded, they embellished it with just enough details to maximize the punch line. Their timing was perfect, almost as if they had practiced the routine during the two-hour flight from Indianapolis to Dallas. It was easy to see why they were the center of attention in their wide circle of friends. They were genuinely funny, played off of each other's lines well, set each other up, and teasingly put each other down. They were the ideal duo, who performed in tandem like a couple of seasoned veterans. After nearly twenty-five years, they had their act down cold.

"You told us to go on a date, remember?" asked Virginia. "You said our lives were so hectic that we had lost some intimacy, and we needed to rebuild it by spending more time together. Just the two of us, you said. Of course, our first problem was finding an open evening. We rescheduled it

1

twice, and on our 'big night' we were an hour late getting out the door because Mike had a long-distance phone call from Los Angeles. His West Coast office always forgets about the time difference." She rolled her eyes in mock disgust.

It was Michael's turn: "We decided to drive over to a little Italian restaurant where we used to eat on Friday nights when we were in college. We ordered our old favorites, and then we traded plates halfway through the meal, just as we always did."

Her turn: "We had such a good time that we thought it would be fun to stop by the campus and get out and walk through the valley. It was so dark that we couldn't see the new buildings. We both felt as if we were twenty years old again, and it was 1960 rather than 1990. We held hands, listened to the chimes, and tried to remember the words to the second verse of the alma mater. Now that I think of it, Mike, I'm not sure there *is* a second verse." She grinned. "No wonder we drew a blank."

"We got home about ten o'clock," Michael continued, in their Ping-Pong style of narration, "and we couldn't get in the garage because of all the cars parked in the driveway. Brian, our son, had invited some friends over to watch one of those pay-TV sports specials on the big-screen television in the family room. Everyone had chipped in a few dollars to take care of the closed-circuit cost, the pizza, and the soft drinks. What a madhouse! Of course, we're used to it; the kids know the welcome mat is always out. Still, after our quiet 'date' Ginny and I weren't ready to face another houseful of company. We had had fun, and we didn't want to break the mood."

"That's when I suggested that we slip in the back door," explained Virginia. "But it was locked. So Mike boosted me up to the bedroom window so I could crawl through and open the door. Suddenly I got to thinking about how crazy it all was. Here we were breaking into our own home while a party was going on. I started to laugh and couldn't stop. Then the dog began to bark. The kids heard the noise, were convinced it was a burglar, and came charging out of the house. Talk about feeling silly! How do you explain to a bunch of teenagers that your doctor had sent you on a date and that you wanted to spend some more time together, so you broke into your own bedroom?"

It was a typical Potter family story, a madcap, "it-could-only-happen-to-us" kind of anecdote. We had heard dozens of them during our weekly counseling sessions, and we had come to enjoy what Michael and Virginia called the "Potter Family Chronicles." Not only were the stories fun, but so were the storytellers. They were a charming duo, the "model couple," who loved each other enough to admit that after so many years of marriage they had a serious problem. They weren't sure what was wrong, but they knew that they weren't as happy as they should be, that something was missing in their partnership and that perhaps a few counseling sessions might restore the spark that had always burned unattended. Michael joked about a twenty-five-year tune-up.

It had taken only one conjoint visit for us to see that the Potter marriage difficulties were far more intricate than the couple believed, and their problems were tangled in a web of their own busyness that threatened not only their relationship with each other, but also their relationships with family, friends, and associates. Convincing Michael and Virginia of the seriousness of the situation was our first challenge. They needed to understand that what they were battling was far more complicated than a few bad habits that should be eliminated or a too-busy life-style that had to slow down. Each of them was struggling with emotional issues that were deeply rooted in their childhoods, and both were burdened with what we call a heavy shame base. Before we could help them solve their problems, we had to help them acknowledge them.

Confronting "Smiling Depression"

The Minirth-Meier Clinic wasn't the first place the Potters had visited in search of help. On the advice of Virginia's family doctor, she had checked into a prominent diagnostic center in the Midwest for extensive laboratory tests a month or two earlier. Her complaints were very real—fatigue, flu-like aches, a lack of concentration, and even some memory loss. Her doctor had suspected either the Epstein-Barr virus, which causes mononucleosis, or chronic fatigue syndrome, sometimes flippantly labeled as "yuppie flu." But results of the tests gave no indication that her immune system was in overdrive, fighting some kind of mystery virus that it couldn't defeat. In both Epstein-Barr and chronic fatigue syndrome the giveaway symptoms are a decrease in cerebral blood flow and an increase in the level of cytokines, which are proteins made by white blood cells to combat infection. Virginia's tests were negative. Physically, she was doing very well. Still, the symptoms persisted.

Another clinic suggested they have a psychiatric evaluation. Since Michael's real estate business brought him to Dallas several times a month, Virginia decided to travel with him and visit our Minirth-Meier Clinic. She had read two of our books, was familiar with our radio broadcasts, and shared our belief that the physical, emotional, and spiritual dimensions are key elements in all healing. Her first appointment was solo, without Michael.

"Fix me," she said simply. "Patch me up so I can get back into my routine and pull my weight again. I don't like feeling this way. Besides, it's not fair to Mike."

Her medical records, sent to us by that Midwestern medical clinic, indicated what her problems were *not,* and her mannerisms hinted at what they could be. Her smile was the first tip-off. It was too bright, too fixed. She was "on" from the moment she entered our office. She chatted nervously with the receptionist, bantered with the nurse, and even found common ground with another patient in the waiting room. They were both sports fans—basketball, in particular —and Virginia could out-dazzle Dick Vitale when it came to ticking off statistics, starting lineups, and standings. The fact that she had been a cheerleader in college came as no surprise—she still was.

Our initial diagnosis was that she was suffering from what therapists sometimes call "smiling depression." On the surface, her life was in perfect order. She was a "people person" who was always willing to take on a good cause, chair a worthy event, host a group, or counsel a friend. She joked that her husband often teased that AT&T invented its call-waiting service just for her. Michael said it was impossible to have a telephone conversation of more than ten minutes with any member of the Potter family without being interrupted several times by callers needing Ginny's always-responsive ear.

But now she was too tired to listen. She asked for help not in slowing her pace, but in stepping up her energy level so she could resume that pace. She talked animatedly about the family compound in suburban Indianapolis, where her husband's parents and brother's family lived within a few hundred feet of her back porch and where no one paid attention to property lines or doorbells. Lately, the come-and-go atmosphere seemed to wear her out. Her enthusiasm for unannounced visits by her adult children also had waned. Setting another place at dinner was more an ordeal than a joy these days.

"Can you get me back on track?" she asked with a smile not quite so bright.

She agreed to the two-step action plan that we prescribed. First, we would admit her to our Dallas hospital unit for what we call environmental intervention. This would physically remove her from the frenzied activity of her home, where the intense family dynamics were literally wearing her out. The hospital stay would immerse her in a setting where she could participate in one-on-one counseling and group therapy. In addition, we could monitor her reaction to a mild antidepressant medication that would correct the chemical imbalance caused by her depression and burnout.

"How soon can I check in?" she asked. "More important, how soon will I be able to check out?"

We reminded her that there was a second step to our proposed action plan. We wanted her and her husband to agree to conjoint therapy sessions. Hospitalization was an intervention technique to halt the emotional drain she was experiencing. Follow-up therapy would address the deeper problems that were causing the drain. We needed to help her discover why she and Michael pushed themselves and their marriage to the limit. As upbeat as they appeared to be, they occasionally revealed an undercurrent of tension. Was it anger? Hurt? It was too early for us to know.

The best way to find the answers was with the two-pronged treatment program we proposed. Both steps were essential to the total healing process. Without hospitalization, outpatient therapy sessions would have to be more frequent and would probably stretch over a longer period of time. Yet, hospitalization alone wouldn't accomplish the permanent results that Virginia and Michael wanted. Without benefit of follow-up counseling, she would make progress toward recovery during her stay in the hospital, but would regress as soon as she returned to the source of her problems at home.

The Epidemic of the Nineties

Virginia's symptoms were typical of what may be the most prominent emotional illness of the 1990s. Technically, it's called compulsivity. We call it drivenness, and we define it this way:

> Drivenness is an insatiable drive to do more and be more. It's a drive that may be masked by charitable and positive motives, but in reality originates in deep, perhaps even unconscious, feelings of inadequacy and shame.

Drivenness often can lead to addictions—a word usually linked with drugs or alcohol. In this case, addiction has a much broader meaning, since we believe that people can become addicted to almost any kind of behavior or activity—work, fitness, perfectionism, sports, collecting antiques, rescuing other people, acquiring financial status—the list goes on and on.

Drivenness. Compulsivity. Applauded addictions. These are interchangeable terms to describe the performance and perfection pressures that characterize this emotional health epidemic of the 1990's.

In some cases the indicators of drivenness are more subtle than Virginia's and are only hinted at during casual conversation. For instance, we recently asked a hard-charging young attorney how she spent her leisure time.

"I read law journals," she told us.

"But how do you relax?" we repeated.

"I track the stock market," she replied.

"But how do you relax?" we persisted, aware that we were beginning to sound like an echo.

Her puzzled expression indicated that she didn't comprehend our question. The truth was that this woman *didn't* relax. She didn't know how. She was blinded by something psychiatrists call denial, the inability to see her own problems, including her drivenness.

According to Dr. Paul Meier, most of us are unaware of 80 percent of our faults. It's human nature, says Paul. We either don't see our flaws, or we choose to look the other way.

Particularly tough to recognize are those negative traits that masquerade as strengths. These are characteristics that appear to be positive on the surface and usually earn us generous strokes and "atta-boys" from the people around us. Such traits might include a relentless dedication to hard work, a dogged determination to stay young and fit, a driving desire to achieve financial security, an intense need to help other people, or a tireless insistence on order in the house. They might even involve such worthy activities as playing full-time cheerleader for our spouses and families, studying law journals, or scrutinizing the Dow Jones Averages in our leisure time.

At first brush, these sound harmless. But carried to extremes, the most positive activity can become a destructive addiction that can cause excruciating pain to its victim and dangerous fallout for its victim's family. One of the difficulties in dealing with addictions that masquerade as strengths is diagnosing the problems in the first place. Often no early warning signs exist, only reinforcement for a continuation of the driven behavior. In other words, more of the same.

7

What motivates a compulsive person? How can one person's healthy dedication to work be another person's unhealthy obsession with a job? At what point does a positive determination to stay fit become a negative urge to beat the clock? And when does the desire for financial security give way to a mania for amassing money?

Perhaps most important is the obvious question: What can be done to help the person who has lost control and is hopelessly at the mercy of an addiction—even one that outwardly earns everyone's approval? If the person is addicted to work, homemaking, super parenting, fitness, or dozens of other necessary functions, how can he or she kick the compulsion without abstaining totally from the activities? Is full recovery even possible?

At the Minirth-Meier Clinics we have a name for these kinds of addictions. We call them "the compulsions America applauds." Judging from the upswing in the number of cases that we treat, they may represent the epidemic of the 1990s. We estimate that as many as 75 percent of the persons who will walk into the offices of pastoral advisors, marriage counselors, psychologists, or psychiatrists this year struggle with compulsivity issues. And a high percentage of patients who will consult doctors for physical problems also suffer from stress-induced fallout.

Some of our patients in treatment for "approved" compulsions refer to them as *positive* addictions. But that label could be confusing to anyone who read William Glasser's book *Positive Addictions* in the mid 1970s.[1] Dr. Glasser's definition of a positive addict was a person who genuinely enjoyed his or her addiction, but kept it comfortably in check and didn't let it dominate his or her life. The "habit" worked *for* the addict rather than *against* the addict because it strengthened him or her and added balance to his or her day. For instance, a jogger might be addicted to a two-mile morning run three times a week, no more, no less. Or an aerobics buff might pop an exercise tape into the VCR each noon and enjoy a pre-lunch workout. Then, after "sweating to the oldies," the aerobics buff feels satisfied for the rest of the day.

Dr. Glasser offered clear guidelines for what a positive addiction is and what it isn't. It is never competitive, and it is always done without self-criticism. The jogger doesn't feel failure if the time isn't faster or the distance isn't farther today than it was yesterday, and the exercise enthusiast isn't discouraged if he or she feels winded before the instructor on the tape runs through the recommended "cool-down" stretches.

Applauded compulsions—1990s style—are different.

The kind of driven behavior that we see on the increase among our patients produces clearly negative consequences. When drivenness crosses "over the border" into negative behavior, which is harmful to the person and his or her family, we call it compulsivity.

Compulsivity is an addiction to achievement and accomplishment. Obsessive-compulsive behavior is based on the mistaken notion that mastery of my body, my performance, and my physical and material environment is the only true source of personal satisfaction and the only answer to my deepest emotional and spiritual hungers.

At its roots compulsivity reflects my inability to appropriately love and value myself apart from external achievement. This inability to accept myself comes from a state of spiritual alienation and from my inability to accept God's unconditional love for me.

Unfortunately, compulsivity is also clearly in vogue. One of the first challenges we face when we begin to work with these addicts is convincing them that their behavior is harmful to their health. Too often people brag about being compulsive and pass it off as a plus rather than a minus. They translate compulsivity to mean that they are top performers, movers and shakers, veterans of the fast lane, and people with a knack for getting a lot done. One self-help magazine even dubbed the 1990s as the "Decade of Compulsive Chic," a time when all baby boomers worth their generous paychecks are workaholics, and all members of the thirtysomething set push for perfection in their careers, appearances, hobbies, sex lives, and families.

The truth is that these "applauded" compulsions were with us long before the baby boomers came on the scene, and they are compulsions that affect persons years younger and decades older than thirtysomething. The greatest mistake of all is to link compulsivity with chic.

The Compulsive Personality

Often when we counsel highly compulsive people like Virginia Potter, we give them "worst-case scenarios" to jolt them into understanding the seriousness of their condition. Especially when dealing with the compulsions America applauds—work, perfectionism, service to others, success, diet, and wellness—we have to convince patients of the negative aspects of their extremism. We use familiar examples to get their attention and convince them that their behavior, if allowed to become more compulsive, could cause serious damage to their physical and emotional health.

"Think of a mainspring on a watch," we sometimes suggest. "If you wind it evenly each day, taking care not to overwind it, the watch will give you years of maintenance-free service. But if you crank it beyond its capacity, it will snap and become useless. Nothing you can do will make the watch function; only expensive repair work by an expert will restore its value."

People can snap, too, we point out. The old complaint "This job is going to be the death of me" contains a lot of truth. Not only is physical ailment a constant threat to the hard-charging perfectionist, but he or she also runs the risk of serious mental fatigue. We know of one driven executive who was dictating a letter on a Thursday afternoon when he suddenly blacked out. He woke up a week later in the hospital, and to this day he doesn't remember what happened between the blackout and his return to consciousness. Diagnosis? Burnout. He had pushed himself so hard for so long that his mind and body simply shut down.

Frightening occurrences such as these aren't restricted to high-level business executives. Many patients, like Virginia Potter, come to us complaining that they can't function usefully anymore. "Fix us" is their request. Then they describe symptoms of anxiety or depression that sap their energy and effectiveness. In our counseling sessions, as we unravel what is going on behind the symptoms, we discover people who simply have pushed themselves to a snapping point.

Often we'll use the illustration of a violin to help them understand the dynamics of keeping stress under control.

"What happens when not enough tension is put on the strings of a violin?" we ask. "What kind of 'music' will it make?"

"Dull and flat," is the answer we usually hear. "Monotonous."

"And what happens when *too much* tension is put on the strings? How does that affect the sound?"

"Shrill and high-pitched" is the typical reply.

We explain that people react in a similar way. If no pressure or no expectations are applied to a person, he or she may feel no motivation to perform. For instance, retirees often complain of a lack of purpose when their job responsibilities are passed on to their successors. They feel dull and flat, much the same as the slackened violin strings. There is no tension, no pressure to succeed. But if a person becomes obsessively caught up in an activity to the point where the activity drives him or her, that person may resemble the violin with the overly taut strings. The person may feel stretched to the limit, propelled out of control, and his or her "music" may be shrill and nervous.

Being vs. Doing

Is there a type of person who is more inclined to be driven than others? Aren't *all* people driven to some extent? Is it possible to be driven at certain points in our lives and not at others?

Good questions. Let's answer them in reverse order.

Is It Possible to Be Driven at Certain Times and not at Others?

It's not only possible, but also it might be advisable to push ourselves very hard during key times in our careers. For instance, when we doctors were in medical school and doing our hospital internships and residencies, we had to drive ourselves to the limit in order to survive. Eighty-hour work weeks were the norm. Fortunately, we knew that our crazy, non-stop schedules were short-term and that graduation would give us a chance to catch our breath.

Somehow we hung on.

A similarly grueling schedule was followed by our associate, Dr. Robert Hemfelt, when he was finishing his psychology degree in Houston. Looking back, he calls this period of his life frantic; at the time, it nearly buried him. Not only was he supervising a large inner-city drug abuse treatment center, but he was also completing his dissertation, preparing for his final exams, successfully interviewing for a position with an out-of-town Fortune 500 company, and courting his future wife.

"Susan practically had to make appointments with me so we could plan our wedding," he jokes today.

But like the rest of us, he hung on.

Aren't All People Driven?

Most likely, yes. It's human nature for each of us to pull out all of the stops when an important deadline looms or a big test is on tap or when we know that we're going to have to perform solo in front of an audience. That's normal. But a more persistent kind of drivenness exists—the kind that isn't short-term and doesn't slacken off when a goal has been reached. That can be the unhealthy kind of drivenness.

Is There a "Classic" Type of Driven Person?

This leads us to our last and most important question: Is there a type of person who is more inclined to be driven than others? Again, the answer is, *yes.*

One of the distinctions between the normal and the not-so-normal kind of drivenness is the difference between *being* and *doing.* Think of it this way: Humans *being* are persons who have a healthy feeling of self-worth, know their value, and have a comfortable sense of how they fit into their families, their work, and their "system." Sure, they feel rattled at times and occasionally overextend themselves, and when they do they get dog-tired as a result. But they *choose* those times. They don't feel driven to say yes to every challenge or opportunity or request that comes along. They don't feel that they constantly have to earn membership in the human race. Like the young doctors completing their graduate study or internships, humans being make a conscious decision to push themselves to the limit for a short time because they believe in themselves and in the activity they have elected to take on.

Humans *doing,* however, are convinced they have to prove their worth every day. They feel that they must always be doing, accomplishing, performing, and perfecting in order to deserve their place in their family, their work, and their "system." Their motives are all wrong. They are driven by deep, underlying, unconscious motives, such as insecurity, fear, anger, and shame.

Humans *being* might jot down fifty chores on their things-to-do list, accomplish only four, and still feel satisfied with themselves. Humans *doing* can complete all fifty tasks and then spend the rest of the day wringing their hands wondering whether they performed well enough, or whether they were too easy on themselves and should have tackled sixty or sixty-five jobs instead of fifty.

If we were to draw a graph of the human being's activity level, the line would go up and down in peaks and valleys as the person made choices and responded to circumstances.

13

But the graph of the human doing would rarely dip downward unless depression or burnout was experienced or an ultimatum was delivered by an unhappy spouse who threatened, "We will take a vacation *or else!*" Only then would the human doing agree to a forced period of rest. Without this kind of intervention—or interference—from the spouse, the human doing would work at such a pace that his or her activity line would steadily climb up, up, up. As it is, even with occasional plateaus of rest and relaxation, the overall activity line inches constantly skyward.

Push-to-Perfection Mindset

We can make several other generalizations about "typical" driven persons. They frequently, although not always, are the oldest children in their families, or at least the oldest son or oldest daughter. On the plus side, they often have higher than average intelligence. Even if they aren't super smart, they earn better grades in school because they work so hard at their studies. When the time comes to make a career choice, they are drawn to three types of professions. First are the entrepreneurial positions that require the self-starter to go out and start a business from scratch. Second are the high-pressure business responsibilities, such as finance, marketing, sales, and administration. Third are the rescuing professions, which include medicine, social work, ministry, counseling, and teaching.

Even after graduation, this push-to-perfection mindset continues as they enter the work force. They are real performers—arriving early at their desks, staying late, and working weekends. They are detailists who cross every "t" and dot every "i." The more driven they are, the more successful. After all, it's the in-the-mainstream "normal" person who wants to knock off work at five, go home, kick off his or her shoes, and watch Monday night football. But not superachievers. They are the ones who snap off the office lights, lock the door behind them, and are the last ones to pull out of the employee parking lot.

The driven personality isn't typically male or female. We see just as many compulsive women as men. It used to be that applauded addictions among women centered on cleanliness, housekeeping, organizing, and parenting. Another predictable compulsion among women has been a consuming concern for appearance, which sometimes has led to eating disorders, such as anorexia, bulimia, and fasting. Or, fearing that they may fall short of those impossible glamour standards, many women turn to compulsive overeating as a means of satisfying their hunger for attention. Still other women have focused on health to such an extent that their preoccupation has evolved into chronic hypochondria.

If these have been typical ways for women to express their drivenness, men have had their own brand of predictable behavior. Often their compulsivity takes on a more competitive flavor. Work or sports addictions have always been particularly common among men. Buying, selling, acquiring, and mastering the art of the deal have a certain macho flair to them. Even today, the ways that drivenness displays itself are different between the sexes, although we've noticed a lot of homogenization since women have entered the work force in such great numbers. Of course, some preoccupations— spending, saving, keeping up with the Joneses, and fitness— have always been taken to extremes by both sexes.

Age is no more a safeguard against drivenness than sex is. We've worked with families—the Potters are a good example —that have multigenerational histories of compulsive behavior. Dr. Minirth recalls a family, the Stewarts (Luci and Richard and their grown son, Bud, and his wife, Rachael) that was driven to such a degree that a third-generation infant, Robbie, was hospitalized three weeks after birth because of the emotional fallout caused by the tension in the home.

Third Generational Fallout

Dr. Minirth learned about this situation when he was counseling the baby's grandmother, Luci Stewart, a perfectionistic woman who suffered long bouts of depression. In describing her family situation Luci explained that her son,

Bud, had become entangled in one get-rich-quick scheme after another, and her pregnant daughter-in-law, Rachael, had been left to wrestle with incredible bills, possible bankruptcy, and the loss of their home. Within the first month of the baby's birth, the tot was diagnosed as having a spastic colon and was rushed to the hospital. The doctor said the condition was caused by stress. Sound impossible? Unfortunately, even though intellectually Robbie knew nothing about what was going on in his parents' lives, he could sense the stress that existed in the home. Pressure was being applied on the entire Stewart family, and every member was reacting in his or her own way. The grandmother battled depression, the young mother felt tense and anxious, and the baby suffered a spastic colon.

How about you? Do you ever feel like that violin—stretched too tight? At the clinic we often suggest that a patient step back and take an objective look at his or her own personality.

Do You Have a Driven Personality?

Many people have addiction-prone personalities even if they currently lead well-balanced lives. Knowing whether you have traits that make you vulnerable to drivenness can be helpful in preventing addiction. Awareness is the key. Check the statements below that apply to you. This will help you to determine your degree of "drivenness."

1.____ "I am a competitive person."
2.____ "I am not very flexible."
3._✓_ "I like to be in control of myself and my environment."
4.____ "I often focus on irrelevant details."
5._✓_ "I am a perfectionist."
6._✓_ "Some of my traits are at odds: I'm tidy in some areas of my life, messy in others. I'm consciencious about some things, negligent about others."

7. ✓ "*I give the appearance of confidence, but I feel insecure.*"

8. ___ "*I set difficult goals and unrealistic expectations for myself, making myself vulnerable to feelings of guilt and failure.*"

9. ___ "*I'm not comfortable 'baring my soul.' I like to keep my emotions to myself.*"

10. ___ "*I don't relax easily.*"

11. ___ "*I often act compulsively. I check and recheck the door at night to make sure it's locked. I return to the kitchen to satisfy myself that the stove is off.*"

12. ___ "*I'm preoccupied with the future, always thinking about what's to come.*"

13. ✓ "*I'm dependable.*"

14. ✓ "*Being on time for appointments is a priority with me.*"

15. ✓ "*I like lists.*"

16. ___ "*I worry too much.*"

17. ___ "*I'm an extreme person—assertive sometimes, withdrawn other times.*"

18. ✓ "*I expect total honesty and loyalty from the people closest to me.*"

19. ✓ "*I don't like spontaneity and surprises. I prefer to know what is going to happen so I can prepare well for it.*"

20. ___ "*On the surface I seem to be emotionally in control, but when things don't go my way, I tend to get irritable and angry.*"

If you checked at least ten of these statements, you are probably highly driven. If you checked fifteen or more, you may be fully addicted to the compulsions America applauds.

Internal Tug-of-War

Strange as it seems, many driven people are in control in some pockets of their lives and out of control in others. That's why a couple of statements in the quiz show such contradictions: "I'm tidy in some areas of my life, messy in others." We've counseled a very successful corporate comptroller who had difficulty balancing his family's checkbook. He was a whiz at overseeing the books of a multimillion-dollar manufacturing organization, but couldn't track his household accounts. His wife was a spendaholic, their credit cards had been frozen by the bank, and their home had been repossessed.

There are many explanations for this. Perhaps the best is that some people feel that if they can't do a job to perfection, they won't do it at all. It becomes an all-or-nothing kind of choice. If they sense they have the ability to control a situation, they will jump in and perform meticulously, but if they feel they cannot gain and maintain any degree of authority, they will slack off or refuse to try. In the case of the corporate comptroller, he had long since given up trying to curb his wife's spending addiction. Instead, he washed his hands of it and suffered the consequences.

This strange tug-of-war is played out with many compulsions. Recently a team of California researchers conducted a study of people who couldn't bear to throw away anything. These pack rats hoarded newspapers, egg cartons, magazines, junk mail, Popsicle sticks—you name it. The results of the study were surprising. First, the project showed that about 10 percent of the population suffers from compulsive saving. Some are well-known hoarders—like artist Andy Warhol, author William Saroyan, and Ruth (Mrs. Billy) Graham, who wrote *Confessions of a Pack Rat.* Second, when these people aren't squirreling away their "treasures," they're leading very normal lives as teachers, writers, ministers, and computer programmers. In other words, they aren't like the eccentric San Francisco woman whose house was so full of junk that it collapsed and slid off of its foundation! Third, most of the hoarders are perfectionists who postpone cleanup duties until they can do a spic-and-span job of it. But that time never comes.

Most hoarders experience an interesting internal battle. They want to hold on to things, but they simultaneously fear that they will never have enough of anything. So while the pack rat is tugging to possess more and more, his or her alter ego is whispering, "You'll never have enough; you'll never *be enough.*" Half of the person is saying, "I want *more,*" while the other half replies, "You'll always be *less.*"

Many pack rats are compulsive in other areas of their lives as well, such as in their spending, eating, and fitness habits. We call this tendency to jump from one compulsion to another "switching addictions" or "addiction hopping." It's very common, and we'll talk more about that in Chapter 2.

We've counseled several take-charge executives—men and women—who are highly structured and organized on the job, but whose personal lives are in chaos. Their employees snap to attention every morning and marvel at their bosses' ability to make quick, effective decisions. But when these CEOs go home in the evening, they're greeted by dozens of unfinished projects, mounds of books they intend to read, correspondence they intend to answer, mates who often ignore them, and children over whom they have no authority.

How can this happen? It's a lot like a law of physics: If you push something hard enough in one direction, somewhere down the road there will be an equal reaction in the opposite direction. It's usually only a matter of time.

Our friend Virginia Potter is a good illustration of this. For so many years she had been the perfect wife, the tireless volunteer, everyone's favorite sounding board and listening post, and the family's most talented cheerleader. Outwardly she was always in control, but inwardly she was slowly veering from her accepted, applauded route and moving in a direction that endangered her physical and emotional health as well as her marriage. What appeared to happen to her overnight actually festered under the surface for a long time before it erupted into visible, treatable symptoms. Fortunately, she and her husband recognized the need for help early enough that we were able not to "fix" her, as she requested, but to help her "fix" herself. A resolution of her problems wasn't immediate, partly because her situation was serious, and partly because she entered treatment the way most people do—with some degree of denial.

"I really love my life," Virginia insisted almost apologetically during her first group therapy session in the hospital. "I wouldn't change a single thing about my home or my family. In fact, I probably should not be here at all. It's not as if I'm sick or anything."

She sensed the warmth of the participants, and she smiled her brightest smile. We had told her what to expect at the session, and we had explained that each of the dozen or so men and women in the circle was at a different point in his or her recovery. It was a friendly, supportive group that gathered daily in the sunny east lounge of our hospital unit in suburban Dallas. No one would judge her, we had promised, but everyone would listen attentively.

On the day of Virginia's introduction we had several "veterans" present who had heard many protests like hers. Still, her delivery was different. Unlike most of our patients, who are noticeably nervous when they talk about themselves for the first time to the group, Virginia took the floor with confidence. After all, cheerleaders are at their best in front of a crowd. Her makeup was perfectly applied, her frosted hair was carefully coiffed and sprayed, and she was wearing an expensive warm-up suit that was as close as she could get to following our suggestion to dress casually.

"The only reason I'm here is that I'm a little run down right now," she explained. "I remember my husband and I once saw a play in New York called *Stop the World, I Want to Get Off*. Anthony Newley was the star." She laughed, and we noticed that her usually melodious voice sounded high-pitched and tense. Dr. Hemfelt scribbled a reminder on his pad to use the illustration of the violin when we met with her later in one-on-one consultation.

"Anyway, that's sort of the way I feel," she continued. "I want to get off the merry-go-round—but just for a little while, just long enough to get my strength back so that I can go home and do all the things I've always done."

She hesitated, then repeated, "I really love my life, you know." This time there was an edge of desperation to her words. It was as if she needed our assurance that, yes, her life sounded truly wonderful. Several members of the group nodded encouragement.

"But maybe it could be even better," Dr. Hemfelt suggested quietly.

Virginia looked at him, her bravado slowly draining away.

"Sometimes patients come to us asking for something that we think could hurt them in the long-term," the doctor said. "What we'd really like for you to do is to commit to a different kind of goal. Instead of trying to become strong enough so that you can go back and do the same things that you've always done, would you be willing to go back and do things differently? Perhaps, do them at a different pace? Or out of different motivations? This might mean making some important changes in your life-style and breaking some old habits. Even more important, it might mean exploring the deepest, most hidden roots underlying your drivenness."

The Driven Society

One of the difficulties in counseling driven humans, such as Michael and Virginia Potter, is to convince them that they can be more effective if they slow down, rather than step up, their activity levels. The whole world may be moving faster, we admit, but the Minirth-Meier message is to buck the trend and ease off. The universal message that is inside all driven people and drives their addictions is this: Do more and be more. More is always better. We counter this universal message with another: More is not *always* better.

Since driven people love to be challenged, we challenge our patients by telling them that leading a balanced life today takes a lot more hard work and concentration than simply going with the flow and picking up the pace. "We live in a driven society," we tell them. "We're bombarded by slogans that warn us that we only go around once, that we should reach for the gusto, and that we ought to be all that we can be. Any way we turn we encounter more information to absorb, new skills to learn, more tasks to complete. We encounter information overload every time we snap on the television or listen to the radio. An average weekday edition of *The New York Times* now contains more data than a person in the seventeenth century was likely to encounter in a lifetime! Somehow we have to consume this volume of information if we want to stay ahead of the pack.

"Even our time limits are gone. We used to be dictated by business hours that told us when we could shop, when we could do our banking, and when we could talk with each other on the phone. But those days are over. Now bank machines let us cash checks at midnight. We shop from catalogues and place orders by calling toll-free numbers twenty-four hours a day. We no longer have to wait until 9:00 A.M. to place a business call, because we can send an electronic mail message or FAX a letter any time we want."

In making patients aware of the endless battle they face against our society's compulsivity, we sometimes tell them about the New York electronics company that introduced a wristwatch that had a "speak" button. When the alarm sounded the first time, a pleasant song played. But if the wearer didn't respond to the first signal, the music was replaced by a programmed voice that repeatedly said, "Please hurry. Please hurry."

That same "please hurry" message plays every day in many ways in our lives. People who aren't compulsively driven can tune it out, but driven humans respond by obeying the message. And driven people are most likely to become victims of applauded addictions.

Stripping the Addiction Mystique

As psychiatrists and counselors, we think it's time to strip the mystique from the compulsions America applauds. That's what this book is all about. Our goals are to help you to identify your personal compulsivity or the compulsivity that plagues your families or organizations. Not only will we teach you to face your addictions, but also we will show you how to break through these addictions and prevent them from recurring. As we walk you around the addiction cycle, we will stop and explain each step along the way. We also will share proven techniques, many of which originated in the treatment of patients suffering from classic negative addictions, like alcoholism and drug addiction, and which we now apply in a pioneering manner to the treatment of applauded addictions.

As Dr. Meier says, most of us are unaware of our faults, but none of us should be a victim of our obsessions. Addictions aren't flaws, but conditions, and conditions can be treated and cured. This book will show you how.

In Chapter 2 we'll survey the scope of applauded addictions. As we look at the many faces of addiction, we'll note the different degrees of acceptability and seriousness attached to each. We'll also take note of the gray area between what is perceived to be right and what is believed to be wrong.

Gambling, for instance, may be legal or illegal, acceptable or unacceptable, depending on who you are, what you believe, and where you live. Gambling is risk taking, and many types of risk taking are thought to be acceptable—and even admirable. What greater risk taker is there than the entrepreneur who pools his or her resources to build and market a better mousetrap? After all, it's the American way to go against all odds bravely and pull out all the stops for a dream. Our society has even coined clichés to describe such situations. We cheer people who "go out on a limb" and "stand up to be counted" and "go to the mat" for what they believe.

Who is to determine what is healthy risk taking and what is unhealthy gambling? We call it gambling when a father's addiction to get-rich-quick schemes causes an infant to suffer a spastic colon, a young mother to be treated for anxiety, and a grandmother to complain of migraine headaches. Yet, the young father might argue that he is only trying to be an entrepreneur when he sacrifices his own security for the opportunity to provide more for the family that he loves.

In Chapter 2 we'll also answer such questions as:

- How widespread are applauded addictions?
- Are accepted addictions finally being taken seriously as the dangerous conditions that they are?
- May I be suffering from more than one applauded addiction or area of drivenness in my own life?

Chapter Two

The Many Masks of Compulsions

Virginia Potter had a secret.

"Not a terrible secret," she quickly assured the therapy group one morning. "It's not as if we're having an affair or anything; it's just that we're seeing too much of each other. And," she hesitated for a moment, "Michael doesn't know anything about it."

The "we" in this case was Virginia and a man thirteen years her senior who was a member of the same church that the Potters attended. Ray was a widower, and Virginia, in her typical good Samaritan way, had befriended him after he had lost his wife to cancer. She had included him in family dinners, had invited him to share Christmas and Thanksgiving at the Potter home, and had directed a steady supply of casseroles to his freezer.

"At least that's how it started," she explained. "But lately we seem to be spending an awful lot of time talking on the phone and arranging to see each other at church meetings or for coffee at the diner. He's lonesome, and I'm afraid he's getting too attached to me." She looked down, embarrassed. "It hasn't all been one-sided, of course. I . . . I really like being with him. But I know he needs to see someone his own age—someone who is single."

"Has there been any, er, physical contact?" asked one of the group members, trying to be delicate.

Virginia smiled. "That depends on what you mean by 'physical,'" she replied. "No, we haven't had sex, if that's your question. But there have been a lot of little things. You know, we touch each other more than we should. He gives me too many hugs, and I reach out for his hand more than I ought to. Sometimes when we're alone he gets a bit too close."

Her face was flushed as she spoke. Virginia obviously was uncomfortable with the topic; yet, she seemed to want to air it to the group. That, in itself, was a breakthrough. She was learning about behavior and how underlying needs and insecurities can motivate people—good people—to act in wrong ways. Sometimes these needs and insecurities can lead to addictions, and one of the most harmful is a relationship addiction. We've treated many patients like Virginia who have become dependent on "special friends" to fulfill needs that weren't being met by their marriage partners.

"Why are you telling us about Ray?" Dr. Hemfelt asked, encouraging her to crystallize her thoughts by putting them into words.

Virginia paused for several seconds before answering. "I think I'm vulnerable to Ray because Mike doesn't always have time for me," she said tentatively. "If it isn't his job, it's one of his community activities that pulls him away. And if it isn't some committee or board meeting, it's his golf or his tennis or his jogging. I feel lonesome, in spite of all the busyness around the house." She looked imploringly at the group members. "Believe me, I'm not the kind of woman who would cheat on her husband. It's just that Ray is a sweet, caring person. He listens to me, asks my advice, and makes me feel important." She laughed. "He even thinks I'm pretty."

Virginia's words told us a lot. Not only did she feel ignored by her husband, but also she expressed surprise that another man would find her interesting and attractive. The undercurrent of her statement hinted at real insecurity. The woman who seemed to have it all was suffering from low self-esteem, and low esteem is nearly always present in cases of addiction.

Most encouraging about Virginia's words was her growing awareness of the tangled web of problems that contributed to her general sense that all was not well in her marriage and in her life. She was starting to recognize Mike's compulsions to work and play too hard. She also was beginning to see how driven she was in her roles as cheerleader and everyone's favorite confidante. More than merely admitting that these compulsions were present in their lives, she was questioning the reason for their presence. What drove Michael? For that matter, what was driving her?

A Nation at Risk

Like Virginia, most people today are tuning in to the compulsions America applauds. The addictive urge to do more and be more is so prevalent that a spin-off industry has evolved to help persons recognize and recover from their addictions. Self-help books are available, seminars are plentiful, and therapy no longer has a stigma attached to it. Major corporations combat stress and compulsivity by providing gyms for their employees, sponsoring races and other fitness competitions, and creating EAPs (employee assistance programs to help workers deal with the problems that go along with living in a fast-paced society).

Addictions are on the upswing. But if that is the bad news, the good news is that more people are aware of the trend. For example, according to *USA Weekend*, New York state racetracks and at least one casino along Las Vegas' glitzy "strip" now post notices that urge compulsive gamblers to seek help for their addictions.

Many people were surprised when a profile of a "typical" gambler was drawn, and the gambler turned out to be neither a high roller nor an international aristocrat. Instead, the typical gambler was depicted as a married man, nearly forty years old, and already $43,000 in debt. To show how typical he is, at some time in his life he must have worn a military uniform because the Department of Veteran Affairs now offers inpatient and outpatient treatment programs at four major medical centers. The need for help is so great that our government is lending a hand.

All this has prompted one executive with the Council of Compulsive Gambling to label gambling as "the hidden addiction of the nineties."

But is it? Therapists at a treatment center in New York argue that spendaholism is another serious contender for the "hidden addiction" title. They say the urge to splurge has its roots in the self-indulgent 1970s but blossomed during the economic good times of the 1980s. The treatment center's files bulge with case histories of persons with tell-tale signs of shopaholism such as having so many pairs of shoes that they have to be alphabetized and stored in the basement. The patients include shoppers who have difficulty choosing which color to buy so they buy one of each. The purchases—called "hits" by compulsive shoppers—often hang in closets with price tags never removed. It's little wonder that popular writer Tom Wolfe has dubbed the current generation the "Splurge Generation."

Despite the shop-till-you-drop stereotype attached to women (the average woman carries *ten* credit cards in her purse), many men also fall victim to chronic shopaholism. We've counseled male patients at our clinics who have felt driven to buy elaborate software programs and to collect expensive computer add-ons known as peripherals. The irony of their spending sprees is that they often can't find the time to snap on their PCs! Then there are the exercise buffs who line their garages with wall-to-wall rowing machines, stationary bikes, trampolines, and treadmills. Another costly habit, often overlooked in discussions of shopaholism, is the compulsion that many people have of diving for the check at restaurants. Every meal has to be their treat.

"We're terribly materialistic in America," concludes Dr. Francesca Kress, director of psychological assessment at the Hapworth Centers in New York, a facility that has an effective treatment program for shopaholics. "We believe there's a God-given right to acquire, to be capitalistic. It's almost a holy thing."

Work is regarded reverently, too. The new wrinkle that we've noted at our clinics is the surge in the number of women who are losing their balance because of demanding careers. The increase in female patients with work-related complaints parallels the increase of women in high places. In the early 1970s only 10 percent of business school degrees went to females; now it's 40 percent. When we were first-year medical students, only about 9 percent of our classmates were women; now 34 percent of the students in classes are female. This equal-opportunity trend will continue, according to projections. By the middle of the 1990s, half of all new businesses will be launched by women. With success can come stress, and from stress can spring obsessive-compulsive disorders. It's no surprise that a national organization called Workaholics Anonymous now exists and advocates a recovery program similar to AA's Twelve Step process.

Out-of-control risk taking? Shopaholism? Workaholism? Relationship and sexual addictions? Rather than tagging a single addiction as the scourge of the decade, maybe it would be more accurate to say that addictions in general are rampant today. Right now, over two hundred support organizations—from Emotions Anonymous to Women Who Love Too Much groups—are functioning across the country. Thousands of meetings are conducted weekly to help shore up the efforts of people who battle dangerous obsessions. What begins as a voluntary action can expand to a habit, then evolve to a compulsion, and eventually erupt to full addiction status.

Of course, some say this is all a cop-out; they argue that anyone who has a bad habit these days can shrug it off as a sickness. "I can't help it," the self-confessed addict might explain. Then he or she borrows a few words from one of the recovery programs: "I'm powerless over my compulsion. It's unmanageable." With that, the person is free to indulge in the bad habit again. After all, it's not that person's fault.

Often people get the wrong idea of addiction therapy programs by the way they are portrayed in the media. Constructive addiction treatment calls the recovering person to a new balanced sense of self-responsibility. It is not a license to practice irresponsibility. Sometimes celebrities who have identified and sought help to overcome addictions tell their stories in a fashion that makes the recovery process sound easy and even glamorous. We read about a television or film star who goes somewhere for a brief thirty-day hiatus and is "healed." In reality, recovery is a long and difficult journey and the side effects of untreated addictions are anything but glamorous. Marriages sometimes fail along the way, businesses are lost, relationships suffer and entire families may disintegrate.

Applauded Addictions Are Kissing Cousins to Negative Addictions

"Applauded" addictions are just as chronic and progressive as drug or alcohol abuse or other compulsions that are perceived to be more harmful. The difference is that the approved varieties are regarded as praiseworthy until they become repetitive, involuntary, and obviously destructive. Only when they start to cause misery to the victim and hardship for the family does the red flag go up and applauded compulsions are recognized for what they are. The treatment required at that point is in many ways identical to programs designed to help drug and alcohol abusers.

Can *any* human activity become an addiction? Yes. When carried to an extreme, any behavior can veer out of control and become the dominant, driving force in a person's life. It can master her. It can consume him.

The Two-Phase Addiction Pattern

Whatever the habit, the two-step pattern is always the same. The first phase is the mental preoccupation—the obsession. The thought of the activity grabs hold of the person and preoccupies him or her to the exclusion of everything else. The person can't shake loose of it. At this point, the shopaholic is absorbed, even *obsessed* with the idea of a buying binge. She wants to acquire, collect, and possess. In the case of the relationship addict, he is *obsessed* with the notion of taking charge of the relationship, and perhaps even taking charge of the other person. After the obsession comes the second phase: acting out the obsessive thought. This action is the compulsion. The relationship addict or the shopaholic loses control, gives in to the mental preoccupation, and is compelled—even driven—to do whatever he or she feels is necessary. She shops. He flirts. Or, in the case of other addictions, he or she might exercise, work, worry, scrub, or gulp megavitamins incessantly.

The list of compulsions is practically endless. The staff of the Minirth-Meier Clinic once attempted to take an inventory of the applauded compulsions that we've treated, but we stopped at number fifty-one. The project grew unmanageable because we had not even begun to categorize all of the compulsions.

We had better success when we divided the more common compulsions into six general groups: money matters; wellness and health; work and play; service and voluntarism; relationships; and the catch-all category of perfectionism.

To illustrate the variety of applauded compulsions that exists, look over our shoulders as we review our files and offer a sample of the cases that we've treated in the past several years.

Money Matters

We've mentioned the shopaholic, the compulsive spender who must have the latest electronic equipment or car or boat. A cousin to this type of compulsion is the insatiable urge to collect rare paintings or jewelry or coins or decorator plates or any number of other valuables. And all of these compulsions are related to the American desire to keep up with the Joneses—to have the biggest house or the most beautiful yard or garden.

Not as easily recognized, but even more destructive, is the addiction to risk-taking. In the last few years we have treated a number of bankrupt millionaires in our clinic in Dallas. Their habit? Going for broke. They experience the same high from teetering on a financial cliff that the drug addict receives from uppers.

What we explain to our patients is that money is a symbol of power and control. Persons who are addicted to taking risks and seeking crises are trying to catapult themselves to positions of power. The irony is that in an effort to seize control, they go out of control. They want the pot of gold at the end of the rainbow, and they are willing to do anything to get it. After all, money equals power, and power equals control.

Risk Taking

One of the most heart-wrenching stories we've heard recently was told to us by a couple who, in five years' time, have gone from having it all to losing everything.

Phyllis and Gary were highly driven young executives in a large Houston-based conglomerate. They were good employees, and their company recognized their performances by rewarding them with "perks," such as stock options, a generous retirement program, and a profit-sharing plan. Phyllis was satisfied with her job and with the life-style that it supported. Gary was happy, too, although he indulged in a lot of "what-if" daydreams. He fantasized about someday being his own boss, launching a construction business, and cashing in on the building boom that was unfolding in Texas at the time. Only then could he truly control his own destiny. Phyllis kept reminding him that they had all the success they needed, so why not enjoy it?

Eventually he shouted her down, quietly. "We only live once," he cajoled. "Let's go for broke."

Unfortunately, that is exactly what happened. Gary wasn't one to test the water with one foot and then decide whether he wanted to go for a swim. He plunged in with both feet with his life's savings tucked under his arm.

His construction business headquarters were so posh that they could have been featured in *Architectural Digest;* his computer system was state of the art; he hired a full office staff rather than adding employees on an as-needed basis, and he bought a corporate membership in the most prestigious country club in town. He had all the trappings of success; the only element missing was the success.

Phyllis was supportive of his effort but worried about how the venture was affecting him. He seemed obsessed with it. She recalled for us one incident that revealed to her just how caught up her husband was in the pot-of-gold dream. They were driving down the freeway one afternoon, and she was asking Gary several legitimate questions about his new business venture. He became so agitated that he nearly lost control of the car.

"This is my business, and I'll do it my way!" he screamed. "I don't want you to interfere with any of it!" From that moment she offered no words of advice, although she knew that he was clearly out of control.

When the economic development of Houston squeaked to a halt, thanks to a faltering oil industry, new companies like Gary's suffered fallout immediately. But his addiction to risk taking overruled his common sense. He elected to weather the storm and to wait until the business climate cleared. Dipping into Phyllis's savings kept him afloat. Cashing in on her stock portfolio bought him a few more weeks. Only when all of the couple's resources were exhausted did he finally declare bankruptcy. The bank not only repossessed his office equipment, but also foreclosed on the mortgage of their home.

Situations like Gary's are played out at all levels of our society. In Texas, where everything seems to be done on a grandiose scale, the stakes are often very high. A much publicized example involved former Texas governor John Connally, a self-made millionaire who served as secretary of the Navy under John Kennedy, secretary of the treasury under

Richard Nixon, and was once a contender for the presidency himself.

With his political career behind him and a personal fortune assuring a comfortable future, Connally was in an enviable position. Everyone expected him to kick back and enjoy the rewards of his hard work. But he formed a new company with a friend, poured his assets into it, and lost everything. The poignant postscript to the John Connally story came in the form of a news photo of the proud elder statesman sitting on the front row at the auction that put all of his possessions on the block. His loving and loyal friends sat beside him, purchasing many of the personal items to sell or give back to him.

Closely linked to the habitual risk taker is the person who thrives on crises. The stakes are equally high, and the applause is equally deafening.

The Crisis High

Americans have always admired the take-charge leader who bursts on the scene, assesses a dilemma, and prescribes the perfect solution. In the corporate world we call such people troubleshooters.

While Dr. Hemfelt was working as a staff psychologist for a Fortune 500 company, he once counseled a top executive who was addicted to dealing with crisis situations. The corporation depended on this troubleshooter to go into a distressed part of the business and to quickly turn failure into success. Each time he worked his "magic," he was lavishly rewarded with praise, a plaque, and a bonus.

The job kept him on the move because the company had operations all over the world. It also kept him on his toes, since he was expected to learn quickly the strengths and shortcomings of all the employees in the troubled division, study the financial records, isolate the problem, and design a solution. Then, as soon as he had applied the bandage, he was off to his next crisis.

The reason he began seeing Dr. Hemfelt was not to learn how to slow his pace—he thrived on it, after all—but to learn how he could help his family members to cope with it. His preoccupation with work, his long hours, and his frequent moves around the country had taken their toll. This man, who had the knack for solving nearly every problem that he encountered on the job, needed help in solving his family's problem at home.

Dr. Hemfelt's first task was to convince the executive that the trouble originated with him, not with his wife and children. Over the years the man had become addicted to the "high" of rescuing ailing business units. His ego was stroked when the corporation's chief operating officer identified a problem so serious that only this gifted troubleshooter was capable of handling it. His orders generally were to do whatever was necessary to fix whatever was broken. He was his own boss, used his own judgment, and spared no expense in the process. When the job was done, the applause was enthusiastic. He was never expected to stay on and manage the rejuvenated company. That would mean settling down to a business-as-usual kind of routine, and that was totally at odds with his breathless lifestyle. Instead, he was off to cope with his next crisis and to anticipate his next high. Fixing became his fix, and as is the case with most addictions, his fixes were destroying his family.

How About You?

Diagnosing addictions that relate to money and control matters isn't easy. We applaud people who are sound financial planners, who live within their budgets, who tuck away savings for rainy days. But when does prudent saving become miserly hoarding? And at what point does investing lapse into unhealthy risk taking? Take this short quiz to see whether you are vulnerable to this compulsion that America applauds. Check the statements below that apply to you.

1.___✓___ *"I never seem to have enough money to meet my needs or the needs of my family."*

2.____ *"I sometimes feel envious of my neighbor's life-style. She (he) seems to have everything."*

3.____ *"I feel exhilarated when a deal closes, particularly a risky deal."*

4.____ *"I fantasize about my investments, real or imagined, in stock and real estate when I'm at work and when I'm relaxing at home."*

5._✓_ *"Sometimes when I feel angry or frustrated, I go shopping. That often makes me feel better."*

6._✓_ *"I seem to be always paying on my credit card. I never seem to be able to pay off my balance."*

7.____ *"Part of me always feels as if I should be earning more, no matter how much money I make."*

8.____ *"My fear that there will never be enough leads me to be 'tight' with money and to constantly search for ways to cut corners."*

If you checked three or more of these eight statements, money may be one of your compulsions.

Wellness and Health

If you don't run a couple of miles a day or spend an hour at the "body shop" doing aerobics, you may feel unfit by today's standards. Health has become America's preoccupation. But a fitness fan can cross the threshold and become a fitness fanatic. Some of us feel guilty if we don't run several miles seven days a week, whether it's snowing, raining, or is a hundred degrees in the shade. We've treated many patients whose marriages and careers have been sacrificed in the name of good health. A common type of drivenness is related to diet. Some people believe their health and happiness will be assured if only they eat enough grapefruit, oat bran, or herbs.

Health Foods

Dr. Meier recently treated a fifty-year-old business executive who was obsessed with health foods. His particular focus was herbs, and he had made an exhaustive study of the healing powers of each root, leaf, and flower that grows in his area of New England. His preoccupation with natural foods had caused him to ignore other aspects of his life, and by the time he consulted with Dr. Meier he was on the verge of losing his wife of twenty-two years. His depression was so severe that he asked to be treated in our Dallas hospital unit.

Shortly after he was admitted, he was told that he would be given no herbs while he was in our care. It wasn't that we felt herbs could cause him harm; we knew they were safe. We merely wanted to break his dependency so we would have his full attention as we concentrated on the larger issue: why he was driven in the first place. As long as he was preoccupied with trying to medicate himself with herbs, he would not look at the deeper problems in his life, such as growing up under the dictatoral guidance of a raging father and living within a cold and loveless marriage.

Although a compulsion to eat herbs is unusual, other diet obsessions are not. The old quip that a person can't be too rich or too thin may be more popular today than it was forty years ago.

Thin Is In

It seems as if nearly everyone is health- and weight-conscious. Up to a point this is a positive trend. But many people take the whole notion of low-fat eating to an extreme. A well-known baby food company polled young mothers and learned that a majority of them consciously regulated the caloric intake of their infants. When asked why, the moms admitted they were concerned about keeping their kids thin. They fed the babies skim milk and formula over-diluted with water. Unfortunately, babies under the age of two *need* fat in their diet for energy.

The "lite" foods market is now a multi-billion dollar industry, a good indication of our preoccupation with staying trim. Once an obsession with diet and fasting nudges out all other thoughts, the healthy concern for wellness has given way to an unhealthy addiction to food deprivation.

In our hospital units we treat three types of eating disorders: compulsive overeating, anorexia, and bulimia. We define anorexia as a compulsive, chronic self-starvation that results in a person's weighing less than 80 percent of what she should weigh according to her height and bone structure. Bulimia is a deadly two-part cycle of gorging great quantities of food and then ridding the body of the food by vomiting or by abusing laxatives or by excessive exercise. Many books have been written about eating disorders, including our own *Love Hunger, Recovery From Food Addiction,* which focuses on compulsive eating.[1] The important thing to note here is that it's possible—even very likely—to become addicted to either consuming food or denying food. As different as these addictions may seem, the cause is usually the same.

Of course, not all "wellness" preoccupations focus on the figure. Some of our patients worry constantly about their health, and they hop from specialist to specialist in search of cures.

Hypochondria

Whenever a client has a first appointment with us, we always begin the session by recording the patient's medical history. This is a routine task and serves as the foundation of the file that will grow with each follow-up visit.

Dr. Hemfelt recalls being surprised by a woman who once waved off his preliminary questions and handed him a multipage computer printout instead.

"Here, this is easier than my trying to tell you all the details," she said, unfolding a seemingly endless cascade of white papers. "I've been keeping my medical record on a disk for years. This will document all of my surgeries, medications, and test results. And here's a list of the specialists I've consulted."

Incredible? Not for a person who struggles with the crippling disorder known as hypochondria. Emotional problems disguise themselves as physical ailments and totally disrupt the victim's life. Typically, the hypochrondriac is most afraid of cancer and heart disease, but his or her complaints may range from headaches to dizziness to gastrointestinal disorders.

Often the hypochondriac uses the preoccupation with disease as a way of coping with stress. If you are sick, after all, you are out of commission and will either be excused from obligations or be pardoned for poor performance. Subconsciously that's saying, *If I am sick, then it's okay for me to slow down, take a day off, ask for help, or go to the doctor.* I know that society has a separate, easier set of rules for sick people. A woman doesn't have to be as loving a wife or as effective a mom if she doesn't feel well. A man doesn't have to be quite as competent or successful if he is hampered by some recurring malady. These people also know that our society finds physical illness far more acceptable than mental or emotional illness.

The irony of hypochrondria is that the victims put themselves in pain as a way of relieving pain. They genuinely suffer the symptoms of an illness, but the illness is conjured up to soothe their insecurities. Like the woman with the computer printout, hypochrondriacs crave the attention of a doctor who asks questions, gently examines their bodies, prescribes medications, exhibits concern, and suggests treatments. As they become totally preoccupied with their state of health they seek the periodic "fix" that comes only from regular visits to doctors. If a doctor shows a lack of concern or hints that the problem might be psychological rather than physical, the patient merely switches to another specialist. Then the cycle repeats itself. More tests, more consultations, more medications, more examinations.

The woman who visited Dr. Hemfelt armed with her lengthy computer printout not only was worried about her health problems, but also was aware that her marriage was in jeopardy because of her obsession with sickness. Every time she and her husband made plans for a vacation, the arrangements were scrapped because of illness. Financial fallout also became an issue when the couple's insurance carrier refused to pay claims for repeated tests and exploratory surgeries.

How can hypochondria ever be considered destructive? Seeking help is a laudable goal, and physical symptoms often serve as tip-offs to emotional issues. (Remember, it was Virginia Potter's persistent fatigue and flulike aches that eventually prompted her to visit our clinic.) However, when a person becomes obsessed with health, it becomes a destructive addiction. This progression from applaudable concern to destructive preoccupation happens in much the same way that an over-the-counter drug habit can be thought of as positive —at first.

Over-the-Counter Drugs

Reaching for a couple of aspirins after a tension-packed day, relieving irregularity with an occasional laxative, or assuring a good night's sleep with a mild sedative is relatively harmless. But sometimes popping pills can become a way of sidestepping serious problems. Drugstore remedies are big business in our society. Currently, more than three thousand medications line the shelves of a typical, well-stocked neighborhood pharmacy. In an average twelve-month span, Americans buy about $15 billion worth of over-the-counter drugs and almost $26 billion prescription medications.

"We resent having symptoms—a slight ache or pain— when we're actually in pretty good health. As a society as a whole, we've lowered our threshold for taking medication," says Dr. Arthur Barsky, a psychiatry professor at Harvard Medical School and author of *Worried Sick: Our Troubled Quest for Wellness.*[2]

Who's picking up most of the 1.7 billion prescriptions filled by pharmacists each year in America? More than half are senior citizens. But here's an interesting fact: Women in their childbearing years have more prescriptions filled than young and middle-aged men. And many of them are doing it for the wrong reasons. Rather than figuring out *why* the chronic headaches persist, the pill popper treats the symptoms. Instead of confronting the issues that are causing the tension at work, the insomniac munches nonprescription sedatives.

When a person depends on any kind of substance to "fix" his or her problems, that person is usually trying to avoid those problems. She or he self-nurtures by swallowing harmless tablets that serve more as a mental crutch than a physical remedy. Often the medications can do real damage. In an effort to lose weight some people take laxatives so often that their bodies rely on the substances to stimulate the digestive tract and cause the bowels to move. Others put so much faith in nonprescription appetite suppressants that they go on food binges. They think they can eat whatever they want because their "medication" will work its magic and cause them to lose weight anyway.

One of the most tragic examples of an over-the-counter drug addiction that progressed into a deadly addictive lifestyle involved billionaire Howard Hughes. As a young man, he often took drugstore pain relievers as treatment for his headaches. He later graduated to using Valium and eventually injected himself with an unknown liquid that caused him to be instantly drowsy.

Hughes was so obsessed with his health that he lived in isolation rather than risk an encounter with germs. His secretaries had to wear gloves when they typed memos that would be routed to his sterile penthouse. He seldom wore clothes because the fabric might be a breeding place for bacteria. Ironically, the richest man in America eventually died of a combination of ailments, one of which was malnutrition.

The example of Howard Hughes is an extreme. To a lesser though still serious degree, millions of Americans do have an out-of-balance preoccupation with wellness.

How About You?

Are you a fan or a fanatic about staying healthy and fit? Check the statements below that seem to apply to you and then honestly rate yourself.

1._____"I've had vague, physical problems for years, but the doctors don't seem to be able to identify my illness."

2._____"I run or engage in other aerobic exercise more than three times a week."

3._____"I look forward to getting that runner's or exerciser's high."

4._✓__"I am preoccupied with food, weight size and body image, and I always feel vaguely guilty after eating a large meal." *NoT !*

5._____"I constantly need to diet to keep my weight down, but I still feel fat. My friends say I don't need to diet, but I think they're just being nice."

6._____"I take more than one vitamin a day and I frequent health food stores."

7._____"I worry about the physical effects of aging."

Now be your own counselor. Do you think that you're carrying your desire to be healthy and fit to an extreme?

Work and Play

"He works hard and plays hard" is a popular adage of our society. Yet, there's no better definition of a driven person.

When Sammy Davis, Jr., died of throat cancer in 1990, all of the tributes that were heaped on him by other performers exalted his non-stop lifestyle. It wasn't enough for "Mr. Entertainment" to be remembered as a bundle of jittery energy who danced himself into a frenzy and sang himself hoarse onstage. Equal time was given to his after-the-show excesses that generally stretched into the wee hours. Alcohol, cigarettes and the night life were all part of his fast-paced scene. Only when his body cried "Stop!" in the form of a tumor behind his vocal cords did he slow down.

We generally think of workaholics as nose-to-the-grindstone types who hold down full-time jobs. But this category also can include those of us who boast that we play as hard

APPLAUDED ADDICTIONS

Money Matters

- Preoccupation with investing, hoarding, amassing fortune
- Gambling
- Risk-taking
- Collecting/acquiring valuables
- Keeping up with Joneses
- Binge shopping
- Controlling other persons through money

Wellness and Health

- Body building
- Exercise
- Diet and weight management
- Medical treatment, tests, surgery
- Personal hygiene
- Hypochondria
- Megavitamins
- Sun tanning

Relationships

- Hero worship
- Worry about others
- Sexual activity
- Super mom and dad
- Friendships
- People-pleasing addiction
- Marital fighting

Work/Play

- Over-achievement on the job
- Busyholism
- Pursuit of academic degrees
- Preoccupation with self-improvement
- Over-zealous homemaking, cooking, cleaning
- Daydreaming, fantasizing
- Music, TV, videos
- Sports

Service and Voluntarism

- Martyr syndrome
- Cause groups
- Charity, church work
- Loaning money to other people
- Rescue relationships
- Rescue professions

Perfectionism

- Cosmetic surgery
- Appearance, clothes
- Order, organization
- Toxiphobia (a fear of contaminants)
- Unrealistic standards of performance
- List making
- House cleaning
- Preoccupation with structures, rules, and rituals

as we work, and even those who seem to lead addiction-free lives. Under this label we find the over-zealous homemaker who is obsessed by cleanliness, the teenager who always has his Walkman "ears" on, and the sports addict who has developed a sport for every season.

There is an old joke about a woman who was so perfectionistic that she always cleaned her house from top to bottom every Thursday, the day before her standing weekly appointment with her cleaning woman. She didn't want the maid to think she was a less than perfect homemaker.

Luci Stewart went one step further. At her husband Richard's request, she hired one cleaning woman after another, but she always ended up terminating the arrangement against Richard's wishes because no one could scrub and polish quite as well as Luci could. Dr. Minirth believes her to be among the most perfectionistic women that he has treated in his more than twenty years as a psychiatrist.

These addictions often receive high praise because they can be worthwhile if not taken to extremes. Who would argue that a woman's efficient touch in the home isn't appreciated by her family? And what's wrong with a teenager's enjoying the music of his generation? And surely a performer as dedicated as "Mr. Entertainment" deserves to unwind after turning in a crowd-pleasing performance.

So what's the problem? Just this: <u>Even pursuits as worthy as homemaking,</u> hobbies, sports, <u>and socializing can be harmful.</u> Let's take a look at a few work/play preoccupations that have slipped over the threshold and into a state of addiction. We'll begin with two education preoccupations: pursuing academic degrees and mastering self-improvement.

Going Crazy by Degrees

Experts tell us that seven out of ten new jobs in the 1990s will be in white-collar professions. This suggests a renewed emphasis on education. So far so good. Few people would argue that education isn't a laudable pursuit. Still, we've counseled students who wonder whether they're going crazy by degrees. Just as they complete requirements for one academic degree, they switch career tracks and take off in another direction. The new goal always has new requirements. More classes. A different major. Additional training. Certification. A license. Preparing for the profession takes precedence over practicing the profession. Happiness is just a diploma away, but first—you guessed it—more classes.

A kissing cousin to the degree-driven person is the self-improvement addict. We might call this habit the quick-fix variation of going crazy by degrees.

Self-Improvement Mania

Some of our patients feel a driving need for self-improvement. Dissatisfied with how they perceive themselves, they search for the eight-hour answer. They want shortcuts to looking better, feeling better, wasting less, and earning more. They become workshop or self-help junkies who hop from crash course to seminar to retreat or read one book or magazine after another, trying to bridge the gap between what they know and what they think they ought to learn.

First it was time management and dress-for-success classes. Then came conflict resolution, team building, and customer service. On the personal enrichment front they have been introduced to marriage enhancement, divorce recovery, and singles seminars. They collect handouts, dominate "breakout" sessions, and buy every book and tape offered at the resource table. If they had their way they would sample all 60,000 of the workshops currently included in the central listing of available seminars.

Don't misunderstand us. We think seminars can be invigorating experiences. Whenever our schedules permit, we enjoy team-teaching at weekend workshops devoted to stress management, co-dependency, or overcoming anxiety and burnout. We believe that workshops and self-help literature can be therapeutic for patients trying to break through denial. Solid information presented by experts in the field can do wonders in convincing victims of applauded addictions that they have a problem and that they need help.

But workshops are "$4 billion per year" businesses, and

much of their success depends on repeat customers. Some people practically make a career of seeking solutions at organized seminars. They anticipate that *this* workshop will be different, *this* one will share the secret that will finally reveal how they can find happiness and peace of mind. The cycle repeats itself weekend after weekend. They are pumped up by the motivational speeches; they feel encouraged as they jot down the tips, checklists, and self-quizzes; and they enjoy the feeling of starting over with a new set of directives as guidelines.

Then comes the letdown. The seminar ends, and they still haven't undergone the dramatic metamorphosis that they expected. They come crashing back to reality. Oh, well, there's always another workshop. Maybe next weekend.

Many driven people are able to "turn off" their jobs and their push for education and self-improvement only by compulsively "turning on" an equally absorbing hobby. Sometimes the hobby can be as harmless as reading a good book.

A Novel Escape

One of our most interesting examples of a hobby addict was a single attorney in her mid-thirties who was seriously addicted to reading historical romance novels. At first, her fondness for the paperbacks seemed harmless enough. After a mentally grueling day in court she enjoyed losing herself in the predictably tangled plots that are at the center of this kind of formula fiction.

What began as a diversion, however, became a substitute for more satisfying relationships that might have developed with actual, not imaginary, people. She preferred to invest her time in fantasy rather than reality. She turned down social opportunities in favor of quiet evenings with her books. As she consumed three or four novels each week, she spared herself the ups and downs of flesh-and-blood emotional involvements. Her social life was nonexistent, and the only kind of excitement she experienced was through the make-believe adventures she vicariously shared with the heroines of the books.

Her recovery was far more difficult than merely breaking her reading compulsion. If we had taken away her books, she would have found another escape. Our task was to determine why she was a victim of an applauded addiction in the first place. Specifically, we had to help her look at her fear of intimacy. During treatment she discovered a long-hidden incident of childhood sexual abuse, which generated a heavy burden of shame. Reading had become her way of avoiding a real relationship that might revive her painful memories.

Flying High

Another example of a hobby that veered out of control involved a couple in their late forties who were experiencing serious marital problems because of the husband's obsession with glider planes. He was an attorney and had been forced into early retirement by the downsizing of the large law firm where he had worked. He was only mildly disappointed by his loss of a job because it meant more time to spend in his hobby, flying glider planes. He even expected his wife to join in the sport by becoming a member of the chase crew that followed the plane across the countryside to pick him up wherever he might land.

The problem? His wife didn't want to chase planes, and she did not feel they could afford the hobby on his modest pension. Her disinterest was equally as intense as his enthusiasm. They were at odds, and their marriage was at stake. In our sessions with the husband, our goal was to help him understand that he was using flying as a distraction from the shame of his latest emotional setback—being cut from the law firm's staff. That recent blow to his self-esteem reinforced old, buried feelings of insecurity, put in place by a mother who always had unrealistic expectations of him. The forced retirement confirmed what she had always implied: He wasn't quite good enough.

What About You?

Are you a work-hard-play-hard kind of person? Take this short assessment quiz by checking the statements that sound familiar and see if you're at risk of crossing the line into the danger zone.

1.____ *"I am continually telling myself I'll be happy when I achieve_____ or when I complete_____ . Somehow the end of the rainbow seems to be just over the horizon, and I remain perpetually discontent."*

2.__✓__ *"I am a perfectionist about my work (my job or my housework)."*

3.____ *"I work so hard, I sometimes burn out."*

4.____ *"I'm always telling myself, If I just had another degree, I'd get that promotion (or be guaranteed success when I graduate)."*

5.____ *"I think of myself as someone who works hard and plays hard."*

6.____ *"I spend most Sunday afternoons and Monday evenings watching sporting events."*

7.____ *"I feel as if I must always have the radio or television on. The house is just too quiet without them."*

8.____ *"I repeatedly tell myself that someday I'll cut back on the busyness of my schedule. Someday never comes."*

Are you addicted to work and play? In upcoming chapters we will tell you how to take two steps back to make this applauded addiction a more balanced part of your life. For now, we'd like you to consider another area: service and voluntarism.

Service and Voluntarism

We once counseled a husband and wife duo who had taken a hiatus from their successful careers as a pediatrician and a nurse to work in a missionary camp in Brazil. The doctor closed his lucrative practice, the nurse leased their lovely home, and for three years they devoted their time and medical skills to the poverty-striken natives of a small village.

Their sacrifice was praiseworthy, but we learned in our therapy sessions that their motivation was unhealthy. They went to Brazil for all the wrong reasons. Like so many persons who are addicted to service and voluntarism, these talented professionals were trying to earn the approval of others through good works and martyrdom. They felt guilty about the success they enjoyed in their professions and felt they had to shun their prosperity and status by imposing this pilgrimage on themselves. They both suffered from strong feelings of inadequacy and were convinced they had to earn their place in the human race by taking on a tough assignment and completing it to everyone's satisfaction.

Such noble action is also typical of the person who devotes himself or herself to rescuing other people. Rescuers can serve in a voluntary role, or they can work within a rescuing profession.

The Professional Rescuer

Whenever we interview young psychologists for positions in our clinics, we ask them several questions that have nothing to do with their professional experience or their academic training.

"Tell us about your life away from the office," we begin. "What kind of recreation do you enjoy? How do you nurture yourself? Do you have a support group? Extended friendship network?"

Our reason is not to invade their personal lives, but to

make certain that they don't depend on their profession to fulfill their innermost needs. No matter how important the counseling function is, it is not a two-way street where the counselor is helped as much as the patient. Solving other people's problems cannot be the way a counselor receives nurturing.

We frequently see patients who suffer from feelings of inadequacy and insecurity and believe that if they give enough of themselves, they will somehow ease their sense of emptiness. But the opposite happens. The more overextended they become, the lower their reserves sink.

How About You?

An unselfish desire to serve others is healthy; a driving need to prove ourselves is not. Which description most accurately reflects your motivation? Check the statements below that apply to you and decide for yourself.

1. ✓ *"I always seem to want to help other people with their problems."*

2. ____ *"I just can't seem to say no. I know I'm overextended, but when someone from my church or community calls me to do something, I feel guilty if I don't accept."*

3. ____ *"I feel important when I'm an active part of my community. It's a status symbol for me."*

4. ____ *"Sometimes I feel as if I help others who are underprivileged or sick because I feel guilty about having money and good health."*

5. ✓ *"Every once in a while I feel that my volunteer work causes me to neglect my family and/or my business."*

6. ____ *"One or more of my friends views me as his or her personal 'counselor' or 'therapist.' I resent the demands this places on me, but secretly thrive on*

the sense of power and importance this role gives me."

7.____*"I always feel a vague need to prove myself, to pay my dues just for being a member of the human race."*

If two or more of these statements sound all too familiar, your service to others and/or volunteer work may be a compulsion.

Relationships

Codependency may be the buzzword of the nineties. In our book *Love Is a Choice*, we defined a codependent as a person who is so enmeshed in another person that his or her own identity is lost.[3] Codependency is based on the mistaken belief that gaining control over another person or allowing another person to control me will somehow satisfy my deepest emotional needs and my love hunger. Not only can someone become addicted to someone else, but he or she can become addicted to certain aspects of the relationship. If this sounds confusing, let's look at a couple of examples from our practice that will show how the intricacies of such addictions work.

Concern for Others

Of course, it's a virtue when people lovingly care for their family members and special friends. However, we once treated a woman who spent so much time agonizing over her children, her mother who lived in another city, and her husband that she ignored her own emotional needs.

When this supermom read about a tragic schoolbus collision in nearby Kentucky, she nearly made herself sick worrying about her children's safety to and from school. She couldn't sell her neighbors on the idea of a carpool, so she gave up and drove the circuit twice daily herself.

Convinced that her widowed mother wasn't eating nutritious meals, she assumed the doting daughter role and prepared double recipes and delivered enough casseroles to fill a freezer each Friday. She wouldn't accept her mother's protests that she was doing quite well on her own.

Worried that her husband might lose his job with a local bank, she was the supportive spouse who cut the household budget in half by canceling the newspaper subscription, turning the heat off for several hours each day, buying clothes at the next-to-new shop, and serving meatless dinners three nights a week. She maintained this pace for several years until her complaints of insomnia, headaches, and depression prompted a visit to the family doctor. All tests were negative. Finally, her too-rapid loss of twenty-seven pounds caused her husband to bring her to our clinic for consultation.

Our diagnosis: She literally was worrying herself to death. She suffered from dual addictions—to her family and to her need to prove herself through nurturing relationships. The paradox was that she was trying to display her love for the people closest to her; yet, she was pushing them farther and farther away. She was so tense that her children didn't enjoy being in her company, and her husband complained of a lack of physical intimacy.

It isn't unusual for marital sex to be adversely affected by addiction. And sometimes it can even be the addictive agent that the driven person reaches for.

Too Much Sex

At the clinic we counsel husbands and wives to communicate honestly to each other what they enjoy or don't enjoy as part of sexual relations. Even this most intimate aspect of marriage can become negative when carried to an extreme.

"Is it normal for my husband to insist we have sex every night?" a middle-aged client asked us several years ago.

She explained that her husband was so dependent on reaching an orgasm before he went to sleep that their lovemaking had become ritualistic rather than spontaneous.

When she occasionally begged off because of a headache, he masturbated to reach his mandatory climax. Unlike most people whose intimate moments are dictated by their feelings, this man was driven by a compulsion. He was convinced that he couldn't relax or sleep without first having sex. He was using sex like a drug to medicate his tension rather than using sexuality as a helpful tool of communication within the relationship. Instead of bonding the husband and wife together, sex was driving them apart.

The sex life of a couple is an excellent barometer of the overall health of their relationship. The fact that Virginia Potter was physically attracted to a man other than her husband told us that her marriage wasn't completely satisfying to her. The more she saw of her friend Ray, the more emotional distance she put between herself and Michael. She invested time and thought in the friendship that she should have invested in her marriage. At the same time, however, she felt guilty about this relationship.

Further evidence of the wedge that was coming between the couple was a discovery that Virginia innocently made one day when she was rummaging through Michael's desk in search of the service warranty on the family's washing machine. She came across several magazines that could be categorized as "soft" pornography. She was shocked and hurt, but she couldn't bring herself to discuss it with him. They rarely fought, and she was afraid that any talk of the magazines would lead to a battle that would be more damaging than keeping the secret to herself. However, the discovery caused her to wonder why her husband felt a need for such material. She assumed that she was to blame because she wasn't a satisfactory partner to him. Her burden of shame became heavier.

Marital Fighting

Couples today sometimes boast that they have totally open communication in their marriages. No secrets. No silent treatment. No pouting allowed. They even follow "fair fighting" guidelines that specify who can say what to whom and under what circumstances. It's all so civilized *and dangerous* if it isn't balanced with other forms of softer, more loving communication.

At least one married couple we counseled became so hooked on their organized spats that the fights served as substitutes for intimacy. Ventilating angry emotions was their way of connecting with each other. The frequent verbal battles were part of a war game that left deep wounds and permanent scars. They could lapse into their adversarial roles on command and would only slip out of the fight mode when one called a cease fire. By that time, both were exhausted and ready to retreat within themselves.

By contrast, Virginia and Michael Potter preferred a more covert style of fighting. Angry words were never exchanged; instead, they got even with each other in more subtle ways. Michael had the irritating habit of forgetting to pay household bills, a practice that caused Virginia much embarrassment. Collection agencies often called, threats of low credit ratings were common, and on multiple occasions the electricity was turned off in their home.

Virginia's mode of retaliation was her emotional entanglement with Ray. Even though Michael wasn't aware of the relationship, Virginia took pleasure in knowing that she was doing something that would hurt Michael deeply if he found out.

How About You?

Each of us develops and nurtures dozens of meaningful relationships over the course of a lifetime. How can we know if our bonds with others are healthy and in balance or if they are unhealthy and addictive? Identifying the statements below that apply to you will help you make a diagnosis.

1._____ *"It feels as if my boyfriend and I have been battling for control since the day we met."*

2._____ *"My husband is like a god to me. He pays all the*

*bills, gets up with the kids at night, even cooks the
meals and cleans the house sometimes. I count on
him for everything."*

3._____*"I spend a lot of time fantasizing about my sexual
desires."*

4._____*"My kids and I experience constant power struggles
—they have all the power; I have all the struggle."*

5._____*"I sometimes look at pornographic films or read
pornographic magazines to feed my sexual
fantasies."*

6._____*"I spend all my time and energy doing all the right
things and trying to please everyone. Yet, at the end
of the day, I still feel guilty."*

7._____*"I periodically act out certain sexual impulses and
fantasies that are in violation of my most deeply
held values."*

8._____*"I vowed I'd never marry a man like Dad. But here I
am married to a man who is married to his job, just
like Dad."*

9._____*"I am constantly pushing my spouse to engage in
sexual activities that he (she) is not comfortable
with."*

10._____*"I become upset and depressed when my spouse
or dating partner doesn't seem to approve of what
I'm doing. In fact when he (she) is in a bad
mood, I blame myself and my own mood quickly
turns sour."*

Be your own counselor. Are you—like one in four Americans
—codependent, addicted to your relationships with other
people?

Let's look at one other area of compulsion, then we'll talk
about how these compulsions that America applauds often
come in twos or threes—or even by the dozen. Most compulsive people have far more than one compulsion.

Perfectionism

One of the reasons that Luci Stewart came into therapy was that she decided she wanted to break out of her dual roles of super homemaker and secretary in her husband's home-based office. At the same time, she craved the double responsibilities because they put her in control of the family's personal finances and of Richard's corporate books. She was excellent at both jobs. Her meticulous attention to detail resulted in every account's being in perfect balance. Although the burdensome tasks weighed her down, they also buoyed her up. She was addicted to the roles. She felt indispensable. At a deeper level, she feared that if she were *not* essential to Richard and his business, he might not love her so much.

People who are perfectionistic, like Luci, often are addicted to control. They have to call the shots. No matter how much they protest, they have to be in charge. One of the difficult aspects of this applauded addiction is that the addict may be commended for practicing this compulsion at certain times of the day and under certain circumstances, but expected to "turn it off" at other times. Let us explain.

We've counseled several patients whose professions require a great deal of precision on the job. Like Luci, these people hold down responsible positions, such as air traffic controller, engineer, pilot, editor, surgeon, accountant, and pharmacist. Attention to detail is a plus in these demanding settings. After all, no airline passenger would object if the captain of a jumbo jet were such a perfectionist that he knew the function of each knob, lever, and gauge in the cockpit and demanded that his crew be equally versed in the equipment.

The dilemma occurs when that same air traffic controller, engineer, pilot, editor, surgeon, accountant, or pharmacist goes home for the evening. Can he or she shed this perfectionistic personality and unwind?

We once counseled a dental surgeon whose perfectionism

was causing a breakdown in his relationship with his wife and eleven-year-old son. His hobby was woodworking, and he was as meticulous about his tools as he was about his surgical instruments. Everything had a place, and heaven help anyone who dared to touch, dust, or rearrange a drill bit or a rasp. His obsession with tidiness spilled over from his basement workshop to every room in the house. He even insisted that there was a right way and a wrong way to open the refrigerator, and he gave frequent demonstrations of both. Jerking it too quickly could break the seals, he would warn his son.

"If you learn to close a refrigerator door properly, it will last two hundred or three hundred years," he would often say. He seemed obsessed with doing everything in such a way as to assure its longevity. Whether he was restoring a piece of antique furniture in his workshop or a wisdom tooth in his office, he fought the aging process. It was his way of exhibiting invincibility.

In spite of constant urging from his wife, this perfectionist refused to consider counseling until he overheard his son's plans for his twelfth birthday party. His wife had suggested having several friends over for cake and ice cream, but the boy preferred a quiet family celebration.

"Why don't you want to invite kids your own age?" pressed the mother.

"Because someone might spill something, and that would upset Dad," replied the boy.

Perfectionism can spill over to all aspects of our lives. Whereas some people aspire to a flawless home or office, others dream of a flawless appearance. They want to be a perfect "10." Thanks to cosmetic surgery, physical perfection may be possible. But, warns Dr. H. George Brennan, a California facial surgeon, "It is unrealistic for a patient to think that by changing her nose or having her face lifted, her failed marriage will be resurrected or she will become more successful. Surgery won't solve life's problems."

Scalpel Slavery

Years ago, doctors often questioned the motives of patients who had what is called elective cosmetic surgery. In other words, if a woman requested a rhytidectomy (face-lift) or abdominoplasty (tummy tuck) for no reason other than to improve her appearance, she was suspected of trying to beat the clock. It was feared that she couldn't accept the natural aging process and that she was making a last-ditch effort to recapture her fading youth.

We know better today. Many of the half million cosmetic surgery procedures that are performed annually are done for professional reasons. People in the public spotlight—such as Betty Ford, and comedian Phyllis Diller—are prime examples.

Cosmetic surgery is sometimes necessary for medical reasons; our concern is not with persons who base surgical decisions on reasonable expectations and constructive motivations. Our concern is with those who are addicted to a quest for physical perfection. These people move from specialist to specialist in search of some improvement in their appearance that will change their lives and make them more acceptable in their own eyes. Several of them have had the same procedure done and undone many times. The unhappy truth is that no matter how many operations they undergo, they will never be satisfied with the results or with themselves. The problem is much more than "skin deep." In therapy they learn to ask themselves, "Am I doing this so I'll look a bit better, or is there some deep shame-based issue that I'm trying to cosmetically change?"

One of our patients, a thirty-six-year-old flight attendant named Suzanne, discovered that the two facelifts she had endured were less for herself and more for her deceased father. Her dad had been so critical of Suzanne that she had grown up convinced that she would never be pretty enough or smart enough to please her dad. She bounced from surgeon to surgeon in search of change. Superficially she succeeded; she was able to change her looks. However, no amount of surgery enabled her to change the way she viewed herself.

Determining a patient's true motive for surgery might require some probing, but at least one perfectionistic addiction is so obvious and dangerous that it requires immediate medical treatment. It's called toxiphobia, and it's on the upswing.

Toxiphobia

In the spring of 1990, a short news item from Langeboom in the Netherlands received worldwide exposure because of its shocking nature. The story told of a twenty-four-year-old woman who was hospitalized after years of living under a plastic sheet and eating only canned foods. Her actions were motivated by her fear of radiation from the Chernobyl nuclear disaster. She had refused to eat any fresh foods since the 1986 explosion in Russia. Her diet and her insistence on huddling on a couch for all that time caused her to suffer from malnutrition and cramped joints.

As outlandish as this example is, many people today are driven by a fear of contaminants. They share a compulsion to cleanse or purge their bodies of anything that might be toxic. They worry about news reports that allege that bottled water might contain benzene or foods might harbor carcinogens. They try to "detox" themselves by fasting, taking enemas, and gulping gallons of fluids to wash away impurities.

In truth, the compulsion to fast your way to health can be dangerous. We've seen patients who have so depleted their levels of sodium and potassium that they've gone into comas. An overload of water can perforate the colon and even cause heart failure. The risk of infection increases, and muscle mass is lost.

How About You?

Is perfectionism good or bad? Like the Olympic gymnast whose ultimate goal is a series of perfect marks from the judges, some of us jump through hoops and turn cartwheels to execute a flawless performance. When is it okay to strive for perfection, and when is it a sign of drivenness? Assessing your personal perspective on perfection will help to provide the answer.

1. __✓__ *"I tell myself that if I had my nose fixed or some other part of my body altered, then I would be loveable in my marriage or dating relationship and maybe I'd be more successful in my work."*

2. __+__ *"My hair must be fixed just right and my clothes the latest designer labels for me to feel good."*

3. _____ *"I've contemplated plastic surgery. Perhaps I've already had one or more plastic surgeries."*

4. __✓__ *"I frequently look in the mirror to check my appearance. It's very important to me that other people think I look nice."*

5. _____ *"I constantly worry about germs and contaminants —and about catching some disease. In fact, I frequently wash my hands to cleanse away the germs."*

6. _____ *"I have an inordinate preoccupation about environmental contaminants (such as water purity, processed foods, and synthetic fibers in clothing and other manufactured goods)."*

7. _____ *"People sometimes say I'm perfectionistic and/or rigid."*

8. _____ *"If I can't do something well, I just don't do it. Or if I've already begun and can't seem to finish the job to my standards, I give up."*

How about you? Are you perfectionistic? If only a few of these statements sound all too familiar, perfectionism may be one of your compulsions.

Many of our patients check statements in more than one of the six categories of applauded addictions—money matters, wellness and health, relationships, work/play, service and voluntarism, and perfectionism. Maybe you did too. In fact, you might be saying to yourself, "I bought this book because I knew I was driven, but I never thought I had that many compulsions. Can I really be that obsessive?"

Our answer to that questions is that you are not alone. If a person is compulsive, he or she often has more than one applauded addiction.

Addiction Hopping

In our collective and separate practices, we three doctors have treated thousands of applauded addictions. The cases we've just highlighted are only samples of the patients who have come to us for help. As diverse as their addictions are, they share several characteristics. Three of their common traits are:

- one addiction often leads to another;
- in the recovery process as we begin to release the addictions often the last addiction is the hardest to break; and
- unless the underlying causes of drivenness are dealt with, addiction relapse or addiction hopping is inevitable.

Too many people perceive applauded addictions to be pesky habits that get a bit out of hand. Their solution is simple: Break the habit, and the problem goes away. If a patient is obsessively concerned with health, fitness, diet, or surgery, a counselor need only to convince the person to lighten up, ease off, and mellow out. If a woman is too perfectionistic about her home, or if a man is overly concerned about his work, the therapist need only suggest some kind of leisure activity to lessen the intensity. Perhaps a vacation is just what the doctor should order.

The truth is that the emotional and spiritual roots behind our addictions run very deep (as we shall see in future chapters) and temporary interruption from one addiction does not always assure the end of addictive behavior. The corporate troubleshooter who travels throughout the country "fixing" broken subsidiaries of the company might be persuaded —for family's sake—to settle down in a permanent management position. He might even start taking a class or two at a local university to keep his mind stimulated to new challenges. Before he knows it, he's working toward another graduate business degree, complete with the pressures of tests, research papers, and class presentations. The stress level cranks up to the same level it was when he was putting out fires as a corporate troubleshooter. His family once again is having to cope with his lack of attention, many commitments away from home, and promises that everything will be fine once this obstacle is surmounted or that deadline has passed.

It's not good enough to intervene and halt a habit. The patient may give it up and then reach out for a replacement. Addiction hopping is a lot like a shell game where the players move the addiction around from one area of life to another without ever discovering what drives them to play the game in the first place. This switching from one habit to another is a lot like switching from a window seat to an aisle seat on the Hindenburg or changing deck chairs on the Titanic. The outcome is still going to be the same. And the last habit is usually the toughest to beat. After so many transfers, addictions often consolidate into one, and when it's time for the patient to surrender that one, the urge to cling to the addiction becomes almost overwhelming.

Most applauded addictions are efforts to mask deep insecurities, both emotional and spiritual. Addictions are not simply bad habits. They are desperately complex attempts to ease universal human fears about our mortality and vulnerability. Applauded addictions become "gods" of performance and achievement in our lives, false gods that dominate us, and false gods to whom we turn to address the most profound questions about the meaning, purpose, and security of life.

These insecurities may have their roots in events that were painful or difficult or missing in early family experiences. In upcoming chapters we'll show you how to get to the core of approved addictions. As illustrations, we'll track several of the patients you met briefly in this chapter. We will give you progress reports on these patients' successes or failures in trying to combat the addictions that America applauds. But first we need to determine the crossover point between normal behavior and compulsive drive. Chapter 3 will explain the threshold and will teach victims how to cry "Ouch!" when they've crossed over the line.

Chapter Three

Learning to Say "Ouch!"

Before Susan Hemfelt, wife of Dr. Hemfelt, "retired" to become a full-time mom, she taught elementary school for several years. At the beginning of the school year, she introduced her students to an idea that Dr. Hemfelt still uses when he counsels victims of applauded addictions.

Susan explained to her class that any time a student was in distress, he or she had her permission to raise his or her hand and say "Ouch!" The distress might be physical, such as a tummy ache, a fever, or a playground bruise. Or it might be emotional, such as feeling lost, confused, or overwhelmed. The point was that if a child was hurting in any way, and if that child needed help in coping with that hurt, he or she could put up a hand, say "Ouch!" and the class would stop whatever it was doing and deal with the problem.

Dr. Hemfelt tells of his wife's "Ouch!" practice whenever he explains the threshold of addiction to patients. One of the indicators that tells us when a habit, practice, pattern or style of behavior—even a positive habit—has crossed over and become an addiction is when a driven person, or someone close to a driven person, says "Ouch!" This happened to Virginia Potter when she first suffered symptoms of fatigue, headaches, lack of concentration, and "smiling depression."

The physical hurts were her body's method of communicating that something was wrong, much like the child who puts up a hand as a way of saying to the class, "Ouch, I'm hurting." Virginia unconsciously was reaching out for help. Her pain first prodded her to check into a diagnostic clinic for a full battery of tests, and it eventually brought her to our counseling offices.

Another crossover symptom is when a family member begins to show signs of distress. In Chapter 1 we talked about a young father—Luci and Richard Stewart's son—who had become entangled in one get-rich-quick scheme after another. The fallout occurred when his wife suffered anxiety, his mother was treated for depression, and his infant son was diagnosed as having a spastic colon. Coincidence? Definitely not. Each of the family members was saying, "Ouch, I hurt!" Each was expressing his or her need for help differently.

Often when a family seems to be deluged by an assortment of problems, well-meaning friends shrug their shoulders and wonder how so many bad things could happen to such good people. "It isn't fair," they say. Or they shake their heads and dredge up the old maxim "When it rains, it pours."

Our reply is: *It may not be fair for problems to compound and multiply, but it's very predictable.* More than one problem within a couple of years is no more a coincidence than rainfall. Problems aren't isolated to their place of origin. As a problem grows in intensity, it spills over and affects the people around it.

The Delicate Family Mobile

When we first met Virginia Potter she said that she felt stretched to the limit. She not only had a driven personality, but she also was married to a driven man who was part of a driven family that was attempting to function in a driven society. Treating Virginia's compulsivity certainly was our top priority, but we couldn't stop there. We also had to treat the *system* that she was a part of. Otherwise, sending her home "cured" would be like successfully bringing an alcoholic through the Twelve Step recovery process and then releasing him or her to a family of active alcohol abusers or a codependent spouse and children who have themselves become addicted to helping the alcoholic cover up his or her addiction.

Understanding how a person's "system" works is essential to effective treatment. Many therapists today liken a family system to a delicate mobile that hangs from the ceiling, each fragile piece suspended by string. If the slightest pressure or stress is placed on any one of the pieces, the entire mobile reacts. The pieces closest to the pressure might move dramatically, while others will barely quiver, but all are affected to some degree by the pressure.

The Potter family mobile was intricate, and its pieces hung very close to one another. The lightest touch would cause the entire system to shiver noticeably. The family business, real estate, had been founded by Michael's father, and was run by Michael, his brother, and his father. The patriarch's rigid work ethic spilled over from the office to the family compound of homes where business was rehashed at the dinner table, and every night was a pitch-in.

A rigid pecking order existed, with Papa firmly entrenched as the aristocratic head of the family, and the sons ranked by age. Because Michael was the oldest, he felt a particular burden to excel. The mantle of power someday would be passed down to him, and he had to be worthy of the responsibility. In addition to putting in long hours at the office, he served on nearly a dozen boards and committees in an effort to maintain the high profile that his father expected. His volunteer roles provided distraction, but they also took him away from his desk. Early in our counseling relationship he hinted that he was beginning to feel a bit fragmented, and his business was suffering because of his outside commitments. Still, he couldn't say no to a good cause. Everyone expected so much of him, especially Dad.

The Potter women also had a carefully designated place in the family mobile. They were to maintain prominent visibility in the community and were encouraged to connect themselves to good works and admirable causes. Virginia had taken hold of this charge with gusto. She was active in church and social circles and was Michael's always enthusiastic helpmate. Her experience as a college cheerleader was probably more beneficial to her than her degree in elementary education. Potter women didn't work, after all, but they were supposed to smile dutifully and applaud from the sidelines.

In her own way and in her own arena, Virginia was just as driven as Michael. Whether her drive was part of her personality before she was married or whether it developed later is anyone's guess. Many times a healthy, well-balanced woman marries a workaholic and, over a number of years, joins him in his compulsivity. Other times, she retreats and becomes an *enabler* of his drivenness by allowing him to be persistently absent from home, by covering up for his apparent lack of interest in his family, and by assuming all the duties that he rightfully should perform as a father and a spouse. Either way, she suffers from the "system" that doubles as her base of operation.

As we mapped out a recovery plan for Virginia, we had to concede that we were helpless to correct this trouble spot in her life. Pieces of the Potter family mobile were broken beyond repair. Michael's father, the source of much of their tension, had no interest in curbing his workaholism or in relinquishing any of the control he exerted over the family and the family business. In addition to his compulsive work habits, he was a long-term alcoholic and rageaholic and, at age seventy-eight, had little desire to change. Michael was going to have to concede that he would never be able to please his father and that, for his own health and happiness, he had to stop trying.

The Rich-kids Syndrome

A tragic example of fallout from an applauded addiction happened several years ago in a wealthy suburb of Dallas. An epidemic of teen suicides swept through an area that otherwise would be considered a model upper income American community. This was a city without slums, where kids

PlANO, Tex.

played in beautifully manicured parks, attended progressive schools, had their teeth straightened by the best orthodontists, wore designer jeans, and were hovered over by doting moms, dads, and nannies in uniforms.

At a time when child psychology experts and educators around the country were worrying about the future of urban latchkey kids and children at risk, the youngsters of suburban Dallas seemed to be the models of how life ought to be. By all yardsticks of success—SAT scores, per capita income, those going on to college—these kids set the standard. Harvard medical school pediatrician Dr. Ralph Minear calls such young people "kids who have too much," and he outlines their dilemma and the treatment of their dilemma in his book of the same name.

When the rash of Texas suicides hit, everyone was confused. How could it have happened? What went wrong? What was making these much loved, much indulged kids take their own lives? Didn't they know that their parents would do anything to assure their happiness and success?

Yes, the kids knew. And in a desperate way, the confused teenagers were responding by saying "Ouch!"

It took a good deal of scrutiny by social scientists and child psychologists to figure out the problem, but when the diagnosis was in, an applauded addiction was fingered as the cause. This model community was a driven society that was addicted to success. Most of its residents were high achievers who were trying to cross the threshold from middle income to upper income. They pushed hard at work, and they pushed equally hard at home.

Because the area was known as being a very good address for people on an upward career track, the community grew quickly. The high school doubled in size and became known for its incredibly high academic standards and its excellent sports teams. Each student was told at home and at school that getting into the "right" college often depends on the student's placement in the high school graduating class. Competition for a top-ten-percent ranking became intense. The pressure also was on athletes not to be merely good, but to be excellent. Otherwise, they wouldn't make the cut and wouldn't be chosen for the various varsity teams.

Without meaning to do their children harm, the parents in this community applied tremendous pressure on their kids to excel. Far from being deprived, these children were pampered. They were picked up after school and carpooled to tennis lessons, dancing school, appointments with tutors, and swim team workouts at the country club.

Although they couldn't express all of the underlying dynamics at work, these rich kids probably picked up on the undercurrents of insecurity in their homes. Newly prosperous people often are tense about their good fortune, since they aren't completely comfortable with it and fear losing it. They value their prestigious addresses and foreign cars and country club memberships as badges of honor. Such trappings cover old feelings of shame and low self-esteem.

Fortunately for many of our patients, their children cry "Ouch!" much earlier and in much more subtle ways than by committing suicide.

With some encouragement from us, the parents describe their life-style. They often can't hide their pride as they talk about their non-stop schedules, busy social calendars, and aggressive goals for the future. If it weren't for the minor problems with the kids, they would be perfectly content with themselves and with their lives.

These parents are caught in a web of denial almost as complicated as any alcoholic or drug addict. The first step in treating those suffering from the compulsions America applauds is to break through this denial, which is also the first step in counseling patients who are addicted to drugs and/or alcohol.

Breaking Through Denial

Different doctors use different methods to break through patients' denial. Stress expert Dr. Larry Dossey convinces patients like Michael and Virginia Potter of their time sickness by asking them to sit quietly and, without counting or looking at a clock, estimate when a minute has passed. Few patients wait beyond twenty seconds before indicating time's up. Their own internal clocks are wound so tightly that they assume the rest of the world plays according to their hurry-up pace.

Ask yourself: *Is my internal time clock racing in this way?* Push the tiny lever on a stopwatch, then close your eyes and estimate a minute. How much time actually passed? Twenty-five seconds? Thirty, maybe? Or try responding to a few diagnostic questions:

- Am I a perfectionist?
- Am I a compulsive rescuer?
- Am I afraid of other people's anger?

Dr. Joan Borysenko, who specializes in working with stressed women like Virginia Potter, asks her patients these same three questions. If the answers are yes the patient probably is measuring her own value by the number of good works she can achieve, says Dr. Borysenko. Over time, such addictions to perfectionism, helping others, and pleasing everyone can lead to serious time sickness and those addictions we categorized under the heading of relationships in the previous chapter.[1]

Dr. Paul Meier often asks patients to keep a time log for one week. He wants to see a minute-by-minute account of how each day is spent. In reviewing the record he is able to gauge a patient's priorities by how much time the patient assigned to such activities as spouse dating, hobbies, helping children with homework assignments, attending church, and enjoying friends. "Or is this person spending hours and hours on compulsive activities that he considers to be important but others don't?" asks Paul. "Show me a person's life-style, and I'll tell you whether he's driven by the right motives or by his insecurities."

Have you ever kept a time log for one week? If your reaction to the idea is "Who has time for that?" or "I could never jot down all the things I do in one hour, much less in a day," you've already diagnosed yourself as being driven by the addictions America applauds.

Dr. Hemfelt sometimes uses a pie chart method to break through his patients' denial. As he walks Virginia Potter through this exercise, put yourself in Virginia's place and analyze your own schedule.

The Times of Your Life

"Draw a pie chart and divide the pie into pieces according to how you spend your time," Dr. Hemfelt told Virginia during one of her early counseling sessions. "Figure out how many hours you devote to your volunteer work. Then think about your family. How much time do they get? How many hours do you sleep in a typical twenty-four-hour period? And how about one-on-one time with your husband? Mark off slivers for church work, golf, shopping, and your other regular activities."

Two sheets of paper later, she was done. "There," she said with relief. "What's next?"

"Do another chart," replied Dr. Hemfelt.

Groan.

"But this time slice up the pie according to the amount of *energy* you devote to each activity. Think of it this way: If you start each day with a certain amount of energy to spend, how much do you allocate to your meetings out of the home? How about your family? After you've fulfilled all of your activities, how much energy is left to devote to yourself?"

Again, Virginia labored over the piece of paper. When she was done she put her charts side by side and studied them.

"What conclusion can you draw by looking at the graphs?" prodded Dr. Hemfelt.

"That I'm a lousy artist."

"Besides that."

She studied the charts seriously, first one, then the other. "There's a real imbalance," she began. "I'm spending hardly any time or energy on Mike."

"Anything else?"

"There's no time—or energy—left for me. No private time at all."

What had seemed so obvious to us in our first counseling session now became apparent to Virginia. The proof was in the carefully drawn circles with the penciled-in wedges.

"What's this?" Dr. Hemfelt asked, pointing to one particularly large slice on her pie chart that she had labeled "C.C.C." She laughed and shook her head as she looked at it.

"An inside joke," she explained. "We live in Carmel, which is a suburb just north of Indianapolis. Ever since our sons and daughter were little, Mike has called our house 'The Carmel Community Center'—the C.C.C.—get it? We've always wanted our kids and their friends to feel they have a place to congregate. A couple of years ago Mike built a huge family room off of the kitchen. My job is to try to keep the refrigerator stocked with snacks and soft drinks. So it's open house seven nights a week and all day on Saturday and Sunday. One of us is always there to chaperone, of course, and if someone has a problem, we take time to listen."

"What happens when *you* have a problem?" the doctor asked. "Who has time to listen?"

Virginia glanced down at her pie charts and nodded. She understood.

Dr. Hemfelt had put a crack in Virginia's denial. "Now draw a pie chart of how Michael spends his time. In the next session you two can compare your charts."

This joint activity didn't take place as quickly as we had hoped. Although on the surface Michael seemed anxious to participate in therapy, in reality he did everything he could to duck it. Appointments were cancelled; excuses were issued. This told us that Michael was afraid of looking at the underlying causes of his drivenness. Perhaps he didn't want to recall the long-buried pain of growing up with a demanding, workaholic father. He, too, was in denial.

Finally, the conjoint session took place. Michael and Virginia traded pie charts and then laid them on the coffee table side by side. They were as revealing as we had suspected they would be. Michael believed he was spending adequate time with his wife and family, but Virginia didn't agree with him. On the chart that Michael drew for himself, he had a large wedge carved out for family togetherness. But the wedge was reduced to a sliver on the chart that Virginia drew for him.

Of course, it worked both ways. Virginia indicated that only a small portion of her time was spent talking with friends on the phone, whereas Michael had allocated a large chunk to the conversations.

The importance of the chart exercise isn't to determine how time actually is spent, but rather how each person *perceives* the time to be spent. The charts graphically indicate the presence and the volume of each "Ouch!" Virginia was saying to Michael, "Your job is causing you to neglect your family." Michael's message was, "You're spending too much time rescuing your friends and not enough time with me."

The looks on Michael's and Virginia's faces showed that Dr. Hemfelt had widened the crack in their denial. The doctor knew that one more piece of evidence would probably complete the breakthrough. The missing piece could only be supplied by Brian, Chip, and Whitney Potter.

We knew all of the Potters' three children had suffered some kind of fallout from their parents' driven personalities. Each had said "Ouch!" in his or her own way. We had become convinced of this by the verbal sketches the couple had drawn of their sons, Chip and Brian, and their daughter, Whitney, during our weekly visits. The amusing anecdotes they called "The Potter Family Chronicles" had given clues about the hectic life at the Carmel Community Center. Each story filled in a few more details of the key players. Within a few weeks, our notebooks were filled with vivid pictures of Brian, Chip, and Whitney Potter. Our observations were recorded in fragments, but the total scenario was becoming more and more clear.

Chip Potter: On the surface, Chip seems to be the perfect son—perhaps too perfect. He seems to be doing everything according to his father's plan for him: He attended the right college; majored in business administration; earned good grades; joined Dad's fraternity; played soccer; married the "right" girl; and now works in the family's real estate business. At his grandfather's suggestion he is becoming involved in community service. He shows signs of having inherited his parents' driven personality—not surprising, since he's the firstborn son. His nickname is no coincidence: He's a real "chip off of the old block."

Chip still spends a great deal of time at his parents' home. He eats many meals with his parents and shares a workshop with his father in the basement of the family's home. Some minor friction is surfacing in his marriage. His wife doesn't share his enthusiasm for the "one big happy family" life-style and refuses to consider Michael Potter's offer of an acre of land in the Potter compound.

Chip seems to be suffering from two addictions. The first is his obvious perfectionism; the second is his addiction to his family of origin. He can't seem to cut the emotional umbili-cal cord.

Brian Potter: Brian has chosen a passive way of saying, "Ouch!" A senior at Indiana University, he has switched his major four times and will have to attend classes an extra year to finish his degree. He's outgoing, enjoys being with chil-dren, and has confided to his mother that he doesn't want to work for his father, but would like to work for an inner-city youth organization. Neither Brian nor Virginia has dared to suggest the idea to Michael, who has always assumed that Brian would join Chip and him in the real estate business. Brian's history of switching majors in school could be his unconscious way of delaying a decision as to what he will do after graduation.

His impulse to avoid being enmeshed in the family system is healthy; however, his fear of competing with his father and brother is not healthy. He finds himself in a push-pull situation. He feels pushed to join the family business, but he is pulled away from that career possibility by his fear that he can't live up to the family's perfectionistic standards.

Whitney Potter: If Chip Potter has succumbed to his fa-ther's strong personality, and if Brian Potter is still fighting a tug-of-war with Dad, Whitney is in full rebellion. At seven-teen, she's figured out Michael Potter's ideal "daddy's little girl," and has taken off in the opposite direction. Her hair is short and spikey, her wardrobe is all denim, and her plans for the future center on a boyfriend who ignores her most of the time. ("Thank goodness!" is Virginia's comment about the on-the-rocks relationship.)

If Whitney's punk image is her way of striking back at Dad, her compulsive eating habits are aimed straight at Mom. Virginia apologizes for her daughter's appearance when she shows us a family photo album. "It's just a stage," she assures us. "I'm trying to get her interested in tennis or aerobics. That will help get rid of some of that baby fat."

Countless "carrots" have been dangled as incentives for her to lose weight, but Whitney isn't tempted. The bigger she grows, the wilder are her clothes. The snapshots document her steady spin out of control. She seems to be trying to grab her parents' attention by looking and acting as unattractive as she can. But even when she is at her most outlandish, she has to wait her turn. There's a lot of competition for Mom's and Dad's eyes and ears at the C.C.C.

As we became more familiar with the Potters and their children, we concluded that each member of the family had suffered a variety of hurts over the years and had cried, "Ouch!" in different ways. But we also concluded that the couple had come for help early, before any major tragedy had occurred. Chip's marriage was slightly shaky, but there had been no threats of separation or hints of infidelity. Brian was waffling this way and that way on what to do with his life, but he was still in school and had made no bad decisions yet. And Whitney, possibly the most at risk, had limited her rebelliousness to ludicrous, but superficial, "ouches."

With a lot of commitment from Michael and Virginia, their family situation could be remedied. But the Potter children would have to help.

"When you go home to Indianapolis, ask Chip, Brian, and Whitney to draw pie charts of how they think you divide your time," Dr. Hemfelt suggested to Michael and Virginia. "See how their charts compare with the ones you've drawn for yourselves."

Virginia nodded her head in agreement, but Michael seemed disturbed by our suggestion. The color rose in his face. Until this point he always had been the quieter of the two, usually content to let his more talkative wife answer for the both of them. But now his eyes narrowed, and he put up an index finger to silence Virginia, who was about to speak. It was his turn.

"Wait a minute, Doctor," he began defensively. "Are you saying that our kids are going to tell us that we've neglected them in some way over the years? Are you trying to tell me that these charts the kids are supposed to draw are going to show us that we haven't spent enough time with them? If that's what you're driving at, you're dead wrong. My job may be strenuous, and I may put in too many hours at the office, but I've always been there when the kids needed me. And when I'm not there, Ginny is."

Michael stood up and walked behind the chair in which his wife was sitting. In an unusual display of gentleness, he protectively placed his hands on her shoulders. "She's chosen not to work out of the home just so she could devote all of her time to being a good mother." He stroked her arms lovingly. "Ginny comes as close to being a perfect mother as you can get, Doctor. Ask anybody who knows her. She's not only counseled our own three kids through some rocky times, but she's also been willing to take on the problems of half the teenagers in our neighborhood. As if that weren't enough, last year she volunteered to lead the church youth group!"

Michael returned to his chair, calmer now, although he still shook his head to indicate that he didn't buy into our suggestion. "If Chip, Brian, and Whitney don't realize what their mother has done for them, well, it's their problem, not Ginny's."

His outburst wasn't all that unusual. He was having difficulty breaking through denial because he hadn't experienced any serious losses yet. There had been no divorce, suicide, or bankruptcy. He even seemed unwilling to admit that several potential crises were just around the corner. His company was struggling with financial problems; Chip's marriage wasn't on firm ground; and he was experiencing an unhealthy interest in pornography.

The earlier we identify an applauded addiction, the louder the cries of denial from the person who suffers the addiction. Why? Because at that point, the fallout hasn't been serious enough to frighten the patient into believing he or she *has* a problem. The patient may not hear the early "ouches" over the din of the compliments he or she receives for his or her behavior. These persons may not sense the hurt they are causing themselves and others because they have been anesthetized by all the warm fuzzies and strokes of approval they have gotten.

If the rash of teenage suicides in the suburban Dallas tragedy had been predicted, the prediction would have met with a chorus of denials. All those cheers and accolades drowned out any early "ouches," and the scholarship awards and athletic trophies distracted the parents from seeing the warnings and symptoms that should have alerted them that something was wrong.

"Think of the dashboard on your car," we sometimes say to patients. "Most cars are equipped with a warning system that alerts the driver when something is malfunctioning. A red light blinks on and off, or a message flashes on the panel and tells you to 'service engine soon.' How quickly you react depends on your personality. Some people panic at the first warning message and turn into the next service station. Others take a wait-and-see attitude. As long as the car seems to be operating all right, the blinking red light is disregarded as nothing more than a minor irritation."

People have warning systems, too. Psychiatrists and psychologists call them primary indicators and secondary indicators.

Primary Indicators

A primary indicator is rare, since it involves a self-diagnosis by an addict. In such a case, a person simply looks long and hard at himself or herself and says, *I've lost my balance. My priorities are out of sync. I need to overcome this destructive pattern of mine before it hurts someone.* The per-

son recognizes in himself or herself the three indicative signs
of addiction:

- Craving
- Withdrawal
- Tolerance

Craving Obsessive-compulsive persons admit that they
have a craving for their *addictive agent*, whether that agent
happens to be work, food, approval from others, exercise,
love, or any of the many applauded addictions. Even when
they aren't involved in their addictive activities, they think
about it to the point of being obsessed with it. For instance, if
they are fitness fanatics, they may be anticipating and planning the next workout. They amuse themselves by setting
goals and laying strategies for accomplishing them. If they
are addicted to pleasing other people, they may be devising
ways to earn recognition or to attract the attention of the
boss or to court the favor of people with clout.

Withdrawal When driven persons deny themselves their
addictive agent (sometimes just to prove to themselves that
they don't *really* need it) they suffer genuine symptoms of
withdrawal. They may become nervous, out of sorts, or depressed. The jogger who decides not to run on Tuesdays and
Thursdays should feel rested on those two days, but instead
feels incomplete and guilty. The workaholic who agrees to
take a two-week vacation spends most of the time sitting on
the beach making lists of things to do as soon as he or she
gets back to the office.

Tolerance As times goes by, these persons require more
and more of their addictive agent in order to feel satisfied. As
they increase the amount of the agent, they note that the
time between "fixes" grows shorter and shorter. They need
more, and they need it more often. Runners push themselves
to run faster, farther, and longer. Businesspersons who already earn more money than they need aren't happy unless

they are in the process of cutting several deals simultaneously.

Take a moment now to break through your own denial.

Are You Addicted to the Compulsions America Applauds?

When does a habit become a compulsion, and at what point does it evolve into an addiction? Focus on the activity that you fear is starting to dominate your life. It may be jogging, working, collecting, dieting, volunteering, counseling, or any of the other applauded activities discussed in Chapter 2. Keeping your activity in mind, check the statements below that apply to you.

1. ✓ *"I experience nervousness or other signs of withdrawal whenever I don't indulge in this activity."*

2. ✓ *"I have deliberately abstained, cut back from this activity just to prove that I can do it."* — *I can't!*

3. ____ *"After I've abstained and felt assured that I can quit, I go back to the activity."*

4. ____ *"I have developed a level of tolerance for this activity, and now I must do more of it to feel satisfied."*

5. ✓ *"I have a false sense of power or <u>comfort</u> when I'm engaged in this activity."*

6. ____ *"This activity allows me to retreat from the real world and all of its emotional entanglements."*

7. ✓ *"I think about the activity even when I'm not practicing it."*

8. ____ *"Well-meaning friends are starting to suggest that I should take it easy."*

9. ✓ *"The activity is harming me because it's taking up too much of my time, thought, and energy."*

79

10. ✓ *"People around me are suffering some unfortunate consequences because of this activity."*

11.____ *"I find myself promising myself and my family that as soon as this project is finished, I'll slow down, but I never do. Another project is always right behind it."*

Rate yourself. A check beside even three or four of these statements means that you are succumbing to the addictions America applauds.

Secondary Indicators

Self-diagnosis by an addict is unlikely if the person isn't reading a book like this one. Denial gets in the way. Much more common than primary indicators are secondary indicators that serve much like those red warning lights on a car's dashboard. We saw a variety of secondary indicators in Michael and Virginia Potter's family. They included Virginia's physical problems, son Chip's driving need to please his father, young Brian's inability to take charge of his life, and Whitney's rebellious attitude and out-of-control eating habits. Each was a symptom, or a warning light, that indicated something was wrong, that help was needed, and that something had to be fixed.

We witnessed similar indicators in Luci and Richard Stewart's family. The Stewarts' grandson, Robbie, was hospitalized for a spastic colon before he was even a month old; their son Bud's marriage was foundering as he fought to hold onto a home that was mortgaged to the hilt. And the grandparents were no better off. Luci Stewart was fighting insecurities within her marriage; and Richard was driven to spend more and more time on the road.

How quickly a person responds to a secondary indicator seems to depend on the individual. Some act immediately, much like the driver who pulls into a service station at the first blink of the red warning light. Others choose the wait-and-see strategy. They vow to keep their eyes on the red lights, but as long as the system doesn't break down entirely, they're going to continue full speed ahead. "Why fix what isn't broken?" is their motto.

Michael and Virginia Potter sought help fairly soon after they became aware of the secondary indicators; yet, there was denial. They knew something was wrong because they had correctly read the warning signs, but at first they couldn't accept the fact that certain parts of their lives were out of control and that their own behavior was responsible for much of their out-of-control state. They both suffered from time sickness, the hurry-up epidemic of having too much to do and not enough time to do it. The trouble was that they were proud of their breathless pace, their non-stop schedules, and all the chaos connected to their open-door style of living.

Not many counseling sessions were necessary before we had identified several addictions that needed to be treated. Michael's workaholism was one. Virginia's perfectionism was another. Their driving need to rescue everyone around them was a major problem that had to be resolved immediately if they were to restore balance in their lives. In our separate meetings with Virginia we had brought to the surface two very negative, secret addictions—one was Virginia's emotional love affair with an older man, and the second was Michael's growing fascination with pornography. (We'll explain more about these compulsions later when we guide the Potters around the addiction cycle and show how it's possible to halt the cycle at several points along the way.)

Asking the Potter children to graphically illustrate on pie charts how their mom and dad spent their hours was one way of breaking through this denial. We knew it would force Michael and Virginia to see themselves through the eyes of the people they love most. And that is exactly what happened.

Whitney, in particular, was hard on her parents. She indicated that most of Michael's week was spent at the office, and she divided all of Virginia's waking hours into tiny slivers of unimportant "busyness" such as reorganizing the hall closet for the third time this season. It was a sobering, revealing picture. Chip's and Brian's weren't very much better. The children's "ouches" came through loud and clear.

If the charts hadn't broken through the senior Potters' denial, we might have used a final technique. It's called intervention.

Intervention

A well-planned intervention involves persons' close to the addict arming themselves with concrete evidence of the addiction and, under the careful direction of a trained therapist, confronting the addict with the facts. Unannounced, the family or friends form a circle of truth around the addict. They lock him or her in, but they also serve as a safety net. No matter which way the addict turns, he or she can't wriggle out with excuses or denial. The truth bombards the addict with specific names, dates, and places where his or her addiction has caused pain. Any argument the addict offers is soundly beaten down with unshakeable documentation. When he or she finally submits to the circle of pressure and admits to the addiction, the circle becomes a support system, which shores the addict up and provides him or her with treatment options.

An example of a successful intervention occurred recently in Dr. Hemfelt's office. The patient was a woman who had suffered serious fallout from her husband's addictions to work, busyness, and travel. Whenever tension mounted at home, Roger, an insurance company executive who could set his own work and travel agendas, would conveniently schedule a business trip. Depending on the size of the crisis on the homefront, the job-related obligation might take him to London for a week, or it might involve an overnight shuttle hop to Detroit from his home in Chicago.

"Sorry, but it's an emergency," he'd say, calling his wife from the airport. Sometimes, if he anticipated an argument, he'd ask his secretary to call his family *after* his departure.

"He's gone," the secretary would tell Linda, our patient.

The most painful incident took place after Linda had undergone a radical mastectomy and was scheduled to have her first chemotherapy treatment. Her doctor had warned her of the possible discomfort attached to the procedure and had recommended that she have someone drive her to the hospital, stay by her side throughout the treatment, and see that she returned home safely.

"Please go with me," she begged her husband. He agreed, but at the last minute bowed out, claiming a crisis in the Detroit office.

She endured the ordeal alone.

Although Linda's pain was the greatest, she wasn't the only one who experienced the fallout from her husband's addiction to work and his need to escape. His reputation for tardiness and his nickname of "No Show" made him infamous. We knew firsthand about his on-again-off-again attendance record. At his wife's urging, Roger visited Dr. Hemfelt's office a few times to talk about his habit of using his job to duck personal responsibilities. The sessions made him uncomfortable, and he often excused himself early because of an "appointment back at the office." At least twice he canceled his appointments altogether, claiming unexpected business trips.

Roger was what we call an "emotional stuffer." On the surface he appeared to be placid and cool—a regular John Wayne. In reality, he struggled to keep his emotions in check; he stuffed them down inside of himself. His inability to show anger, tenderness, sadness, remorse, or happiness caused pain not only to his family, but to himself as well. His body was beginning to cry "Ouch!" in the form of acute colitis. With Linda's approval we planned an intervention.

Our purpose was to confront Roger with undeniable proof that his preoccupation with his job and his inability to "connect" with the people around him were causing harm to his family. With Dr. Hemfelt serving as the orchestrator, Linda, the couple's daughter, Melanie, and two close friends gathered in our office one afternoon. Members of the group were asked to recall specific incidents when Roger's work or travel habits had been the source of pain. Each person rehearsed his or her memory out loud, with Dr. Hemfelt timing the recollections and arranging them in an order that would assure maximum impact. At the appointed time, Roger arrived, totally unprepared for the encounter. One by one, the members of the group shared their pain. Linda, for instance, relived the trip to the hospital for her first chemotherapy treatment.

"I needed you, but you weren't there for me," she said through her tears.

There is nothing fair or equitable about an intervention. We purposely include several friends and family members as a way of outnumbering and overpowering the person who is the subject of the intervention. We play on that person's sense of guilt by emphasizing how his or her loved ones have been victimized by his or her addictions. The person is pelted by example after example of the pain that his or her behavior has caused. In a military setting an intervention might be called an ambush. The purpose of the intervention is not to blame, shame, punish, or condemn the addict. Rather, the purpose is to use confrontation and guilt as constructive tools to break through the thick barriers that surround most addictions, especially applauded ones.

Like all sneak attacks, interventions are risky. The timing is important, as is the element of surprise. The first reaction of the subject of the intervention is shock, and then the person is swept up in the bombarding messages that are directed at him or her, the target. The entire event resembles Ralph Edwards's old television show, *This Is Your Life.* The "guest of honor" had thought he or she was routinely keeping a doctor's appointment, but suddenly he or she opens a door and is greeted by a sea of faces. Then, one by one, his or her loved ones start taking turns sharing long-buried memories.

Even ambushes have rules. The purpose of an intervention is not to burden its target with intense shame. If that were to happen, the person might withdraw even deeper into the addiction in an effort to numb the pain. Rather, the purpose is to make the addict aware of the trauma his or her compulsion is causing. The motivation is to break through the wall of denial.

Also, lectures and sermons have no place in an intervention. Participants are not trying to extract a promise from the target that he or she will give up the addiction immediately. The truth is, the addict can't live up to such a promise. The goal is more simple: The addict agrees to seek treatment. In Roger's case, he agreed to enter the hospital for inpatient therapy, and he agreed that after he was released from the program he would continue with outpatient counseling. Our intervention had accomplished its mission. We had broken through the wall of denial.

The Consequences of Continued Denial

Sometimes the techniques that we've described aren't successful, and valuable time is lost because of long periods of denial. One of the most complex cases we've handled in the past two years involved a young Houston couple, the Jansens, and their four-year-old adopted daughter, Kim.

Paula Jansen first came to us for help in curbing her compulsive spending habit. Her shopping binges had nearly led her husband into bankruptcy twice, and the family attorney and financial advisor had suggested that her sprees were cyclical and seemed to be more like an addiction than a normal activity.

Unfortunately, we had only limited success in treating Paula's shopaholism because she often cancelled appointments and would miss her group therapy sessions for long stretches at a time. Whenever she found her way back to us she was like a child with guilt written all over her face. She had suffered another setback, she'd tell us, and it had caused all sorts of problems at home. Her husband, Hank, became understandably angry after such sprees, and he punished her by withdrawing into his work. If she complained about his absence from home, he'd retort that he had to work long hours just to service her debt.

The red warning light flashed on one day at the Jansen home when Paula and Hank received a note from Kim's nursery school teacher. The teacher explained that no one at school was sure whether Kim was simply misbehaving, had some sort of learning disability, or was suffering from what the school psychologist called an "oppositional disorder." Whatever the reason, Kim had a problem and needed help.

"What does that mean, Dr. Minirth? What on earth is an 'oppositional disorder'?" Paula asked during one of our sporadic sessions.

"It's a euphemism for unworkable behavior," Dr. Minirth explained. "For instance, if a teacher were to say to her class, 'Take out your crayons and open the box,' the child would close his or her box of crayons and put it away. The child does the opposite of what he or she is told to do."

Having counseled Paula for several months for her compulsive spending habit, we were of the opinion that little Kim had no learning disability at all, and she certainly wasn't suffering from a true classic oppositional disorder. Instead, she was merely saying, "Ouch!" And Kim was saying the "no" that Mother was unable to say to her own spending and that Dad was unable to say to Mom. Mother could not say no to her spending compulsion. Dad's workaholism enabled the spending. Dad was emotionally incapable of saying "No" to Mom through the imposition of a budget. Kim was carrying the boundary-setting responsibility for both Mom and Dad by saying "No" to all authority figures and to the world at large.

The stress at home was taking its toll on Kim. The tension between her parents was obvious, and Kim was reacting as many children do, by misbehaving at school. In her own childish way, she was saying that something was wrong and that she needed help in coping with it. She couldn't do it alone.

The logical solution would have been for Paula and Hank to commit to breaking their shopping and working addictions, and then to concentrate on repairing their husband-and-wife relationship. If they could accomplish those goals, Kim's problem would solve itself.

But denial set in instead. True to her compulsive personality and her addiction to spending money, Paula overreacted and vowed to hire a variety of experts for Kim. In addition to coming to our clinic for family therapy, she set up a regular schedule of appointments with a psychologist whose specialty is to coach parents of problem children. Then she engaged a play therapist to work directly with Kim. This expert observed Kim's behavior in game situations—she watched how Kim competed, how she interacted with playmates, and how she related to dolls and other toys. Finally, Paula arranged for Kim to see a speech therapist in case the little girl had a hearing impairment.

The result of all this flurry of activity was a compounding of the original problem. By denying the obvious, Paula made the situation so much worse. She ran up a tremendous debt as she hurried from one doctor's office to another. This meant that Hank had to work harder than ever to pay for the additional services. The new financial obligations touched off more tension at home, which caused Kim to react to the tension by stepping up her disruptive behavior. Of course, the worse her behavior became, the more determined Paula was to find and to buy the right expert to treat it. And so the cycle continued to turn, around and around and around. The cause of it all was denial.

Fortunately through the tools of recovery and therapy, many of our clients see through their denial, as the Potters did. Before they are able to look toward full recovery, however, they had to take a second step: They had to abstain from and balance their addictive activities.

Chapter Four

Riding a Bike Without a Chain

We could not counsel the Potters effectively unless they abstained from some of their compulsions. Dr. Hemfelt made that very clear to them at a conjoint counseling session.

"How do we begin, Doctor?" asked Virginia.

"By fixing a broken door," Dr. Hemfelt answered.

He explained that before they could understand how the addiction cycle works, how they had become slaves to their applauded addictions, and how they could break out of the cycle, they had to rid their lives of their many distractions. This was necessary because one of the major functions of an addiction is to distract the addict from the true source of pain. The Carmel Community Center, a major distraction to the Potters, had to be shut down for internal repairs.

"For too long, you've operated with a broken front door," we said. "People have burst in on you unannounced and uninvited at all hours of the day and night. Now it's time to take control of who comes through that door. Of course, we're talking about much more than an actual door. We're talking about the need for barriers and boundaries in your lives that will allow you privacy and tranquility."

Virginia looked as if she were going to argue our point, but her husband reached over and covered one of her hands with his and gave it a reassuring squeeze. She shrugged her shoulders and finally nodded in agreement.

With a lot of willpower and determination, Virginia and Michael Potter could establish boundaries in three other major areas. Michael could force himself to put in a forty-hour work week—and not a minute more. Virginia could stop being everyone's sounding board, adviser, and cheerleader. They could also try to work around Michael's father and to set boundaries on the areas where the patriarch would be allowed to wield his power. Everything else would be off limits.

Kicking the Habit

Cold turkey. Taking the cure. Coming clean. Staying sober.

It's impossible to live in the 1990s and not understand the language of addiction. Unfortunately, we often concentrate on two parts of addiction and disregard the third, and perhaps most important. Sure, we can understand the pain of an active addiction, and yes, we can imagine the blessed relief that comes with abstinence. But that's as far as we go. We believe that going cold turkey is the major hurdle, and once that has been accomplished, all of the problems attached to the addiction disappear. The family "mobile" that was so violently shaken by one family member's dependency hangs serene once again. The chorus of "ouches"—some of them whimpered, some of them shouted—is silenced at last. The system is safe, and the ending is strictly the happily-ever-after variety.

The truth is, the first year after an addiction has been surrendered usually is the hardest for the family of the former addict. Why? Because the addiction is gone, but the problems that caused the addict to reach for the addictive agent are still there. Not only are the problems present, but also they're sharper, louder, and bigger than before because they aren't muffled or clouded or hidden by the addictive agent.

Life After Abstinence

Kicking an addiction is not the same as recovering from it. The word abstinence *isn't interchangeable with the word* recovery. The reason is simple: By merely abstaining, the addict hasn't gotten down to the deep fears, angers, and insecurities that motivated the dependency.

No one knows this better than Barbara Ryan, a thirty-year-old sales executive, currently on an extended leave of absence from her job because of a depression so intense that her husband was afraid she might commit suicide. In the course of our counseling with Barbara, she described vivid memories from her childhood both before and after her alcoholic father stopped drinking. Both recollections were equally painful.

"My dad is a dry drunk," explained this burned-out yuppie. "He's been sober for almost twelve years and miserable for the same amount of time. He knows he can't drink because alcoholism is a disease for life—it never goes away. What he hasn't figured out is that the problems that led to his drinking *could* go away if only he would confront them. But he refuses. He won't get involved in any kind of recovery program, such as Alcoholics Anonymous. He just concentrates on staying sober. And staying miserable."

Author and counselor Earnie Larsen divides recovery into Stage I and Stage II. He describes Stage I as breaking the addiction. This is an enormous step, but it's only the first step. Stage II is rebuilding the life that was saved in Stage I. The former addict successfully deals with his or her addiction in Stage I, then in Stage II successfully deals with the problems that caused him or her to take up the compulsion in the first place. That's true recovery.[1]

The experience of Barbara Ryan and others who have lived with "dry drunks" is exactly why we told the Potters, "There is much more to this process than just rolling up the welcome mat at the Carmel Community Center and passing the word around town that the Potters are going to spend less time entertaining the world and more time getting reacquainted with one another."

That sounds good. It's a step in the right direction, but it's only the second step of Stage I (the first was breaking through their denial). Unless Michael figures out what drives him to *want* to work long hours, and unless Virginia discovers why she so desperately *needs* to be needed, the Potters' "recovery" will be superficial. Like riders on a chainless bike, they will be going through the motions but getting nowhere in their quest for happiness and inner peace. They will give the appearance of seizing control of their lives as they cut the distractions and spend more time together, but their efforts will only be for show. Staying home and playing Superspouse isn't going to feed Michael's insatiable ego. And canceling Virginia's call-waiting service and curbing her club schedule will only give her extra hours of solitude to question her self-worth. Actually, the Potters may experience *more* pain after they've halted some of their compulsions.

Remember Paula Jansen, the compulsive spender introduced in Chapter 3? Lavishing money on herself had been Paula's way of numbing reality since she was a little girl. Although she had grown up in a wealthy, politically prominent family, she had received very little attention from her busy, always-on-the-road parents. Gifts often were substitutes for quality time with Mom and Dad, and shopping sprees were used to make up for cancelled family outings and missed birthday celebrations. Paula recalled for us one particularly painful experience in college when, at the last minute, her father ducked out of Dad's Weekend festivities at her sorority. To make amends for his absence he sent his charge card and a note authorizing her to treat her roommates and their fathers to dinner. Such incidents were so common in her family that Paula came to see money as an anesthesia for emotional pain. It was the bandage that covered the hurt for a little while.

Years later, whenever Paula felt neglected, unloved, or insecure, she reached for a bandage in the form of her checkbook or charge card. Got a problem? Throw money at it. Unhappy? Go buy something pretty. Need a lift? Splurge, pamper yourself, prove to yourself that, of course, you *are* the best because you *have* the best . . . of everything.

Convincing Paula not to spend money compulsively would have been a major victory, but it would have been only a Stage I victory. Helping her to confront her feelings of insecurity and unhappiness would have been more than a victory; it would have been a Stage II recovery.

Full recovery encompasses both stages and must be achieved progressively. An addict must first abstain from the compulsion and, second, must learn to deal with the underlying psychological issues causing the compulsion. Reversing the order—understanding the issues first and then halting the compulsion—seldom is successful. As long as a person is practicing an addiction, the brain is too preoccupied to grasp the problems that led to the addiction.

The Risk of Being Stalled at Stage I

A former addict who is stalled at Stage I is like a person riding a bicycle without a chain. From a distance the person looks as if he or she is performing very well—going through all the motions, looking the part of a fully functional member of the human race. In reality, these persons aren't going anywhere. They aren't making any progress. They are wearing themselves out doing what they are supposed to do. They are so busy taking the cure, coming clean, or going cold turkey that they have little energy left to nurture themselves and to build lasting relationships with their loved ones and with God. They have all of the work and the pain of life's journey but none of the rewards.

One of the risks of being stalled at Stage I is the possibility of swapping one addiction for another. If the underlying problems aren't solved, the person might successfully give up the addiction, but not the need for an addiction. Take away the painkiller, let the person feel his or her pain, and before long the former addict will reach for a different pain-killer, merely trading one addiction for another.

Someone whose addiction-hopping made headlines in recent years is Kitty Dukakis, wife of former presidential hopeful and Massachusetts governor Michael Dukakis. In 1987 Kitty publicly revealed a longtime dependence on diet amphetamines. But the addiction cycle had been stopped, she assured the media. She had recovered. Then, in 1989, she declared that she was an alcoholic, and she agreed to enter a treatment program. When she was released several weeks later, she assured everyone that the cycle was broken. Once again, she had recovered.

Although drug and alcohol dependency are negative addictions, Mrs. Dukakis also showed signs of applauded addictions during the times when she had "recovered" from the negative addictions. Her perfectionism and her drive were well known. Her energy was legendary. She was a whirlwind of activity and enjoyed being "on." As soon as she was released from the alcoholism treatment facility she began a rigorous campaign against substance abuse. She criss-crossed the country speaking out against addiction. Simultaneously, she worked to meet the demanding deadlines of her soon-to-be-published memoirs. There was little time to work through the problems that caused the multiple addictions.

Several months after being treated for alcoholism, she was rushed, semiconscious, to a Boston hospital. Her stomach was pumped to rid her system of the rubbing alcohol that she had swallowed. The alcohol, plus the antidepressants she had been taking, proved to be a nearly deadly mix.

The Barreling Wheel of Addiction

Like a wheel set in motion on a downward decline, the cycle of addiction has forward momentum. Its natural tendency is to keep moving until a greater power exerts enough strength to stop the momentum. To understand how the cycle turns, let's take a quick trip around the wheel, noting each of its nine stopovers. Then in part two of this book, we'll spend time fully exploring the stops.

Initially, the cycle is kicked into gear by some event or situation in the addict's past (Point 1). This might be the trauma of growing up in an alcoholic family where children somehow blame themselves for Dad's unhappiness and excessive drinking. Or it could be the horror a daughter experiences when she is sexually abused by a family member and feels she is somehow responsible for the male relative's violating her sexual boundaries. Or it might involve a workaholic's child who is convinced that Mom or Dad wouldn't invest so much time in a job if only the child were more significant.

Such an event or situation in a person's past could have been so traumatic that it touched off a flurry of negative internal messages that caused the person to question his or her self-worth. "What's wrong with me? What terrible thing have I done to deserve this?" (Point 2). Since there is no statute of limitations on feelings, these negative internal messages play on and on over the years. Even though the person might know intellectually that he or she wasn't responsible for Dad's drinking or for Mom's preoccupation with her job, the feelings remain entrenched.

Shame builds as the person becomes convinced that he or she is responsible in some way for the traumatic situation (Point 3). With the growing shame comes sinking self-esteem, and this causes the cycle's forward momentum to gain in intensity (Point 4). Emotional pain is the offshoot of low self-esteem (Point 5), and the person reaches for a painkiller (an addictive agent) to dull the pain, which acts as anesthesia (Point 6). In cases of negative addictions, this painkiller might be alcohol, drugs, sex, or gambling. In cases of applauded addictions, the addictive agent might be work, voluntarism, rescuing others, cleaning, serving, or being the perfect mom, dad, student, or employee.

The person uses the anesthesia to provide relief from all of the emotional hurt. The relief doesn't last long, but for a while, the senses are numbed, attention is diverted, and—in instances of approved addictions—the applause is reassuring.

Eventually fallout occurs (Point 7). After years of being pushed to the limit, the addict's body cries "Ouch!" by developing symptoms of physical or emotional illness. (Remember Virginia Potter?) Children shout "ouch!" by becoming rebellious or withdrawn. (Remember Whitney Potter?) Spouses say "Ouch!" by asking for divorces or by becoming entangled in extramarital affairs or by suffering from illness or by developing their own addictions.

At this point of the addiction cycle the addict realizes that the dependency has caused him to violate the value system (Point 8) that she or he has championed. Perhaps a businessperson has always considered himself to be a good Christian, and now realizes that quest for professional achievement has distracted him from God and has sapped the energy that he should have devoted to strengthening faith and even lead him into ethically questionable business practices. Perhaps a mother's need for accolades has caused her to spend precious time in high-visibility community work while her family was left to shift for itself. Much like the woman who sees the truth in the pie chart that her child has drawn for her, she now recognizes that she has turned her back on what should have been her priorities.

With this violation of values come staggering feelings of guilt (Point 9). This adds to the expanding shame base, and the addiction cycle goes around again. The self-esteem dips even lower, the emotional pain escalates even higher, and more of the addictive agent is needed to dull the pain. Work distracts the addict from thoughts that hurt. Applause drowns out the "ouches" that seem to come from every direction. And so it goes, on and on and on.

If this series of stops around the addiction cycle sounds uncomfortably familiar, don't despair. The proven recovery plan that we will unfold in Part Two will combat each devastating point of the cycle. However, if you aren't convinced that the addiction cycle fits into your life, remember that the reaction of most people is either to deny or to minimize the existence of the cycle. Only after they've delved into their pasts do they understand how precisely on target it is.

The Addiction Drivers

We've talked about the addiction cycle's being like a wheel traveling downhill. The momentum is in place, and until someone slams on the brakes, the wheel keeps turning around and around. Now let's put the same wheel on a flat surface. Momentum propels it forward for a while, but it gradually runs out of power, slows, and stops.

Once the addict kicks the habit, the addiction cycle might also stop if it weren't for several built-in drivers that provide plenty of energy to push it forward. Picture a child who wishes to push a wheel on a flat surface. The child uses a big stick to keep the wheel moving. Each addiction driver is like that stick, pushing the addiction faster and faster. Most persons' addictions are powered by multiple drivers, and that is why stopping the addiction momentum is monumentally more challenging than merely "breaking a bad habit."

Even if a former addict gives up the addiction (a Stage I victory), the drivers remain in place and can propel the cycle onward. The addict, struggling to deny the painkiller, still hears negative messages in his or her head ("What's wrong with me?" "What did I do to deserve this?"), still suffers from shame, still has low self-esteem, and still feels emotional pain. The fact that the addict has stopped using an addictive agent doesn't mean that the addict has stopped being buffeted around the cycle. With or without the original painkiller, the cycle churns, fed by the addiction drivers. It's little wonder that Barbara Ryan described her father's "dry drunk" status as twelve years of miserable sobriety.

Addictions are chronic; they don't go away unless we deal with the deeper causes and the drivers. They also are progressive; over time they pick up speed and momentum. They only get worse.

At the Minirth-Meier Clinics we've identified several drivers that keep the addiction cycle turning. In a sense, these drivers arise as a desperate effort to satisfy healthy, God-given human needs. However, these drivers tend to be *coun-*

terfeit means of meeting those needs. Here's how we explain it to our patients: We suggest that they think of a person, dying of thirst, who reaches for relief by drinking salt water. The thirst is a legitimate need, and the effort to quench the thirst is a legitimate reaction. But the salt water is a counterfeit means of satisfying the need.

Addiction drivers are like salt water. They are illegitimate means of satisfying our very real needs. We become addicted to the services they perform, and that's the reason we keep reaching for our addictive agent. An addict who truly understands addiction and who has worked through the cycle might explain the benefits he or she receives from the addiction in the following ways.

Driver #1: "My addiction seems to justify my right to exist. It gives my life meaning."

Virginia Potter needed the busyness of the ringing phone, the requests to serve on committees, and the obligations to provide counsel and advice to friends and students because all of these demands on her time and talents assured her of her worth. Every request fed her sense of value.

When a driven person is high on accomplishment, that person feels happy and competent. But if you talk with this person during the low part of the cycle, when the person is depressed or burned out, she or he will make such statements as, "I don't deserve to be alive. Why am I even here? What good am I to anyone? If I died tomorrow, it would be no loss to the world."

Driver #2: "My applauded addiction seems to anesthetize my emotional pain and serve as a form of hypnosis."

Have you ever gotten "lost" in a good book? Are you a music fan who can pop in a compact disc, close your eyes, and shut out the rest of the world for a few restful minutes? There's nothing wrong with being lulled into a sort of dreamland as a respite from the breathless pace of the 1990s.

Unless, of course, you become addicted to your fantasy world and begin to prefer it to the real thing.

The attorney who was addicted to romance novels used her addiction to pull her into a near-hypnotic state. The books didn't rejuvenate her; instead, they anesthetized her. When she slipped between the pages of a formula romance she built a wall around herself, and no one could penetrate the barrier. The more time she devoted to her books, the more time she wanted to spend with them.

Michael Potter used the pace of his job to hypnotize himself and put a wall around him so he didn't have to deal with the problems of his children. Work also became a way he could avoid connecting with his spouse.

Driver #3: "By practicing my applauded addiction I feel as if I am punishing myself and, at the same time, making installment payments on my guilt."

If you've ever read the classic *The Divine Comedy* by Dante, you remember purgatory, his imagined way station between hell and paradise where sinners were detained to work off the sins that they had committed in their lives. In repetitive fashion the sinners did penance so they could earn their way out of their shame and be allowed to pass into heaven. Their punishments were linked with their sins. For instance, greedy souls were shackled in such a way that their hands were outstretched and motionless; souls that were guilty of envy were forced to wallow on the ground with their eyes sewn shut with wire; and gluttons were positioned under trees with their hands raised up to the delicious fruit that was out of reach.

People who carry around a great deal of guilt and shame often put themselves into a voluntary state of purgatory. They sentence themselves to performing certain activities over and over again to make up for what they believe to be their sins. Unlike a revolving charge account where, after so many installments, the debt is paid off, the "sinner" in this case never settles the account.

Counselor and author John Bradshaw is an excellent example of a man who spent too much time in a self-imposed purgatory. Bradshaw speaks and writes candidly about his alcoholic father and grandfather and about his personal role as his family's redeemer. As devout Roman Catholics, the Bradshaws believed that the highest achievement a young man could attain would be to become a priest. With this in mind, young John studied for the priesthood. Such an honorable profession not only would delight his mother and grandmother, but also would atone for the "sins" of his father and grandfather.

Young Bradshaw dutifully took his vows of poverty and chastity and earned three master's degrees while living a life of denial. By trying to measure up to the perfectionistic standards of a priest, he also tried to square his family's debt. He personally assumed the huge Bradshaw burden of shame. He drove himself to excel in the classroom and in his church work as a way of making up for his father's and his grandfather's alcoholism. As he put more and more pressure on himself, his own need for alcohol escalated. He was the model student until he came home for vacations; then he'd shed the demands of religious life and break all the rules of priestly conduct. After a binge, his shame base would expand, and he'd sentence himself back to purgatory to do more penance for his sins.

"Shame begets shame," he says. "The more I drank to relieve my shame-based loneliness and hurt, the more I felt ashamed." Only after working through his deep, shame-based problems was Bradshaw able to stop making installment payments and fashion for himself a full Stage II recovery.

Michael Potter is another good example of someone who made a career of paying off the shame debt accumulated by his father's volatile personality, alcoholism, and work addiction. Michael tried to offset his father's shortcomings by being all things to all people. He served on the local school board, was involved in a number of service clubs, and was considered one of the leaders of the church he and Virginia attended. His wall of fame in his office was covered with plaques, certificates, and other "hardware" that recognized his contributions to improving the quality of life in his community and state.

If Michael carried the burden of old shame for his father's rageaholism and alcoholism, he added new shame because of his dalliance with pornography. He knew the explicit sex literature was wrong; yet, he was strongly attracted to it. The emotional tug between right and wrong—what he knew he *should* do and what he knew he *wanted* to do—caused him real inner turmoil. Whenever he slipped into his growing addiction to the questionable material he offset it by simultaneously plunging into more public service.

His ongoing need to pay off his expanding shame debt was beginning to cause problems. He had difficulty saying no to pleas for money. Playing the role of generous benefactor was another way to balance his shame burden. For example, for several years in a row he had hosted an elaborate steak fry for his alma mater's football team in his backyard. According to Virginia Potter, the event cost thousands of dollars, but he refused to either break with the steak fry tradition or scale it back. It served a purpose—it lightened his shame, at least for a little while.

The Whipping Post of Addiction

At the same time an addiction can ease shame, it also can also serve to inflict terrible pain on the driven person.

In earlier periods of Christianity, self-abuse rituals were common. People wore hair shirts to inflict pain on themselves. Men would carry small whips with them, and if they entertained a sinful or lustful thought they would take out the whip and hit themselves. Today, we have more subtle ways of inflicting pain. If we need to punish ourselves, we take on three or four more responsibilities at work. Or we set impossibly aggressive goals. Or we volunteer for yet another committee.

Or, like one weary young patient told us during a counseling session: "Even though it's the last thing in the world I feel up to doing, and even though it means robbing me of

The Seven Addiction Drivers

1. "My addiction seems to justify my right to exist. It gives my life meaning."

2. "My applauded addiction seems to anesthetize my emotional pain and serve as a form of hypnosis."

3. "By practicing my applauded addiction I feel as if I am punishing myself and, at the same time, making installment payments on my guilt."

4. "My addiction is a way for me to say 'Ouch!' "

5. "My addiction attempts to restage a painful situation from my past and gives me the illusion that I can correct it."

6. "My addiction lets me express my anger."

7. "My addiction assumes almost spiritual dimensions and creates the god-like illusion that through practicing the addiction I can suspend time, be invincible, become transcendent, achieve immortality, and find the perfect union."

what little recreational time I have, I've decided to home school my three kids." While home schooling can be an appropriate option when pursued for the proper motives, in this case what she really was saying was that she didn't feel she deserved time for herself. She purposely deprived herself of any enjoyment by taking on the enormous task of educating her children at home.

Driver #4: "My addiction is a way for me to say 'Ouch!' "

Think of an addiction as a mouthpiece, a warning signal, or an indicator that something is wrong that needs immediate attention. The hypochondriac who is addicted to regular visits to the doctor may be using various complaints as a way of saying, "I crave attention. I need to be nurtured." Perhaps the person's self-esteem is so low that she or he can't candidly express hunger for love to the people around her or him. The person may fear that she or he will be rebuked. Instead, the person uses aches and pains to secure the attention she or he craves. Luci Stewart's headaches and depression, for instance, were the last straws in a series of lesser complaints that finally caused her to pick up the phone and arrange a consultation with Dr. Minirth.

Again, it's important to remember that addictions are illegitimate ways of addressing legitimate needs. There is nothing wrong with expressing feelings and grieving over our pain. The woman who craves attention should be encouraged to ventilate her needs to her spouse or friends. It would not be healthy, however, to express needs in a counterfeit way—by conjuring up one illness after another and by going from doctor to doctor as a hypochondriac often does.

Driver #5: "My addiction attempts to restage a painful situation from my past and gives me the illusion that I can correct it."

If you were to visit any substance-abuse clinic in the country and survey the staff, you'd probably find that at least 75 percent of the counselors who are treating patients for alcohol and drug addictions are adult children of alcoholics. Although there are many excellent reasons for entering such a "rescuing" profession as substance-abuse counseling, a common motivation is the desire to fix situations similar to those that the counselors couldn't fix in their own families when they were children.

When Dr. Hemfelt was training to become a psychologist, a favorite mentor and teacher explained his own experience this way: *One of the greatest career crises I ever faced was after I finally had made peace with my alcoholic parents. I had been a successful substance-abuse counselor for several years and had "rescued" many patients and families from the traumas of alcoholism. But I had never worked through the grief that I had suffered personally as a child in an alcoholic home. When I finally ripped off the old scars and confronted the pain that had festered under the surface most of my life, I was faced with a new dilemma. Suddenly, I had no driving need to solve the problems that plagued other families. I no longer had to remember my own miserable childhood and "fix" it by fixing their situation. I didn't need to spend eight hours a day listening to people in pain in an effort to relieve my own pain. It took a lot of time and prayer to keep me in my profession after I had discovered why I had entered that profession in the first place.*

Many times we've counseled women who have had long histories of unhappy relationships with the "wrong" kind of men. It's an old story: A battered wife frees herself from an abusive husband and then, within a year or two, is married to an equally cruel man. Family therapist Robin Norwood, author of *Women Who Love Too Much,* says she recognizes the familiar pattern whenever her clients explain that, in their opinion, being in love means being in pain. It's the same thing, they surmise.[2]

"I've dated every man in North Dallas, and they've all been cads," announced an attractive secretary at one of our outpatient group therapy sessions. "It's almost as if I have radar. I can walk into a crowded room, pass by a hundred healthy men, and pick the one with all the problems. Then it starts all over again."

103

What we have to explain to such patients is that picking the wrong mate has nothing to do with luck. Usually women who are prone to bad relationships grew up in homes where the dominant male was abusive. Rather than avoiding such men, the women gravitate toward them in an unconscious effort to correct what went wrong when they were children. They feel a strong urge to replay the awful scenario, but this time to fix it and make it right. Only then will they feel free of their painful past. Of course, they don't succeed, but like any addict, they keep repeating the process.

Although driven people hesitate to admit it, they often adopt the same negative traits that they so strongly disliked in their parents. Occasionally we counsel people who have grown up in legalistic homes where parents constantly have reminded the children to cross their *t*'s and dot their *i*'s— "And don't slouch at the dinner table!" As a way of coping with this barrage of criticism, the children take on the same critical characteristics as their parents. Psychologists call this "internalizing the aggressor" (the victim copies the aggressor). Instead of rebelling against the critical parent, the child becomes just as critical as the parent. The child adopts Mom's or Dad's high expectations and joins them in making impossible demands on himself, never satisfied with his performance, and relentlessly pushing himself to do better.

Michael Potter's workaholism was alarmingly like his father's, and his son, Chip, was already adopting this trait from his father and grandfather.

Driver #6: "My addiction lets me express my anger."

Compounding Paula Jansen's problem with shopaholism was her husband Hank's addiction to work. Of course, Hank argued that he *had* to work sixty hours a week to support her spending habit. The truth was that Hank felt tremendous anger toward his wife for her compulsive shopping. One way he could get even and express his furor was to say to her, "Don't make any plans that include me. I'm going to the office, and I don't know when you'll see me again." Such defiance was his manner of lashing out and hurting her.

Along similar lines, we once counseled a woman who was a compulsive cleaner. Her husband wasn't allowed to walk on the living room carpet unless he first kicked off his shoes. If he put his car keys on the kitchen counter, she would scoop them up and hang them on the special peg she had created just for that purpose. Her obsession with keeping a perfect house was driving a wedge in their marriage.

What did this have to do with anger? It didn't take us long to pick up on the strong negative emotions of the duo. The wife was well aware that she was driving her husband away, and that was her subconscious goal. She was paying him back for being unfaithful to her several years earlier. She had never forgiven him, and now she used her compulsive house-keeping to goad him and frustrate him.

Driver #7. "My addiction gives me the illusion that I can suspend time, be invincible, become transcendent, achieve immortality, and find perfect union."

Every addiction, every compulsion—yes, we said *every*; this is the one driver that is always present—has behind it a quest for spirituality and more specifically a quest for God and the attributes of God. Almost fifty years ago Bill Wilson, founder of Alcoholics Anonymous, realized that the only lasting answer to an addiction had to be spiritual. Wilson was a pioneer in recognizing this and in developing the how-to of recovery. His Twelve Step program and the "Big Book of" *Alcoholics Anonymous* have changed the lives of millions of people who are addicted to alcohol and drugs and are now being used with obsessive gamblers, smokers, spenders, and workaholics.

Bill Wilson makes the necessity for spiritual help very clear in the second chapter of the "Big Book:"

If you are as seriously alcoholic as we were, we believe there is no middle-of-the-road solution. We were in a position

105

where life was becoming impossible, and if we had passed into the region from which there is no return through human aid, we had but two alternatives: One was to go on to the bitter end, blotting out the consciousness of our intolerable situation as best we could; and the other, to accept spiritual help.[3]

Wilson knew from personal experience that spiritual help was the necessary "how" for recovery from his addiction of alcoholism, but he may not have fully appreciated the "why." Now, through the modern science of addictionology, we better understand the "why." The addiction—be it alcoholism or drug addiction or a compulsion America applauds —fulfills the addict's need:

- to suspend time (the "Stop-the-world-I-want-to-get-off" desire);
- to be invincible;
- to become transcendent;
- to achieve immortality; and
- to find perfect union.

It doesn't take much imagination to see how all five of these needs can ultimately be answered only by God. Our everyday compulsions give us the false illusion that they can answer these needs.

Intellectually I know that my becoming president of the corporation is not going to make me immortal or invincible, but way down inside—emotionally—the magical thinking, which operates on this level, says, "If I only do more, I will become immortal."

The Prototype of Drug Addiction

During Dr. Hemfelt's years as a graduate student, he was supervisor of counseling for a large opiate addiction treatment center in Houston, Texas. As he worked with those patients, he realized that the addiction was providing the false illusion that the addicts were meeting these needs:

To Suspend Time

The patients often reported a sense of time slowing down. "What was only fifteen minutes seemed like ten hours," they said. They felt that they could slow the rush of time and ultimately create a sense of immortality.

In our ordinary day-to-day drivenness we are also pursuing this spiritual quest. The driven, compulsive person is searching for the special anesthesia of transcendence, immortality, invincibility, perfect union, and suspension of time. That's why the addictive agent is so compelling. It creates the false illusion of meeting these needs.

Once Michael Potter began to recover, he could see that his drivenness was motivated by these spiritual needs. "I realize now," he told us, "that I thought, *If I can cram more into an hour, I'm stretching that hour.* The same for a day —and a week. I was trying to suspend time by compression."

His regimen of afternoon jogging also allowed him to step out of his tension-packed work environment and, for an hour a day, concentrate on nothing but the rhythmic beat of his feet as they hit the pavement. His secretary knew that for sixty minutes every afternoon she was to take telephone messages and invite clients to be seated and to wait. Everything stopped. Time was suspended. Mr. Potter was not available.

We all know people (or are ourselves) like Michael Potter. Pushed by their goals and objectives, these ambitious and successful folks are obsessed with pruning the waste from their days and replacing it with even more productivity. They play beat the clock, not as a game but as a preoccupation. Outfoxing time becomes the driving force in their lives. Their goal is to suspend time.

To Be Invincible

Often the drug addicts would also feel invincible. "When I'm high, I feel as if I could fall off the roof and not hurt myself," they said. Often people who have used cocaine feel as if they are supermen. "I can perform anything. I can think faster." And we all know kids who drink alcohol and then get in a car and drive 100 miles an hour, only to slam into a telephone pole. They feel as if, "Nothing can harm me when I'm high. I'm invincible."

It was no coincidence that Michael was a compulsive jogger who ran three to five miles every day, seven days a week. Michael's jogging gave him a sense of invincibility. In recovery he realized that he had been unconsciously telling himself, *If I just jog enough, I won't age. I won't get sick. My body will stay as it is.* (I'll be invincible.)   *Not II*

Another way to feel invincible is to "be in control." Driven people play a lot of "if only" games. It's a fill-in-the-blank kind of pastime with the addict completing this sentence: "I could achieve complete mastery of my life if only_____ (my business were perfectly organized/my house were spotless/I hit the jackpot in the state lottery/I'm chosen by the boss for the big promotion)."

During therapy, Virginia Potter came to realize that her effort to oversee the chaotic life-style of the Carmel Community Center actually was her way of creating a certain environment that she could dominate. However, the ongoing activity and the open-door policy actually were taking her out of control. She was having to react to whomever or whatever entered her door. She never knew what to expect. Life was unpredictable and, therefore, was characterized by a certain looseness.

To Become Transcendent

All of the mood-altering drugs are addictive because they induce a sense of getting "high": "I rise above myself. I get out of the ordinary level. I'm above it all." Drug addicts often talk about drugs as a god in their lives. (And all of us, in fact, refer to alcohol as a spirit.) The addicts in that treatment center in Houston told Dr. Hemfelt: "When I get high, I feel as if I'm transcendent. I feel as if I've been lifted off the ground and out of reality."

We've all heard of runners' high, caused by a self-generated chemical in athletes' bodies that pumps them up to a dreamy, elevated state. They feel wonderfully in control, as if they could conquer the world—at least until they come "down." Yet, Dr. Kenneth Cooper, whose books on running, aerobics, and nutrition have touched off a wonderful awareness of preventive health, has commented that if a person jogs more than three or four times a week he or she may be jogging for reasons other than health.

Even if you're not a runner, you've probably experienced the effects of one of the most powerful mood-altering chemicals known: adrenaline. In many ways, adrenaline mimics pharmaceutical stimulants like speed, cocaine, and crack cocaine. Some people feel adrenaline kick in when they close a big deal, make an important sale, perform well in front of an audience, win an election, or solve someone's problem. Applause can touch off a rush of adrenaline.

These compulsions America applauds give people a false "high," which makes them feel as though they're transcending to a lofty level. Like many risk takers, Michael Potter achieved a natural high when he closed a particularly risky deal. He felt that same high as he moved deeper and deeper into his flirtation with soft pornography. In a very unhealthy way he was moving out of his conservative little world into an exciting and "forbidden" arena. The fact that he was doing this on the sly only added to the excitement of it all. It was unlike him; it was dangerous; and that feeling of being naughty was part of the reason it was so appealing.

The problem with becoming addicted to any kind of high —even the natural high of adrenaline—is that "normal" seems very bland by comparison. In Chapter 2 we talked about the corporate troubleshooter who was addicted to the high of saving distressed divisions of a very large company. The pressure in his work life was incredible since his speciality was crisis management. The adrenaline started to flow as soon as he arrived on the scene of a pending disaster. He immediately was put in charge, and the rules were suspended as he seized control and made all of the judgment calls. Long hours, missed meals, emergency strategy sessions, too much coffee, and too little sleep became the norm. Finally, as the exhausted key players in the corporate drama held their breath, the tension built to a climax. When the company was saved everyone cheered, and our troubleshooter experienced a high that practically sent him into orbit. No wonder everyday life at home seemed bland by comparison.

There's an even more dangerous side of becoming addicted to a compulsion America applauds. Every high has a down side. The higher the high, in fact, the lower the low. Michael Potter experienced periods of depression after he closed one of his risky deals. Normal was not just bland and boring; normal was unbearable. And the lower Michael felt, the more he felt pushed to find a riskier deal to take him back up again.

To Be Immortal

Many people, especially those on LSD or acid back in the 1960s, often reported, "I saw God. I touched God. I'm immortal."

Michael's search for immortality was even more obvious. His dream was evident in the rolls of blueprints that often were tucked under his arms when he arrived, between business appointments, at our clinic. He told us the documents were plans for a series of shopping centers—"Huge projects," he boasted—that would establish his real estate firm among the largest in the Midwest and Southwest. Once developed, the centers, many bearing his name, would provide guaranteed revenue for his children and grandchildren. The family name would be revered long after he had passed on the baton of power to Chip, Brian, and Whitney.

To Find Perfect Union

Finally people who are high on heroin report a sense of their body boundaries disappearing. For them, the ultimate sense of union is for two people to "shoot up" together and then just sit and stare into space. In the fantasy of the drug high and illusion, they feel as if they are perfectly united. Intimate sex seems like a nuisance or a bother.

We can see the same phenomenon in a singles bar. Once men or women drink enough beer, they walk up to someone they wouldn't ordinarily speak to and propose marriage. Irrational, yes, but the alcohol has created the illusion that "You and I are destined by fate to be together." We can find perfect union.

Sex and relationship addictions offer the false promise of achieving complete oneness with another human being. For example, Virginia Potter's growing dependence on her friend Ray is a quest to finally capture the kind of unity that she never was able to accomplish with Michael.

Jokes sometimes are made about the unfaithful husband who attempts to seduce women with the old line, "My wife doesn't understand me." Hardly original, the words sum up the man's belief that somewhere out in the great unknown is his perfect mate. He's willing to break promises, trample on relationships, and thumb his nose at his marriage vows in order to finally meet his match. He becomes addicted to the quest, and the quest is never ending. He's being propelled by the illusionary belief: *I can achieve perfect union.*

Michael Potter's desire for relationships—for union with other people—caused Michael to enter into codependent business deals. Instead of making practical, objective decisions, Michael was swayed by his emotions. If he liked someone—and wanted the person to think well of him—he decided to go into the deal (to rescue the person). Michael also made many personal loans to friends and business associates, which had not been repaid, and the family real estate conglomerate had suffered because of the bad IOUs.

He was also driven by his need for love in his relationship with his wife. Unconsciously he thought, *If I just earn enough money—if I'm a good enough warrior in the battle —when I come back to the cave, my wife will love me.*

His sexual fantasies were also driven by this desire. Pornography gave him the false sense of being physically intimate with an anonymous person in a glossy photograph.

The Potters truly liked—loved—one another. Yet, they were often too busy to be intimate. (Remember Michael's boosting Virginia up to climb into their bedroom window so they could have some privacy from the group of teens at the Carmel Community Center?)

These five spiritual drivers arise out of healthy, God-given desires, that may move us closer to God if we are open to having a relationship with Him. Yet, if we have moved away from God or become skeptical about God or out of touch with the spiritual dimension of our lives, we unconsciously lean more and more firmly on other people and activities and things to try to fill our spiritual needs. We turn to the applauded addictions instead of turning to God.

Stepping onto the Cycle

There may be more addiction drivers than the five we've listed. And, it's important to remember, not all five are present in every addiction case that we treat. As you became acquainted with the explanations, some drivers might have seemed uncomfortably familiar if they applied to your own situation. You may have seen yourself in several of the descriptions, since it's possible for a single applauded addiction to be powered simultaneously by many of the drivers.

At the Minirth-Meier Clinics, we tell our patients that the only way *out* of an addiction is *through* an addiction. What we mean by that is that a person who is in emotional pain needs to work through the pain, step by step, if the person truly wants to be rid of it. No shortcuts are allowed. It's not enough for addicts to make changes in their lives. Instead, *they must change.*

This takes commitment and participation. Patients have to accept active roles in their recovery; it can't be done *for* them or *to* them, only *by* them. It also may require the help of a good friend or the professional services of a therapist, a pastoral counselor, a psychologist, or a psychiatrist. Recovery that includes Stage I and Stage II is a participative process. Who participates and how many people participate depend on the nature of the problem and its seriousness.

One of the purposes of this book is to be a self-help guide for you to walk through the recovery process. We hope that by combining the contents of the book with the support of good self-help groups, you will enjoy full Stage II recovery. However, if at any point you feel overwhelmed by emotions and issues, or if you can't move your addiction into a temporary state of abstinence or balance, then we suggest outpatient therapy or inpatient hospitalization. From this point on, as we move around the addiction cycle, we will be sharing information that will serve four functions:

- prevention;
- diagnosis;
- support; and
- hope.

Prevention

Familiarity with the addiction cycle can arm readers with valuable knowledge so they will be less likely to fall victim to dangerous addictions. By making readers aware of how easily applauded behavior can slip over the threshold from positive action to negative addiction, we hope to decrease the incidence of crossover.

Diagnosis By describing the ten points of the addiction cycle and by explaining what takes place at each point, we will offer readers a yardstick for measuring their own behavior and the behavior of the people and organizations around them. If they diagnose themselves as being at risk, we'll teach them several self-help techniques and direct them toward professional help if they need it.

The major purpose of diagnosis is not merely to understand that a compulsion is present, but also to diagnose the causes, the root issues, that are deeper than the addict might have originally suspected. Unless the underlying foundation of the addiction is identified, there is no possible hope for long-term healing and recovery.

Support For persons suffering either from a compulsion America applauds or from the fallout of this compulsion, understanding the cycle will offer support. If you are in treatment, much of what you find in these pages will be familiar and will underscore what you are experiencing in your own recovery program. We hope it also will ease the burden of family members who are hurting directly and indirectly as a result of addiction.

Hope Explaining the various points of the addiction cycle would be of limited value if we also didn't explain how to halt the cycle at each of these key places. It's not enough merely to intervene at a certain point, like Point Six, which is the critical time when the addict reaches for his addictive agent. We're convinced that *every* component of the cycle needs to be looked at and dealt with if a true Stage II recovery is to be achieved. With that in mind, we'll offer suggestions on how to interrupt the addiction cycle at all nine of its points.

As we prepare to step onto the addiction cycle, we'll keep the drivers in mind. But as varied as the drivers are, the stops around the cycle are constant. They have the same launching point: the family of origin. That's where we'll begin our ride.

PART TWO

Breaking

the Cycle

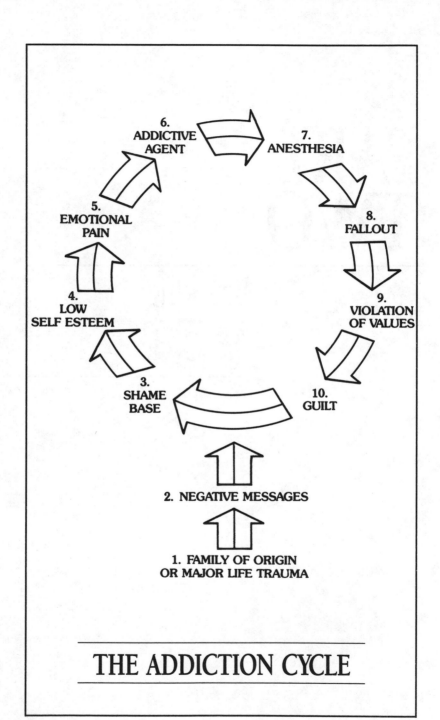

6.
ADDICTIVE
AGENT

7.
ANESTHESIA

5.
EMOTIONAL
PAIN

8.
FALLOUT

4.
LOW
SELF ESTEEM

9.
VIOLATION
OF VALUES

3.
SHAME
BASE

10.
GUILT

2. NEGATIVE MESSAGES

1. FAMILY OF ORIGIN
OR MAJOR LIFE TRAUMA

THE ADDICTION CYCLE

Chapter Five

Events That Set the Cycle in Motion

Point 1: Family of Origin or Major Life Trauma

Like father, like son. Like mother, like daughter. You probably have noticed that throughout this book we are quoting old adages. Why? Because there's a lot of truth in those old sayings; people throughout the ages have noticed these tendencies and put a handle on them. Now we've begun to understand why those old sayings are so true.

As we mentioned earlier, drivenness is often multi-generational. The spastic colon of an infant, like Robbie Stewart, can be traced back to its origin in the childhood of his grandparents, Luci and Richard Stewart. Their son's addiction to get-rich-quick schemes actually was rooted in two generations of shame and poverty. His parents grew up in families that had little ambition beyond paying their weekly grocery bills and making installment payments on their secondhand cars.

Luci's parents, in particular, didn't understand her drive to excel in school. They didn't share her vision of someday qualifying for a job other than as a clerk or a waitress. Luci knew that college was out of the question, but she thought if she picked up enough marketable skills in her business education classes she might be able to earn a position as an executive secretary after graduation.

Her natural assertiveness attracted the attention of the high school debate team sponsor who recruited Luci to join the club. The only catch was the financial obligation that was attached to the honor. She would be expected to buy certain study materials and share in travel expenses to out-of-town debate meets. Her parents saw no value in the extra-curricular activity and turned thumbs down on her participation.

"Not only did I not get to join the team," Luci told us through tears many years later, "but I had to make up an excuse to explain why I had decided against it. No one believed me."

Richard Stewart's childhood was equally poor, although for different reasons. His father was seriously handicapped with arthritis and had to support the family on a small government check. Like many teenagers, Richard dreamed of a professional football career. The only way he could have earned an athletic scholarship to college would have been to have a stand-out high school career on the field, but that was impossible since his parents insisted that he quit the team in his junior year to get a weekend job. He resented their lack of support—both emotional and financial—and he secretly resented his father's disability.

When Richard and Luci married three weeks after high school graduation, both were quietly determined to succeed. Each carried into the marriage a tremendous amount of shame, anger, and drivenness. Richard plunged into a door-to-door sales job, and Luci doubled Richard's effectiveness by overseeing the books, inventory, and record-keeping. By the time that Bud was born, Richard was spending Monday through Friday on the road, and Luci was preoccupied with managing the home office. Bud grew up hearing his parents discussing deals, investments, and expansion. He picked up on their determination to show the world that they were just as good as anyone else. Money became the proof of their worth, and their goal was to accumulate as much "proof" as possible. Bud inherited that goal.

Negative fallout like Bud Stewart's financial collapse is common in families where applauded addictions run rampant. The reason is simple: Applauded addictions aren't recognized as problems until something goes terribly wrong. They're encouraged rather than discouraged. They fester and grow and spread and infect other parts of the family system until finally someone shouts "Ouch!" Only then is the addiction recognized as being harmful.

Luci and Richard Stewart were constantly used as examples of the American success story until Bud tried, but failed, to follow in their footsteps. Even then the link between his addiction to risky schemes and his parents' drivenness was ignored. He merely was passed off as the "black sheep" in an otherwise exemplary family.

"Who else could be to blame?" Luci Stewart asked Dr. Minirth one day.

When we answer that question, we often borrow a phrase from author-counselor John Bradshaw. "In families, no one is to blame," says Bradshaw. "Everyone is responsible." Rather than cast blame on anyone, we try to help families to understand where responsibility genuinely rests.

Addiction Prone Families

In this chapter we are going to begin our walk around the addiction cycle at point one: the family of origin or a major life trauma. In our years of counseling driven people, we've found that nearly all of them come from one of four types of family backgrounds, or they've experienced what we call a "major life trauma." The adult compulsivity is an effort to compensate for the old family shame and/or an effort to anesthetize the memory of deeply buried family pain. As we describe each setting, recall the backdrop of your own growing-up years and see whether it resembles one of the following scenarios.

The Low-achieving Family

Luci and Richard Stewart and yuppie executive Barbara Ryan both came from low-achieving families. Often, however, when we try to talk about a client's childhood, we run into that old adversary denial.

"I've already told you that my dad is a dry drunk," said Barbara Ryan when we brought up the subject in one of her counseling sessions. "Frankly, I've never understood why you doctors insist on starting with the old 'tell us about your family' routine. Is it really necessary to go digging around in the past? I made peace with all that years ago. My problem is the depression I feel *now;* it has absolutely nothing to do with my parents. Besides, we've gotten along better these last couple of years than we ever did when I was living at home."

Barbara shook her head and rolled her eyes upward to let us know that we were being predictable and that she was two jumps ahead of us. Finally, with a shrug of her shoulders she indicated that she would humor us. "Okay, okay," she said. "What do you want to know?"

To put her at ease, we half-joked, "Tell us about your family."

Barbara was right. Psychiatrists and psychologists are predictable when it comes to probing a patient's past, but they do it for a reason. Understanding what we call "the family of origin"—the family the patient grew up in, whether biological or adopted—is essential if we are to explain why patients act and react the way they do. By looking at their past, we can explain their present and foresee their future behavior.

If we were predictable in our early questions, Barbara also was predictable in her denial that her childhood experiences affected her current depression. Denial lurks at every stop around the addiction cycle, and the first stop—"family of origin or major life trauma"—is no exception. Many patients refuse to place any blame on their parents. It's almost as if Mom and Dad are off limits, and the patients would rather shoulder the blame themselves than to point the finger at their families. One of our challenges as we guide our driven patients around the addiction cycle is to help them face and forgive mistakes made in their pasts.

Barbara's family was typical of the low-achieving family, we later learned. Here, the atmosphere is almost chaotic and loose, with the family members often disorganized and underachieving. Like a rocket, the driven person catapults out of this kind of system as a way of breaking with the past. It's as if driven persons look at their family members and say, "No way! I want more than this; I'm going to be different. Just watch me." These are the self-made men and women who are praised for their up-by-the-bootstraps efforts. They're applauded as American success stories.

A well-known woman who was driven by this kind of family background is the actress Meredith MacRae. Until she was ten years old, she enjoyed a picture-perfect childhood with her sister, two brothers, and her famous parents, Gordon and Sheila MacRae. Then, her father lapsed into chronic alcoholism, and everything changed. As the oldest child (remember, firstborns are most likely candidates for drivenness), Meredith assumed more and more adult responsibilities.

"I was the rescuer," she once told an interviewer. She vividly remembered her many trips to the country club and local pubs to drag her father home. Everyone else in the family was too upset to take control. Meredith was forever trying to pick up the pieces and put the old, happy picture back together. "I got straight A's in school. I thought the better child I was, the less he would drink."[1]

Although her father had many happy years of sobriety before he died, Meredith admits that she still suffers fallout from her difficult childhood. She diagnoses herself as a borderline workaholic, a super-achiever, and a die-hard worrier. She adores her father's memory, but, like most driven people, she carries the scars from her past. There is no time clock, no expiration date, no statute of limitations on pain. Emotionally, it is always there. And Barbara Ryan was no exception.

Even though Barbara insisted that she had made peace with her parents, it was necessary for her to look back before she could understand the reasons for her current struggle with depression. We knew she was driven and perfectionistic —she admitted that—but we didn't know how deep her pain really was. When we explained the various kinds of family situations that most often produce driven people, she reluctantly agreed that the low-achieving family background was very close to her own. Then she shared some painful memories. Her tears confirmed that not all of the wounds had been healed by time.

"When I was a little girl, there were nights when my mother and father simply didn't come home at all," she recalled. "I'd wait for the phone to ring with the news that they had been in an accident and were hurt or even dead. In the morning, Dad usually would call from the police station where they had been locked up on DWI or disorderly conduct charges."

The trauma of growing up in an alcoholic home was particularly acute for Barbara because her father hadn't always been a practicing alcoholic. She remembered the good years and how it used to be before Dad got "sick." Until she was eight years old, Barbara led a relatively normal life. Her father was a good provider and was even active in the church. However, as he moved into midlife, he began drinking more and more. By the time she entered her teens, his alcoholism was severe. Barbara witnessed her father's descent into the pain and chaos of addiction. The family descended with him.

The Ryans quickly lost all touch with normalcy. Sometimes there was food to eat, sometimes there wasn't. Sometimes Dad went to work, most often he didn't. The only "sure thing" in the family unit was Barbara. She studied hard because she knew the only way she would get to college was with the help of a scholarship.

Even as she excelled in the classroom, so did she shine in extracurricular activities. She joined the high school choir and was the featured soloist by the time she was a senior. Performing made her feel good; it was the only way she could earn the approval that no one had time to lavish on her at home. As a high school senior she automatically took on the task of researching colleges, applying for financial aid, and taking all the required entrance examinations. It never occurred to her to ask her parents to participate in this important process. She had become so accustomed to being an overachiever and being her own parent that anything else would have seemed strange to her. She was smart enough to know, even as a child, that if she ever were to break away from her unhappy situation, she was going to have to do it alone. It was at that point that she became driven.

The Family That Expects Too Much

The second type of family background that nurtures driven people is the opposite of the Ryans' chaotic life-style: the perfectionistic family. Dr. Paul Meier is the first to admit that he grew up in a perfectionistic home and that his loving but strict German father believed that no matter what young Paul did, he probably could have done more. Not only was the Protestant work ethic followed to the letter around the Meiers' home in Michigan, but it also was translated into German. *Arbeit macht das Leben süss*—"work makes life sweet"—was the family motto, and the senior Meiers believed in leading a very sweet life.

Not wishing to disappoint his dad, Paul pushed himself to the limit. He was a straight-A student in college, played two sports, worked nights as a private nurse for an elderly man, was the president of two campus organizations, read a book a week, and did charity work on weekends. In short, he was driven.

Paul is quick to explain that time has mellowed his dad, and at age eighty, Alexander Meier is generous with his hugs and compliments for his son. Many people aren't as fortunate.

Driven families are as easily found in fantasy as in real life. For example, in the popular film *Dead Poets Society*, one of the young students at the elite boys preparatory school is Neal, the driven son of a perfectionistic middle-income couple. Neal's parents have his life mapped out for him: He's to graduate as valedictorian of his class, attend Harvard University, and eventually become a surgeon. Neal is like a robot, programmed to agree with his mother and to say "yessir" to whatever his father suggests.

The family's perfectionism is depicted in subtle ways in the film. When Neal's father goes to bed, his slippers are placed side-by-side exactly in the spot where his feet will touch the floor in the morning. Neal's mother lays out her son's carefully ironed clothing for him every evening and has his toothbrush spread with just the right amount of toothpaste.

The climax of the story comes when Neal defies his parents for the first time in his life by secretly accepting the starring role in a school play and studying harder than ever so his straight-A record won't suffer because of his daring fling into acting. His father finds out and, in a belittling lecture, emphasizes how Neal has disappointed him, how his action has let down the family, and how his defiance proves his ingratitude to his parents and all of the sacrifices they've made for him. The burden of shame is heaped so high that Neal punishes himself by unlocking his father's desk, taking out a pistol, and shooting himself.

Recently, former film star Kim Novak resurfaced after twenty-five years of self-exile. When she was interviewed and asked why she fled a successful career so many years ago, she talked about the trauma of growing up in a family that expected too much. Her father in particular believed in hard work and little praise. He was demanding, and nothing his daughter did—even being selected as the most popular star in the world in 1956—quite satisfied him. Or, if it did, he refused to let his pleasure show.

"My parents were very strict, very Old Country," she explained. "I wanted my father's approval more than anything on earth. I worked so hard to get it, and I never did."

Neither could she earn the approval of several of Hollywood's power brokers, who resembled her perfectionistic father. Whether or not she was naturally drawn to these controlling moguls in an addictive way is anyone's guess. In any case, she scrambled to earn their favor and failed. She was rewarded with star status and money, but little positive feedback. "All I wanted was for them to tell me that I was doing something right," she recalls. They didn't, and eventually she chose to run. Today she says that she ran *to* a new life rather than *from* an old one. She stepped off the merry-go-round and out of the cycle that had driven her since her early childhood.

This old story is repeated in our counseling offices nearly every day. Details vary, but the theme is the same. Often the high expectations of driven parents are compounded by their other addictions. In Michael Potter's family, his father not only was addicted to work, but also was an alcoholic and a rageaholic. Whenever he drank too much—from Friday afternoon to Sunday night—he would become loud and abusive. His favorite target was Michael. Any mistake that Michael made during the week, whether it was a bobbled ball on the Little League diamond or an A-minus on a test, was stored and dealt with over the weekend after a few rounds of drinks. One by one, the boy's shortcomings of the previous week were dredged up, replayed, and hashed over. The conclusion was always the same.

"You've got to do better," was the message that Mike heard for years. "You've got to work harder or else you won't —make the team; be accepted into the best college; be invited to join the right fraternity; date the best-looking girl on campus; earn a place in the family business." The "or else" varied, depending on Michael's age and situation.

To all children, parents assume the status of "gods," those who literally possess the power of life and death over a child. If a child is convinced that he or she has not lived up to the parents' inflated expectations, the child may gradually and even unconsciously come to believe that God is also a parent who can never be pleased. Therefore, the driven person turns to perfectionistic standards as false gods and jumps on the performance treadmill in a vain belief that demonstrations of invincibility and superhuman achievement will someday secure the approval of an earthly father or a heavenly Father.

The Preoccupied Family

A third type of family that often produces driven children is what we call the "preoccupied family." In this situation, one or both of the parents have some emotional, mental, or physical preoccupation that distracts their attention away from the children. On the surface, the preoccupied family seems far less dysfunctional than the low-achieving, alcoholic family. But the damage that results can be very similar.

Richard Stewart grew up in a family that was absorbed with illness. Richard's father didn't intentionally inflict harm on his son, but he was genuinely in pain and suffered from bitterness about his inability to work and provide for the family. In addition, Richard's mother was preoccupied with the financial strain of making ends meet on a small government disability check. The parents had little emotional energy to invest in their children. Very early in life Richard realized that he was on his own. With little guidance and no encouragement from his parents, he decided that he somehow would find a way to have all the material advantages that he never enjoyed at home. He became driven to succeed.

Often when we try to explain the concept of passive neglect to patients we suggest that they envision a balance beam. On one side of the beam is the parents' emotional investment in the children; on the other side is the parents' preoccupation with some mental, emotional, or physical concern. The greater the parents' concern, the less energy they have available to devote to the children.

In recent years, the most common preoccupation that we have encountered among patients has been work. A child can emerge as a very driven adult if he or she grows up in a workaholic home where Mom and Dad are frantically enmeshed in their jobs. Typically, career-minded parents neglect their children in a passive sort of way. So the children are driven not by their parents' expectations of them, but by the children's expectations of themselves. The sons or daughters become driven and compulsive in order to win the parents' attention.

Virginia Potter grew up in a preoccupied home where the head of the house, her father, was an emotionally distant man. Quiet and reserved, he never did anything abusive to his daughter other than withhold affection by burying himself in his newspaper in the morning and the television in the evening. His lack of concern for Virginia probably contributed to her desperate need for her husband Michael's approval. She craved attention from the dominant men in her life. In her middle years she became drawn to Ray when he indicated that he was more than willing to lavish affection on her.

In some ways, Michael Potter endured the worst of two worlds. As far back as he could remember he had been subjected to the high expectations of his domineering father. That led to his drivenness. But there was a secondary contributor as well. His mother, meek and passive, was so overwhelmed by her husband that she suffered frequent problems with her emotional and physical health, which was her way of forcing the family to slow its pace. When Mom had a "nervous breakdown," everyone was expected to pause and patronize her for the duration of her illness. The family's squabbles were suspended, and a sort of unity descended until Mom could be patched up, delivered home, and the battles could continue. These "breakdowns," however, caused her to be constantly preoccupied with how she felt. The result was that Michael was pushed by one parent and ignored by the other.

We stated previously that a child's experience of biological human parents may dramatically shape that child's unconscious perception of a spiritual Father. If the child's human parent has been preoccupied, self-absorbed, and basically unavailable to meet the child's needs, the child may project those same attributes to God. The child's subsequent adult compulsivity may be self-directed efforts to gain security, love, and even immortality, since the adult child seriously doubts whether God is sufficiently interested in him or her to meet those innate needs.

The Family With Unfinished Business

The fourth type of family which can transmit drivenness is the family with unfinished emotional business. The premise of what we call unfinished business is this: A major goal, need, or expectation that was left unfinished by one generation is pushed on to the next. Unfinished business is Mom's or Dad's business that was never completed. One or both may have had some area of their lives in which they always felt discontent. The children picked up on these unresolved goals and made them their own. The pressure on the second generation is often intense; to fail to reach the goal would be to disappoint Mom and Dad. That becomes unthinkable.

The awareness of the unfinished business concept usually surfaces during midlife. A woman like the burned out yuppie Barbara Ryan may wake up some morning and suddenly say, "Wait a minute. Is this all there is? Is this why I've been knocking myself out all these years?" She realizes that she has accomplished the things that her mother was unable to do. She is self-sufficient. Her financial future doesn't depend on a man who might disappoint her at any time. She is a successful person in her own right, rather than a homebound, submissive hausfrau. But—and here is the irony—she isn't happy. She may have resolved Mom's unfinished business, but she's created some of her own.

Major Life Trauma

Whenever we search for the roots of drivenness, we start with the family of origin. If we don't find the cause there, we discuss with our patients any major life traumas that occurred in childhood or might have been experienced later, during their adult years.

When we say "trauma," we don't mean a minor setback or disappointment that taught the person that he or she should work harder next time. Instead, this is a life-changing event or series of events that causes the person to totally reshuffle priorities. For example, we've worked with men who have lost everything in a business failure and from that point on have become obsessed with amassing a fortune that will assure financial security. They spend hours studying their profit-and-loss spreadsheets, and they record every expenditure right down to the thirty-five-cent postage stamp that they personally affixed to their wife's birthday card.

We've counseled women so traumatized by a midlife divorce that they've become driven to stop the clock and hold onto whatever is left of their youth. They experiment with new hair colors and styles, consult with cosmetic surgeons and ask for "the works," buy youthful wardrobes, and they frequent singles bars for affirmation that they still can attract members of the opposite sex.

Sometimes a major life trauma can appear to be an unfair twist of fate. When Frank Minirth was a young boy growing up in Arkansas, he was diagnosed as having diabetes mellitus. His life changed immediately. Overnight he faced the ongoing discipline of a very restrictive diet. He had to deal with the reality of taking insulin shots every day for the rest of his life. He had to cope with the fear of dying young. And, at his doctor's insistence, he had to take very good care of his frail body if he was to battle successfully the chronic disease that he would never conquer. Any doubts he might have had about the seriousness of his condition were put to rest three years after the initial diagnosis. He nearly died when pneumonia set in and his blood-sugar level shot up to an alarming level.

As serious as diabetes is, it has helped Frank to lead a very disciplined and healthy life. It also put him in early contact with the medical profession. He was fascinated with the field, and during his teenage years he declared that he wanted to be a doctor. He overcame difficult odds to make good on his dream. Some life traumas can bring positive, rather than negative, results. Yet, Frank openly admits that he has to battle his obsessive-compulsive tendencies every day.

A major life trauma may not be a single, jolting event, but it might be a series of events that occur over a period of time. That is what happened to Virginia Potter. Her father's preoccupation planted the seeds of drivenness. But there were other, later, contributing factors. Remember, signs of compulsivity didn't appear until several years into her marriage to Michael.

"Could that be it, Doctor?" she asked us one day after we had talked about her growing-up years and how different they were from her husband's. "Is Mike partly to blame for how I feel?"

Virginia was onto something. We encouraged her to talk out her idea. We knew she had been in therapy long enough to understand how delicate the family mobile is and how each part affects the others. If she could come up with the answer to her own question, that answer would be more meaningful than if we supplied it.

"How could Michael be responsible for your need to be constantly busy?" we prodded. "What did he do to encourage you to be everyone's cheerleader, listening post, and problem solver?" We watched her as she bit her bottom lip, looked down at the floor for a moment, and tried to piece together the clues.

"Mike has spent his whole life trying to please his dad," she began thoughtfully. "That's why he always worked so hard in school, in sports, and now in his job." She paused. "Come to think of it, his drive is probably what attracted me to him in the first place. Mike was everything in college— first-string quarterback, president of the student senate, and he made the dean's list every semester but one." She laughed at the memory. "That was the semester we got engaged. His dad still won't let me forget it. I ruined Mike's perfect record, he says."

We nodded. It was easy to trace Michael Potter's drivenness. But Virginia's?

"I think I've been trying to keep up with him all these years," she said. "I've always been a strong person, so I'm not going to react to a workaholic husband in the same way that Mike's mom has reacted. She withdrew and became passive. But that's not my way of dealing with things. No, somewhere over the years I must have decided that the best way for me to win Mike's attention and affection was to be as busy and involved as he is. Since he didn't want me to work out of the home, I had to push myself in other areas—community service, church work, clubs, and the C.C.C."

Virginia was exactly on target. We summed up her assessment this way: "Mike has been driving himself to win his father's approval, and you've been driving yourself to win Michael's approval."

"And neither of us has gotten what we need," she finished.

Healing the Wounds of the Past

Most people assume that their family of origin was normal. After all, they never knew any other way. A comparison might be if you grew up in a Third World country and never had indoor plumbing. Dipping water from a river or pumping it from a community well might be part of your daily routine. It would be normal by your standards.

One of our early tasks in working with driven patients is to point out that some aspects of their pasts may not have been normal by most standards. A common technique we use is to interrupt them from time to time as they tell their life stories and say, "Do you realize that was abusive?" Sometimes they don't agree; their tendency is either to deny or to minimize the trauma they endured.

Often members of a patient's therapy group will help to break through this new wall of denial. Typically, when patients join the circle, we ask them to share their life stories. Then we might turn to the group and say, "Barbara has just told us about her childhood and her family. Is there anything we can tell her?" The responses might unfold this way:

"Your parents used to stay out all night without letting you know where they went? You must have been scared to death! If that's not a form of child abuse, I don't know what is."

"Since you were the oldest child, you probably had to keep all of your fears bottled up so your little brother wouldn't worry, right? That's a lot of stress for a kid to han-

131

dle. Not only were you filling the role of big sister, but of Mom and Dad too."

"And yet you still managed to go off to school in the morning, concentrate on your classes, and get straight A's? You must have been a very strong little girl. It's no wonder you have a hard time trusting people today. The only person you could count on when you were growing up was yourself."

And so it goes. The patient listens and learns.

Even without the help of a professional counselor or a therapy group, a person can gain insight about his or her drivenness in a couple of different ways. First, she can identify a trusted friend and ask that friend to listen as she relates her life story. Even though the friend is not a trained therapist, he can react to the story and point out incidents of abuse or events that wouldn't seem normal by most people's standards.

Insight also can be gained by doing what we call a relationship inventory.

Relationship Inventory

Take a piece of paper and list all of the significant people in your life. These should include family members, friends, neighbors, teachers, authority figures, and any others from your past or present who have had some degree of influence on your life. At the top of the list put your parents, whether they were your biological mother and father or adoptive parents.

Think about your relationship with each of the names on your list. As you try to capture these significant people on paper, think in terms of your senses. What was the *sound* of Dad's voice? Loud? Angry? Critical? Try to remember your mother's *touch.* Warm? Soft? Caring? Picture your little brother's face. Is he laughing? Does he look tense or frightened? Smells can be important. We recall one patient who became very anxious whenever she encountered the scent of a popular aftershave. Her abusive stepfather had worn it for years, and the smell brought back a rush of frightening memories. If you had to describe each person using two or three adjectives, what words would you choose? Don't deliberate too long over your descriptions; jot down the first words that come to mind.

Now think of several important days from the past. These might include a birthday party, Christmas, graduation, a family vacation. Were those days marred in any way? Did you look forward to holidays? Was the mood in your home happy and relaxed? Or was it tense and out of control? Try to imagine yourself driving up to your family's home after a long absence. How do you feel just as you are about to reach for the doorknob, knowing that Mom, Dad, your sisters, and your brothers are waiting inside? Are you excited at the prospect of a family reunion?

After you have completed your inventory, review all of the major relationships and then concentrate on your family of origin. Ask yourself these questions:

- Did my parents expect too much of me?
- Was the atmosphere in our home chaotic and loosely out of control?
- Did I experience some major life trauma during childhood or later?
- Was there something going on in our home that grabbed my parents' attention away from me?
- Did I inherit any significant unfinished business from a family member?

We encourage our patients to pour out their memories on paper because events from the past seem less fuzzy and more concrete when they are visible in black and white. Often patients are surprised at what they have written.

As you review the relationship history, look for repeating patterns. For example, Barbara Ryan discovered that in all of her life relationships, she only had emotional permission to give to others. She had no permission to receive and no permission to have her own needs met. She always had to be the caretaker for others.

These recurrent patterns are important because they identify codependent relationship addiction patterns. These codependent patterns further reveal what may be an underlying spiritual hunger for perfect union. We all desire to be close to a family. If that need was not adequately satisfied in childhood, we may compulsively push for unrealistic union in later adult relationships.

Understanding the roots of drivenness is essential to a full recovery. Sometimes exploring this first stop along the addiction cycle is difficult because we uncap volatile feelings of anger and sadness. But accepting the past can lay the foundation for a happier future. Stop Two will move us closer toward that goal.

Chapter Six

Sinister Whispers from the Past

Point 2: Negative Messages

Except for her soft Southern drawl, burned-out exec Barbara Ryan bears no resemblance to Scarlett O'Hara. She doesn't have red hair, didn't grow up in a wealthy family, and certainly never lived through a war —although as a child she endured more than her share of battles. Still, when she first told us her life story and described her unhappy family of origin, a part of it sounded very much like what we describe to patients as the "Scarlett O'Hara turnip speech." Within the counseling profession, this is generally known as an "inversion."

We explained it to Barbara this way: In the classic book *Gone with the Wind*, Scarlett returns after the Civil War to find the family plantation Tara to be little more than a shabby, war-torn reminder of its former beauty. A particularly poignant scene shows the once elegant and spoiled Scarlett out in the fields, trying to harvest a crop of turnips with her bare hands. In frustration she grabs a turnip and simultaneously shakes a fist at God. "As God is my witness," she promises, "I will never be hungry again."

In similar acts of frustration and determination, many of our patients have vowed to pull themselves out of their unhappy family situations and never, never suffer again. Often they won't verbalize the promise as Scarlett did, but they make a decision to do whatever is necessary to assure that they will never be hungry again. They usually don't mean physical hunger, but instead, the hunger for security, love, money, or the material goods that have been denied them. From that point on, they become driven to fulfill their promise to themselves. These identifiable hungers may be further reinforced by the unconscious spiritual hunger for transcendence, invincibility, and perfect union.

Psychologists call this an inversion because the patients are promising to turn upside down—invert—the situations that currently surround them. For example, Scarlett hates the grit under her fingernails and the hunger in her stomach, and she vows to beg, borrow, manipulate, or steal to get herself out of poverty. She is driven to turn her poverty state upside down—to invert it.

At some point in her childhood, Barbara Ryan experienced an inversion. For years she watched her mother silently put up with her father's drinking. She knew that her mother felt trapped because of her lack of job skills. From her mother's point of view, a confrontation, separation, or divorce was out of the question. She simply couldn't manage financially without him. So, even though the children suffered, the situation continued year after year after year. Instead of sympathizing with her mother, Barbara disapproved of her. Mom became a role model for what Barbara was determined *not* to be.

If Barbara had verbalized her Scarlett O'Hara speech, it would have sounded like this: "I will never, never trust any man to provide for me. I will always control my own life and take care of myself. I will do whatever is necessary to make sure I will not be victimized the way my mother has been victimized by my father."

Barbara made good on her promise. By the time she entered our hospital unit for treatment of depression she was the vice-president of sales for a large furniture chain and was making nearly twice the salary of her husband. She also was unhappy, and her marriage was in trouble. Part of her wanted to stay home with her young son, and part of her was afraid to surrender the independence that her job assured. The tug-of-war had left her tired, confused, and burned out.

An echo from Barbara's past reminded her to protect herself, to be self-reliant, and not to give in to anyone. This old message conflicted with her current feelings, but it had been playing in her mind too long to be turned off.

Tuning in to Old Messages

The stereotype of a deluded mental patient is one who walks around in a daze and complains about hearing voices. The truth is that we all are subjected to voices, especially those from our childhood. These voices and the content of their messages play over and over in our heads. They may not be audible, but their effect can be devastating, especially for driven people. Like a broken record that drums and throbs the same bar of music, the same messages follow these people through the years. No matter how hard the people try, they can't get away from the sound. The voices repeat: "You don't measure up. You fall short. You are worth *less* than everyone else. Who do you think you're kidding? You'll never amount to anything."

We mentioned these negative messages when we briefly walked you around the cycle of compulsion in chapter 4. Now let's trace the four common sources of those negative messages. As you rummage through your past and try to locate the root of your drivenness, tune in to the messages that have played in your head since childhood. Distinguish how you "heard" them. Most likely, you picked up on them in one of four ways:

1. The messages were spoken directly to you.
2. You experienced the messages firsthand through situations that happened to you.

3. You witnessed the messages as they were delivered to someone else.
4. You intuitively "felt" the messages.

Michael Potter grew up with a variety of negative messages that came from all four sources we've listed. For example, some were audible, spoken directly to Michael in the loud, abusive voice of his father. "You've got to make better grades, or you won't get into college. You've got to try harder, or the coach will cut you from the varsity football team," his dad constantly reminded him.

As harmful as these were, the messages that caused even more pain were the unspoken ones that he experienced. When Mr. Potter chose to work rather than to attend Michael's Little League game, young Michael interpreted his dad's decision to mean, "I'd rather spend my Saturday at the office than watch you play ball. You're not as important to me as my job." Michael later unconsciously assumed that same message from God. "You're not a priority to me, Michael. Unless you perform at a superhuman level, you are not worthy of my notice. By comparison, Michael, you simply don't measure up."

Whenever a negative message such as that is received, a silent dialogue begins to Ping-Pong back and forth in the receiver's mind. Michael's unspoken reply to his dad was, "Why do I always fall short? *What's wrong with me?*" This "What's wrong with me?" response is the most common question that plagues driven people. It is what nudges them toward the compulsions America applauds. Their impossible mission becomes to prove their worth to themselves and to everyone around them. It is their way of saying, "There is *nothing* wrong with me. See how successful I am, see how much money I have, see how hard I work!"

The third way the driven person intercepts a message is by witnessing it being inflicted on someone else. For example, Michael Potter frequently watched his father treat his mother as if she were an emotional and mental invalid. Over the years she lived down to those expectations. Mr. Potter never had to have a man-to-man talk with Michael and say,

"Son, I view women as being inferior, and I want you always to treat women as subordinates, too." Simply by watching his father's behavior toward his mother, Michael "heard" the message.

Much later, as a married man with a family, Michael knew intellectually and spiritually that men and women are equal and that he should esteem his wife. But the old message was still playing somewhere beneath the surface, and on an emotional level a part of Michael looked toward women with the same kind of disdain that his father had exhibited. This was probably why he felt driven to involve himself with soft pornography. The message witnessed from Dad was: "Women are not persons worthy of respect. Women are merely objects—sex objects."

Finally, the fourth way a message can be transmitted is by feelings. For instance, a child can walk into a room and intuitively sense the emotional atmosphere that he or she has entered. To use a slang term, the child can "pick up on the bad vibes." This is what happened to Virginia Potter, whose parents weren't openly hostile toward each other, but were coolly aloof. Virginia could sense that something important was missing in her mom's and dad's relationship. She didn't know exactly what it was, but she knew an element was lacking. For this reason, when she and Michael were married she was subconsciously determined to compensate for the vacuum that she had felt in her family of origin. When Michael, a captive audience of his own messages, didn't respond to her liking, she was driven to try harder and harder to create the kind of relationship that she craved.

What's Wrong with Me?

When we counsel driven people we ask them to tune in to the messages from their past. You can do the same kind of exercise. To prod your memory, answer the questions that we ask our patients. Put yourself in Barbara Ryan's place for a moment and recall the "voices" that whispered messages to you in your childhood.

"In your line of work you do a good deal of traveling," Dr.

Meier began his discussion with Barbara. "So you know that in the pocket of every airplane seat is a plastic sign that says 'occupied/occupado.' Passengers who decide to leave the plane briefly during a stopover can put the plastic cards on their seats to indicate that they will be back soon."

Barbara nodded, obviously curious about where Dr. Meier was going with the conversation.

"Think about your parents," Dr. Meier continued. "Were there times when you were a child that your parents seemed to be wearing signs that said 'occupied'? Did you feel when you looked in their eyes that their attention was somewhere else? Did it seem as if their bodies were there but their minds were a million miles away?"

She nodded.

"How did that make you feel?" Dr. Meier asked.

"Sometimes I wanted to pound on Daddy's chest and say, 'Hello, in there! Is anybody home?' I wondered what was wrong with me. Why didn't anyone have time to listen to me? I knew I couldn't be very important to Mom and Dad since they never paid me any attention."

"And when your father drank too much and your mother was wearing her 'occupied' sign, did you ever blame yourself for what was wrong at home?" Dr. Meier asked. "Did you ever think that if you worked a little harder at school, made your parents a little prouder, and helped out around the house a little more that your mom and dad might be happier and everything would be all right?"

Again Barbara nodded. "Pretty silly, huh?" she said. "I had this crazy idea that if I did my part to make everything perfect, somehow the perfection would spill over to Mom and Dad. Especially to Dad."

Barbara's reaction wasn't silly at all. It was normal. Remember Meredith MacRae's similar words: "I thought the better child I was, the less my father would drink. So I was the one who, when he was home, made him peanut butter sandwiches. I was the hero, the rescuer."

Young chldren are typically self-centered. They peer out at their small world and see everything as being connected to themselves. If Mom is depressed, the daughter wonders,

What did I do to make her feel this way? If Dad drinks too much, the son is convinced, *If I were a better person, Dad wouldn't do this to himself.* Children watch as their parents fight, separate, and finally divorce. The message that is replayed over and over in their heads is, *If we had tried harder this never would have happened. It's our faults.*

Negative messages can kick in later in life, too. Not until after Virginia and Michael Potter were married did she start to decipher silent messages from her husband. He often wore an "occupied" sign as he thought about his business, making money, and building his reputation in the community. She interpreted his workaholism as a message that said, "My job is more important than my marriage. You are worth less to me than my career."

What Virginia didn't realize was that Michael was still reacting to the old messages that he had fielded from his father so many years ago. He was still trying to prove his value to his dad. Like a child, Virginia connected Michael's lack of attention with something she had done. *What's wrong with me?* was the familiar question that haunted her. Then, as if to prove to herself and to her husband that there was nothing wrong with her and that she had a great deal of value, she plunged into community service, club work, and acting as everyone's favorite cheerleader.

One of the problems with these silent negative messages is that they tend to be whispered from one generation to another. When Virginia set out to prove her worth to herself and her husband, she began wearing an "occupied" sign of her own. It wasn't until her children, Chip, Brian, and Whitney, participated in the pie chart exercise that she realized how preoccupied she was and how neglected they felt.

How to Silence Negative Messages

Turning down the volume on negative messages isn't easy, but it can be accomplished. We tell patients that there are three steps to silencing the "voices" of the past: overcoming your denial that these messages existed, admitting that the messages are still there, and forgiving whoever put them there. In a sense, you have to let all of your childhood pain bubble to the surface, confront it, and then let go of it forever.

Overcoming Denial

As you can see, denial plagues driven persons at each point on the cycle. Only the object of that denial changes. Now the patient is denying the negative messages from the past. One of our most difficult cases of workaholism involved a successful executive who fought all of our efforts to trace the roots of his drivenness. He never became angry when we probed around in his past; he simply denied that there was anything there. Even his wife couldn't shed any light on his early years. She told us that she knew David's parents had divorced at some point in his childhood, but he had never wanted to talk about the details. That reluctance was a strong clue that a pocket of pain existed somewhere under the surface. We knew we had to help him to confront it and get rid of it.

One afternoon, when he was telling his life story to members of his therapy group, a remarkable change came over him. His voice became different—almost like that of a little boy—and he started to sob. For the first time, he allowed himself to relive the awful night when he was five years old and he watched his father walk out on the family, never to return. Even his facial expression changed, and he took on a childlike despair as he begged his father, "Please don't leave us." He tried to strike a bargain: "If you will stay, I'll always do what I'm told to do." No reply. The door slammed shut, and the child was left with the haunting messages: "What's wrong with me? What did I do to make him go away? Why didn't he love me enough to stay?"

Eventually David responded to the messages with his own version of a Scarlett O'Hara turnip speech. He vowed to become so strong, so tough, so self-sufficient that no one would ever hurt him the way his dad had hurt him. Work became his obsession. It provided him with the money and success that he thought would insulate him against pain. It also occupied his mind so he didn't have time to think about how much he still hurt. He became so addicted to work that it became a source of pain in itself.

The day David confronted the negative messages from his childhood he cracked the door to recovery. What followed was predictable: He had to grieve his past pain before he could be rid of it once and for all. For several days he was on an emotional roller coaster. More than once he half-jokingly commented that if this was part of recovery, he thought he preferred the work addiction.

David's roller coaster had the usual highs and lows. Initially, he was shocked by the realization that he had endured such a horrible trauma. He had buried the incident so successfully for so long that it was like a revelation when it finally surfaced. When the truth sank in, his shock turned to anger.

"How could he do that to me?" he demanded. "How could any father be so cruel and insensitive as to walk out on his five-year-old son without an explanation?"

This stage of the grieving process can be difficult for our hospital staff—and for us. Patients who are finally venting years of pent-up anger often look for whipping posts. They carp at the nurses, rage at the doctors, complain about the food, beat the walls, kick the chairs, and threaten to leave. Eventually, when they realize that they can do nothing to change what happened so long ago, they turn their anger inward, and depression sets in.

What we call "true grief" is next, and is characterized by waves of tears that leave the patient exhausted. Sometimes men fight the urge to cry, although we assure them that this is the purging part of the grieving process and is normal and healthy. Letting the tears roll is a cleansing exercise that clears the way for forgiveness. If the patient doesn't reach a point where he or she can accept and forgive the past, he or she may never break out of the addiction cycle. The person may put a stopper on one addiction, only to turn to another, equally harmful, habit.

The danger of confronting negative messages and grieving

old pain is the temptation to dance the Texas two-step. Here's how it works: Patients successfully break through their denial of the messages, and they face the pain head-on. So far, so good. But then, rather than working their way through the anger, depression, and tears, they do a quick two-step all the way to forgiveness.

"Okay, okay, so my parents weren't like Ozzie and Harriet or the Cleavers, but I'm a good Christian, so I forgive them," they say too quickly. Spiritually and intellectually they make amends, but emotionally they haven't worked through the hurt. They settle for a bandage kind of forgiveness that simply won't stick. The pain residue remains in place, and they continue to ride around and around on the addiction cycle. Only when the negative messages truly are faced and grieved are the patients ready to move on to the second step of silencing the voices forever.

To help patients confront their old negative messages we suggest that they complete two easy "purging" exercises. You can do them, too.

Take four sheets of paper and on each sheet list the negative messages that you intercepted as a child. Trace the messages to the four sources that we've talked about. Have one sheet devoted to messages that were spoken directly to you; a second for messages that you experienced; a third for messages that you witnessed; and a fourth for messages that you felt.

Phrase each message in the words someone might use if he or she were speaking to you. For instance, you might remember a spoken message like Michael Potter's, "You've got to try harder or you_____ (won't get into college, won't graduate from high school, won't be good enough to be my son or daughter)." When you have completed this task, the result is a mosaic of all the messages that you may have heard or felt in your childhood. One or two of the lists might be lengthy, the others may be short, but at least one negative message probably will be written on each of the four sheets of paper.

Next, we ask our patients to take their lists of negative messages and go to a large mirror, look at themselves, and

start repeating each of the messages out loud at their reflec-
tions. As you go through this process, you may be startled by
the intensity of the words that you speak. The messages,
buried in your subconscious for many years, finally surface
in raw form and harsh terms. Hearing them spoken will help
you to break through any denial that you may be experiencing. Among your messages might be these:

- "You're no good."
- "You won't amount to anything."
- "We didn't want another child, you were an 'acci-
  dent.'"
- "Your father was so disappointed that you weren't a
  boy."
- "If I hadn't quit my job to have a family, I'd be a
  district manager by now."

Regardless of how you first received these messages—
whether by hearing, experiencing, witnessing, or feeling
them—they have been trapped inside you for so long that
they have become a part of you. After so long, you have
actually fed them to yourself. At some subconscious level,
you have been cast in the role of being your own dysfunctional parent, and in that role you have continued to admin-
ister these old messages.

As you look at the mirror and repeat each negative statement, think about the specific person who originally sent the
message and try to identify exactly who was the rightful
target of the message. For example, suppose a persistent statement that you heard from your father in your childhood was
"You'll never amount to anything." In reality, the message
was about Dad and his sense of failure, frustration, and inadequacy. He had projected it onto you, but you weren't the
legitimate target of the words. The message didn't belong to
you. Now you have the opportunity to give it back.

"Dad, the message that you sent to me, the one that said,
'You'll never amount to anything,' is about you and not
about me," you should repeat into the mirror. By doing this,
you are depersonalizing the toxic message. Remember, a

child who grows up in a dysfunctional family intuitively overpersonalizes negative feelings and messages. The person claims them as his or her own, even if they are directed toward someone else. Now you are clearing the air, refusing to accept the message. You are directing it back to the sender.

Another example might be the daughter who grew up with constantly bickering parents. The message the child heard from her dad was "All women are self-centered nags." The little girl assumed the assessment was correct, and she has a very low opinion of herself. In therapy as an adult, she learns to shed the label by looking at herself in the mirror and saying, "No, Mom and Dad, that message had nothing to do with me. It was all about your conflict with each other and Dad's anger and fear of women. It is not a message that I choose to carry with me anymore."

The mirror exercise not only breaks through the harshness of the original messages, but it also helps you to realize that as long as you carry those messages, you will continue to feed them to yourself. After you have become comfortable with the concept of refusing messages and sending them back to their originators, you don't need the mirror as a prop. If you encounter a grumpy, out-of-sorts sales clerk who verbally snaps at you when you ask a simple question, you can refuse to accept the negative communication. Internally you reply, *That rude statement by the clerk might have been directed at me, but it really has nothing to do with me. The clerk obviously is upset with herself or with something that is going on in her life. I refuse to carry her unkind words with me.*

Replacing Old Messages with New

Negative messages that have been playing for decades can have an almost hypnotic effect on the listener. As we try to stop the flow of these messages and turn the tide in the other direction, we often use a saturation technique.

"What are these?" asked Virginia Potter one morning as we doled out a handful of paper cutouts.

"What do they look like?" we replied, answering her question with one of our own.

She looked down at our gift and grinned. "Paper hearts? Hmmm, I know time flies when you're having fun, but I didn't realize it was February fourteenth already." She nodded her head knowingly. She had been in our hospital unit long enough to be familiar with our techniques. "Okay, what's my assignment?"

We told her we wanted her to distribute the hearts to the other patients on the floor. Each patient would then write something positive about Virginia on the scrap of paper and return it to her during the next day's group session. She would be asked to lead off the session with a reading of her paper hearts.

Although the exercise may seem silly, it's one small way that we can help a patient to alter her or his perspective of self. The positive messages give balance to the negative voices that have played like a background chorus for so long. The patients who scrawl notes on the hearts choose their words carefully. They're very specific and sincere in their comments, and they hone in on the person's character and personality rather than on attractive clothes or jewelry or family.

"You're a wonderful listener," was a compliment that was repeated on three of Virginia's hearts.

"I liked it when you teased me the other day. It didn't hurt; it just made me feel special."

"Great smile!"

"I wish we lived closer. I've never had a friend like you before."

These messages usually have a profound effect on the receiver, even one as sophisticated as Virginia Potter. Although she had fielded many compliments in her life, she was visibly touched by the genuine love that was expressed in the penciled sentiments of the group. A few tears were blotted during her "reading," and a round of hugs wrapped up the session.

"Want us to get rid of those notes?" we asked Virginia after everyone else had filed out of the room. We were kidding, of course. She looked at us and smiled, then carefully wrapped the paper hearts in a tissue and tucked them in her pocket.

"I think I'll hold on to them," she said.

Virginia didn't know it, but in the next several days she would have the opportunity to collect many more affirmations of her worth. Some of them would be provided by herself.

"We'd like for you to start a list of positive messages that you want to give yourself," we announced to her the next day. "Include characteristics that you particularly enjoy about yourself and then jot down several new 'permissions' that will accompany the messages."

She look confused. "I understand the positive characteristics—things like my dazzling personality, toothy smile, and dynamite body," she joked. "But 'permissions'? That's the part I don't get. Give me an example, and I'll take it from there."

"Okay," we agreed. "You might give yourself permission to set boundaries on when your friends and family can and cannot visit your home unannounced. You might decide that Saturday and Sunday afternoons are fine, but during the week you want your privacy. Or you might give yourself permission to express appropriate anger when Michael chooses to work six nights out of seven. Or you might give yourself permission to resign from all of the out-of-the-home activities that you don't enjoy and to concentrate on the few that you find rewarding."

"I think I'm going to like this exercise a lot," she said, nodding in a way that told us she understood. "And the purpose? What does it accomplish?"

We explained that she had reached a point in her therapy where she needed to begin to reparent herself. She had to start sending herself appropriate, positive, and nurturing messages.

"Now I *know* I'm going to like this exercise," she said with a wide grin.

Her response didn't surprise us. People who have been driven by negative messages have an insatiable hunger for positive feedback. We were giving her the green light to create such feedback. Prior to this, she subconsciously had sought activities that guaranteed her lots of applause. Among the benefits of her role as cheerleader and listening post had been the many spoken and unspoken messages of gratitude and approval.

For this same reason, many driven persons who work outside of their homes choose to enter professions that give generous strokes in addition to salaries. Applause is one of the perks of being in the public arena of politics, theater, and other high-profile jobs. If you trace the backgrounds of several successful entertainers you'll find echoes of negative messages and more than a few Scarlett O'Hara turnip speeches. They choose show business because of the applause they receive from their enthusiastic fans. A good example of such a performer is country crossover singer Ronnie Milsap, whose blindness hasn't prevented him from winning six Grammy awards and selling more than twenty million records.

Milsap's negative messages were put firmly in place during infancy when his mother rejected him and his blindness. She saw her son as some kind of punishment from God. She spent most of Ronnie's first year crying and blaming her husband for cursing her with a blind child. Finally, she demanded to be rid of the baby, and Ronnie's father took him to live with his own mother and stepfather a few miles away. Even the love Ronnie received from his grandparents couldn't erase the pain of being rejected by his mother.

New negative messages were added the few times that he encountered his mother. Once she brought her baby daughter to visit him. She put Ronnie's hands on the little girl's eyes and said, "She's not like you, and she didn't shame me. She can see."[1] Although he claims to hold no bitterness for the pain his mother inflicted, he admits today that the lingering effects still haunt him. He explains it this way:

> I have heard psychologists claim that ninety percent of a child's personality is formed by the age of seven. If this is true, my psychological scars are deep. I was taught to feel

guilt and inferiority because I was blind. Sometimes, instead of trying to compensate for blindness, I tried to punish myself. I was a small child trying to achieve atonement for an affliction over which I had no control. My mother actually made me feel, in my young mind, that I was responsible for my own blindness.[2]

Today he calls music his vehicle for acceptance. Not only does it give him personal independence and financial security, but it also provides waves of positive messages in the form of applause, sell-out concert dates, and industry awards. On a grand scale, each request for an autograph, every fan letter, and each hit record is similar to receiving another paper heart that contains a positive message.

Recognizing God's Validation

As comforting as applause and paper hearts can be, they aren't the ultimate source of validation. The foundation of drivenness is unmet spiritual needs, those needs for transcendence, immortality, and perfect union. These needs must be addressed at a spiritual, as well as human, level. Ultimately, every driven person has to recognize that his or her worth isn't validated by other people alone, and it doesn't have to be proven through kind scribbles, soft strokes, or hard cash. All these gestures merely reaffirm a person's worth and bolster his or her feeling of self-esteem. Sometimes we ask patients to repeat these sentences: "I deserve to live because I am here. The fact that God made me proves that I have value. All other 'proof' is circumstantial."

Not only did God create you, we tell them, He values you so highly, "the very hairs of your head are all numbered," according to the Bible (Luke 12:7).

Often our patients will question the combination of therapy methods that we use. They say for a team of doctors determined to silence negative messages, we sometimes send mixed signals of our own.

"You tell us our worth comes through God," said Virginia Potter. "But if God's validation is all that we need, why do you also tell us to develop a support network, healthy family relationships, and good friends? Why isn't God's assurance enough?"

It is. However, any positive message gains volume and strength when it is repeated in various voices at different times and from all corners. A healthy, well-balanced person might classify, by importance, the sources of validation this way:

1. God's validation.
2. Self-validation.
3. Validation from others.
4. Validation from material possessions.
5. Validation through self-sacrifice or self-destruction.

As we've said, we need no other acceptance than God's. The fact that He put us on this earth assures us that we are worthy of being here. Of secondary importance is our self-validation. We are aware of our self-validation when we feel good about ourselves and when we experience inner peace. Third, as humans, it is helpful to us to be uplifted and encouraged by feedback from people around us.

The final two validations—the kind that comes from material possessions and through self-sacrifice—are of little importance to the well-balanced person. However, they are of extreme importance to the unhealthy, driven individual. In fact, the list of validations, as shown above, is inverted—turned upside down—for the driven person. Knowing that God loves us unconditionally is of little importance to the compulsive person. Of highest importance is the feeling that the only way the person can prove himself or herself worthy is to push almost to self-destruction (validation through self-sacrifice). Only if she works herself into a frenzy, performs as the perfect mom, has the most beautiful home in the neighborhood, wins the "teacher of the year" honor, or gets a standing ovation for her speech, will she feel fulfilled and worthy.

151

The Validation of a Support Group

As we lead our driven patients through therapy and help them to recognize their true source of validation, we encourage them to tap into the fellowship and strength of a support group. Not only do group members help one another to gain insight into past experiences, but they also assist in sorting out the conflicts that occur every day. Burdens aren't as heavy when they are shared, and a good support group willingly assumes part of each member's burden.

We recommended the support group called Al-Anon to Michael Potter since it is an organization geared to persons who have an alcoholic in their family. It includes a Twelve Step recovery program based on the very effective Twelve Step program of Alcoholics Anonymous. We also suggested that Michael might see whether his community had an active Workaholics Anonymous chapter. Other groups that could offer support to Michael and Virginia would be Emotions Anonymous and Adult Children of Alcoholics (ACOA). Even though Virginia didn't grow up with an alcoholic parent, she was at a point in her recovery where she recognized that her family was dysfunctional. She had suffered passive abuse similar to the kind endured by children of alcoholics. Members of an ACOA group would understand her childhood experiences, and she would understand theirs.

A support group is an opportunity to be re-familied, to receive the fellowship, love, and support that may have been missing in the family of origin in the past or that may be missing from a dysfunctional marriage in the present. A support group is also a flesh-and-blood symbol and reminder that we are all members of God's family and that we do not have to seek human immortality or chase false performance gods as a means of gaining membership into His family.

One of the purposes of a support group is to add to the stereophonic chorus of affirmations that is building around the driven person and is drowning out the negative messages from the past. This blending of "voices" can work together to diminish what we call the "shame base," which we'll encounter at Stop Three of the compulsion cycle.

Chapter Seven

The Shame That Blinds
Point 3: The Shame Base

No one was surprised in 1984 when superstar Liza Minnelli checked into the Betty Ford Center in Rancho Mirage, California, to get help in kicking her two-decade dependence on Valium, alcohol, and what she referred to as "party drugs." She was just the latest in a string of celebrities who had gone public with an abuse problem in our unhealthy, driven society.

Sometimes addictions are very predictable, like Liza's. After all, she had been in and out of treatment centers since she was a toddler—not as a patient, but as a visitor. Her mother, Judy Garland, had publicly and privately battled addictions for years and had died of an accidental drug overdose in 1969. Although the genetic link of addictions is still unclear, most people aren't surprised when abuse spills over from one generation to another. Neither are they surprised when well-known people suffer from addiction. Somehow it seems to go with the territory. Life in the fast lane apparently requires a lot of speed.

Four Shame Factors Lead to Addiction

Although we were not a part of the medical team that helped Liza to achieve her healthy recovery in California, we've counseled scores of patients whose addictions have been equally predictable, although far less public. In our work with these people we've identified four factors that make their addictions predictable, all of which arise from shame and the threat of failure. Any of these factors, when present in a person's childhood or current life, make him or her extremely susceptible to addictions. When we become aware of the factors, we start looking for the addiction. We call the first factor "living legends."

Living Legends

The pressure of living up to a legend can be overwhelming, whether that legend is a famous entertainer like Judy Garland or a local version—a successful and prominent businessperson, doctor, attorney, educator, or pastor. Everyone is watching, making comparisons, and repeating clichés, such as "Like father like son" or "She's certainly following in her mother's footsteps."

We once counseled a third-generation attorney who had been married and divorced four times by the age of thirty-six. He was addicted to what we call serial marriages—a rapid succession of brief (but legally binding) relationships. His addiction was costly, embarrassing to his family, time-consuming, and emotionally draining for himself and his train of brides.

As we talked to this man about his past, he recalled for us his junior year in college when he was toying with the idea of becoming an elementary school teacher. He wrote to his father, a lawyer, about his career aspiration and promptly received a box of very expensive stationery via parcel post. The letterhead read: Logan, Logan, & Logan, Attorneys-at-Law. Our patient, the third Logan, read the future and felt the pressure. He could forget about a career in education; his father was counting on him. His destiny was engraved in script on expensive, watermarked paper. Insecurity engulfed him. *What if I can't match the high standards of Logan I and Logan II?* he wondered. If he failed, how could he possibly cope with the inevitable shame?

His fears were similar to those that Liza Minnelli once expressed to an interviewer: "Oh, how am I ever going to live up to everything everybody's thinking?"[1] In cases of "living legends," an addictive agent can ease the pain of insecurity and medicate the shame that is attached to failure—real or imagined. A succession of intense relationships, complete with the "highs" of courtship and conquest, can soothe low self-esteem and divert attention away from a demanding profession.

Eleven Going on Thirty

A second shame factor that makes addictions predictable is the lack of a childhood. Sound confusing? Here's what we mean: Many of our patients admit that their mom's or dad's behavior forced them to take on adult roles when they were still children. They were deprived of their right to be young. As kids, they were kept too busy mothering Mom or fathering Dad. There was no time for them to act their age.

Barbara Ryan was only twelve years old when she assumed responsibility for cooking her family's meals, cleaning the house, and watching over her young brother. She had no choice. Her mother was wearing an "occupied" sign as she tried to care for her alcoholic husband and then became an alcoholic herself, and her father's attention was dominated by his addiction to Scotch whisky. Barbara did her best to compensate for her dysfunctional home by performing all the duties that would make it appear normal, at least on the surface. She took charge.

Situations like Barbara's are repeated in many families, even very prominent ones. In his biography *Judy*, author Gerold Frank told the revealing story of a husband and wife duo who once arrived at Judy Garland's home to be interviewed for positions on the household staff. The couple was slightly nonplussed when a pre-teen Liza answered the door, matter-of-factly asked to see their list of references, and then excused herself to use the telephone to check the names. She was in charge. In fact, Judy is said to have told Liza, "You are now the head of the house," when the child was only eleven.

Children who are forced to grow up too fast often reach for addictive agents that give them a feeling of control. By "being in charge" they feel they can compensate for the shame that surrounded them during their childhood, when their lives were so clearly out of control.

All in the Family

A third shame factor that makes addictions predictable is one that may be out of the victim's hands but could be in the blood. As we've said earlier, the jury is still undecided as to whether or not some addictions are inherited, but the evidence is mounting in favor of the idea. In 1990, a team of researchers announced that it had pinpointed for the first time a gene on a chromosome that may make people prone to alcoholism. If verified, the discovery will represent the first specific identification of a genetic root for alcoholism.

Even without such conclusive proof, certain addictions seem to run rampant in some families. Several studies have indicated that four times as many adult children of alcoholics (ACOAs) as non-ACOAs become substance abusers. The reason for this could be genetic, or it could merely be behavioral. In other words, parents model certain behavior for their children, and the kids are quick studies. They learn by example. They watch Mom and Dad turn to a substance to fill unmet needs, and they do the same. Like father like son, again.

Kids may or may not reach for the same substance as they saw their parents use. Liza Minnelli followed in Judy Garland's footsteps when she developed habits similar to those that contributed to her mother's death. This isn't always the case. Sometimes a parent may exhibit an applauded addiction that is not passed on to a child; instead, the child develops a negative addiction. This might have been what happened in another legendary show business family—the Bing Crosby family. Bing, in addition to being very successful, was a straitlaced, perfectionistic father who laid down the rules and expected everyone to follow. His troubled son Lindsay chose to break the rules that his father had valued, including moderation in the use of alcohol, a legalistic adherence to the Catholic faith, and hard work. In treatment for alcoholism two weeks before Christmas in 1989, Lindsay committed suicide after he learned that the inheritance that had provided support for his family had run out of money.

Another example occurred in the Bill Cosby family when Cosby's daughter Erinn checked into a drug rehabilitation center for treatment of cocaine, marijuana, and alcohol abuse. Her dad is not only America's favorite television father and author of the book *Fatherhood*, but is also well known for his hard-charging, highly driven approach to work.

We frequently see this same generational flip-flop—an applauded addiction passed on as a negative addition—in our counseling practice. For years, young Bud Stewart, son of Richard and Luci Stewart, witnessed his driven parents plotting their hard-earned success. Evenings were spent with both parents huddled over financial ledgers, and the only friends who were entertained at home were steady clients or prospective customers. Everything was done for a purpose, and the purpose always was related to getting ahead professionally. Although the Stewarts put far too much emphasis on succeeding as a business team, they accomplished their goal through legitimate hard work. Bud, on the other hand, inherited his parents' desire for success, but tried to achieve it by taking shortcuts. He fell victim to any promise of quick money. He couldn't turn down a deal, no matter how risky or costly.

In part, Bud was merely living out the logical extension of his parents' unchecked ambition. Since the family message was "There will never be enough," Bud leapfrogged over legitimate business approaches into the realm of the super-risky and the borderline ethical. Bud's unconscious message may have stated, "You can never do enough or be enough in the mainstream. Therefore, go to the fringe in your quest for superhuman achievement."

Of course, the opposite can occur as well. Often a parent's *negative* addiction resurfaces in the second generation as an applauded addiction. This is what happened to Barbara Ryan, one of an estimated twenty-eight million Americans who grew up with at least one alcoholic parent. Barbara wasn't drawn to alcohol as her father was or to a codependent relationship as her mother was. Her addictive agent was work, which probably caused her and her family a comparable amount of pain. Many adult children of alcoholics become overachieving workaholics and perfectionists. They bury themselves in work or busyness so they won't have time to dwell on the pain and shame of the past. Their addictive agent serves as means to escape and compensate for the family shame. Eventually, like Barbara, they burn out in middle age.

The Heavy Burden of Shame

The fourth and final factor that makes an addiction predictable is the one we've touched on as we've talked about the other three factors: the presence of shame. *Without exception, all addictions are based on shame.* People become addicted to a substance or to an activity as a way of dealing with or covering up their shame. Every person who suffers from an addiction carries an enormous—although often secret—burden of shame. For that reason, whenever shame is present, addiction is predictable. If we encounter one during our counseling sessions, we look for the other. And we usually find it.

Shhhh: Learning to Say the "S" Word At a recent workshop on shame, the joke among the participants concerned the single characteristic that they found they all shared. When they compared notes as they introduced themselves to the group, they discovered that not one of them had told family members or friends the nature of the workshop they were attending that weekend. Why? The topic was shame, and they were ashamed to admit it! At least one woman preferred to call shame the "S" word rather than to name it. Others simply lowered their voices whenever they spoke of their (shhh) shame.

Even though shame is a basic emotion that all human beings experience, it often is so personal and so secret that no one wants to discuss it. However, as we work our way around the addiction cycle and try to understand each progressive step, we can't bypass the third, and perhaps most important: the shame base. To effectively halt an addiction and build a healthy Stage 2 kind of recovery, each of us has to locate and understand his or her shame base. In cases of addiction, it's always there, although it may be forgotten, hidden, buried, or in disguise.

Addictions that are predictable—such as those of Liza Minnelli, Lindsay Crosby, Bud Stewart, and Barbara Ryan— are based on shame that is obvious. It's easy to see the shame attached to a child whose parent is alcoholic, especially if the alcoholism is no secret. It's understandable, too, for a child to suffer shame about inadequacies when she or he is trying to live up to the great expectations of her or his parents or "audience." But what about shame that isn't so visible or obvious?

Often patients in treatment for applauded addictions are confused by our flat, unequivocal statement that *all* addictions are based on shame. These people take a quick look back at their childhood, survey their school years, scrutinize their current family, and they find . . . nothing. They shake their heads and question our diagnosis. The family tree is well pruned of any embarrassment or shame, they tell us.

"Maybe you're looking in the wrong places," we reply. Then we explain the not so obvious hiding places where shame can accumulate out of sight. We suggest that they envision their shame bases as great holding ponds that are fed by springs trickling down from the past as well as those feeding in from the present. We tell them that the shame base can be so broad and so deep that it not only can engulf its victims but it often can drown them as well.

Sources of Shame If you have recognized your applauded addiction, but you can't locate your shame base, we can help you in your search. Imagine, for a moment, that you are a participant in one of our workshops on shame or that you are a part of a therapy group that is discussing the shame base. As we describe the various sources of shame, take a pencil and put a check mark next to the ones that might apply in your life. Read each description carefully, since your addiction may have more than one source of shame.

_____ *Carried Shame* Sometimes shame trickles down from generations far beyond your parents' generation. The source of shame might date back to your grandparents, great-grandparents, or even great-great-grandparents. A dramatic example of this is the self-help group that currently meets regularly in Germany in an effort to heal the wounds left by a past generation. The group's members? The adult relatives of Nazi officials. These people are still haunted by the horrible acts committed by their now-deceased family members.

Of course, the "sins" of your relatives may not be very sinful at all. To qualify as a source of shame they need not be serious or frowned-upon acts, such as a bankruptcy, an illegitimate birth, or a bonafide crime. Instead, they could be nothing more than nagging little feelings and doubts that whisper to you, for whatever reason, that your family isn't as good as other families.

In the popular Broadway classic *Showboat,* one of the main characters is a beautiful entertainer who is a favorite with everyone on board ship and with the audiences along the riverbank. However, her secret shame is that she has an African heritage. She tries to hide the truth, but when it is made public she is so disgraced that she leaves the ship and retreats into the degrading life of an alcoholic.

Although the *Showboat* story is fictitious, a similar kind of shame was experienced by many immigrants who came to the United States from Europe in the first half of this century. Rather than being proud of their ethnic roots, they tried to bury them. They Americanized their names and style of dress, and they quickly forgot the traditions of their homeland. They adopted the language, standards, and trappings of their new country, but they often couldn't shake the underlying doubts that they were as good as persons who had been born in the States. These doubts formed a quiet shame base that spilled down from generation to generation. The unspoken shame probably motivated many determined immigrants to prove their value by working incredible hours, amassing fortunes, building businesses, and becoming famous.

A well-known example of this is Chrysler Chief Executive Officer Lee Iacocca, who recalled in his book *Iacocca* the prejudice he faced as one of the few Italians growing up in Allentown, Pennsylvania. When classmates would mock him and make fun of his name, he tried to follow his father's advice: "Use your head instead of your fists." He used his head so well that he generally was the second-best student in his class. The top scholar was another child of immigrant parents, a Jewish girl.

_____ *Shame of Addiction* Parents who suffer from an addiction are usually ashamed of their dependency. Even if they deny or defend the addiction, at some level they feel real guilt about it. Dad may be addicted to getting himself entangled in extramarital affairs, and when confronted with his actions he rationalizes, "It's normal. Some men have to act out their sexuality, and I happen to be one of those men."

Or Mom may be a compulsive overeater who minimizes her addiction by saying, "Oh, I just love to cook, and I love to eat, so I don't mind being a little heavy." In reality, she is a lot like the man with the sex addiction. In spite of their protests, these people feel considerable shame about the lack of control in their lives. They offer excuses, but they don't believe their own words—not for a minute. Neither do their children. The kids sense the shame, and they share it.

___✓___ *A Child's Feelings of Embarrassment* Sometimes children are tremendously ashamed of their parents, and for good reasons. We once counseled a woman whose father's rageaholism constantly embarrassed her in public. She recalled times when he would treat the family to dinner at a fancy restaurant, but by the end of the meal all of the children had fled to the restrooms or to the car in tears. Dad would argue with the manager about the quality of the food, or he would rant at the waiter and refuse to leave a tip because the service wasn't up to his standards.

It took many therapy sessions before our patient realized that her father was addicted to rage because of his own shame: his deep sense of inadequacy. Only by "pulling rank" and picking on a person in a subservient role did Dad bolster his sagging self-esteem and medicate his feeling of personal worthlessness. The actions that medicated his shame caused a tremendous build-up of shame for his children.

Jacqueline Kennedy Onassis is a good example of a well-known personality who has suffered embarrassment because of a parent's dysfunction. Jackie's handsome father, called "Black Jack," was famous for his good looks and his well-publicized womanizing. Even after marriage to Jackie's mother, he made no attempt to curb his appetite for non-stop love affairs. Because of the family's social standing, the eventual divorce made headlines. Everyone knew that Black Jack was being charged with adultery by his angry and embarrassed wife. Details of the scandal were the talk of the town.

Such a source of shame can make addiction predictable. Jackie's shopping habit raised eyebrows when, during her first year in the White House, she engaged Oleg Cassini to design over one hundred dresses for her. In 1961, a bill for $40,000 covered the cost of gloves and other incidentals. Her compulsion to splurge continued in her years of marriage to millionaire Aristotle Onassis.[2]

Another shopaholic whose shame can be linked to embarrassment over a parent's action is Princess Diana of Great

Britain. Diana Spencer suffered real trauma at age six when her mother fell in love with a married man. Two well-publicized divorces (her mother's and her mother's lover's) and a child custody battle resulted before the headlines finally ceased. Later, when Diana was a teenager, her father fell in love with a married woman, and another divorce (this time the "other woman's") and a second custody battle were played out in the British tabloids.

After Prince Charles and Diana were married and had their first son, the princess suffered from what may have been depression and a dramatic loss of weight. Unconfirmed reports raised the question of anorexia. A psychiatrist, not employed by the palace but one who watched as the royal drama unfolded, predicted that Diana might develop an obsessive-compulsive illness or an addiction. Not only was she burdened by "great expectations," but she was also coping with a very large shame base that was formed by her embarrassment about her parents' actions during her childhood. Shortly after that, Diana began the series of buying binges that touched off a deluge of criticism from the British subjects. The psychiatrist's prediction seemed to have been on target.[3]

_____ *Parents' Lack of Identity* Psychologists call this an "identity vacuum," but the pop term is an "identity crisis." Either way, the meaning is the same. Some parents have difficulty in deciding who they are and what they are all about. Dad may hop from job to job or from location to location trying to "find himself." Mom may look for her answers in yoga class, transcendental meditation, or in the study of Eastern religions and reincarnation.

Children have a comfortable sense of pride and security when they know that their parents like themselves just as they are. Growing up with a dad who drives off whistling every day to his job as a janitor is healthier than watching a dad agonize over an executive position he hates.

Whenever parents are unhappy with themselves or don't have a clear vision of who they are, an air of uncertainty and shame permeates the home. Children grow up unsure of

163

what to expect next. They know only that Mom and Dad don't like the way things are. The status quo must be bad, the kids surmise, and, therefore, it becomes a source of shame.

_____ *Separation from God* As Christian counselors, we believe that all persons have an inner need for God. We also think that people are aware of this need, even though they may deny it vehemently.

How does this become a source of shame? In two ways. First, children may be ashamed of their parents' lack of connection with God. They witness the presence of religion in their friends' homes, and they compare it with the absence of religion in their own family. No one says grace around the dinner table; Sunday school and church services aren't a part of the weekly routine; vacation Bible school isn't anticipated in June; and no one named Pastor This or Reverend That ever comes to call. Something is missing, and the absence of that "something" is a source of shame.

A second way that shame can spring from a separation from God is when victims of applauded addictions allow their addiction to take the place of God. One of the by-products of all addictions is that the compulsion—whatever it is—becomes a mini-god. When this occurs, the person worships the compulsion and becomes even more detached from God. Although she may not be able to stop her addiction, she still feels shame about the wedge it places between herself and the true God.

Recall that one of the most virulent addiction drivers is the unmet spiritual need for union. If that union is missing with the authentic God, driven persons will place jobs, bank accounts, fame, or other mere mortals in that role as god-surrogates.

Examples of extreme rebellion against religion often mask a deep unmet hunger for God. The rebellion itself may be an upside down or inside out expression of the profound yearnings for union with God, yearnings that are universal. Tragically, anger or rebellion against an overly rigid human parent can become confused with rebellion toward a heavenly Father. The end product of such rebellion is alienation from God (the ultimate source of our shame reduction and shame resolution), and spiritual alienation only compounds the already existing shame base.

_____ *Emotionally Divided Marriages* Along the same lines, another source of shame is what we call fractured marriages. This occurs when the children in a family are ashamed of what they see as a weakness or division in their parents' relationship.

We once counseled a man who suffered a great deal of shame about his parents' platonic marriage. Simply put, they had stopped sleeping together years earlier and had even occupied separate bedrooms. Although nothing was ever said about the arrangement, the young man felt the deep split in the union. Long before he understood what a normal husband-wife sexual relationship entails, he knew that something was missing in his parents' marriage. It wasn't the same as the marriages he had witnessed all around him, and the difference became a source of shame.

_____ *The Shame of Poverty* Poverty is probably the most common source of shame that we see among patients in treatment for applauded addictions. We recall one workaholic who told of attending elementary school in his bare feet because his only pair of shoes was being repaired. The shame of that awful day haunted him for years, causing him to have an inversion (Scarlett O'Hara turnip speech), and directly resulting in his drive to achieve phenomenal success in business.

Bess Myerson, the beauty queen who grew up in a Bronx housing project, was driven to succeed far beyond the standard of her impoverished Jewish family. At times, her compulsivity was applauded—she earned the title of Miss America, became a television personality, was a spokesperson for a huge corporation, ran for the United States Senate, and was a well-known consumer advocate. But her drivenness also had a negative side. She was a convicted shoplifter, had a track record of volatile relationships with married men, and has been the subject of at least two books that paint her as a

165

neurotic, insecure woman who would stop at nothing to get what she wanted.

An even more tragic story of poverty involves Imelda Marcos, the former first lady of the Philippines, whose shopping addiction was confirmed when her closet was raided and found to contain 508 gowns, 1,060 pairs of shoes, vats of expensive facial cream, and 71 pairs of sunglasses.

Like all addictions, spendaholism is based on shame, and Mrs. Marcos's shame trickled down from a childhood that was unbelievably poor and dysfunctional. Her father was irresponsible and did nothing to provide for the brood of children he had brought into the world. His second wife, Imelda's mother, was so submissive that even though she threatened to leave the chaotic home, she never got farther than the garage. It was there that she finally escaped with her children, to live without lights or ventilation. The mother slept on a table, and the children made beds out of boards that were balanced by milk boxes. Since Imelda was the oldest, she was expected to beg for the family's food.

Even after her mother's death, when she moved back into her father's house, Imelda's life didn't improve by much. She attended a school that regularly posted the names of the students whose tuitions hadn't been paid. Imelda had to endure the shame of seeing her name listed on many occasions. Her humiliation drove her to experience an inversion. She promised to never, never be poor again. And, as we know, she made good on the promise.

Poverty isn't the only source of shame that is related to money. Rigid control of a family's funds is another. If Mom is stingy or Dad is a Scrooge, a child can translate their message to mean, "You don't deserve to have money." We once treated a young executive whose spending sprees could easily be traced to the shame imposed by his father. Dad made a good living, but he would only buy items for his children if they begged him for them. Our patient remembered many times when he would cringe at the thought of having to ask Dad for school books, a baseball glove, or new clothes. The boy's requests usually were granted, but only after a long lecture about the value of money.

Another source of shame connected to money is grandiose spending. Children can sense if parents are overdoing their spending habits. Shame and embarrassment result when Dad tries to "buy" friends for his son or daughter by lavishing money on expensive gifts, tickets to special events, or dinner at fancy restaurants. One of our patients, in treatment for bulimia, said that her workaholic father never would give of his time or his affection, but he would slip cash into her wallet without telling her. Rather than pleasing her, his generosity made her ashamed.

"I felt like a prostitute," she told us. "My dad was buying my emotional love."

_____ *Shame Caused by Family Secrets* At least three kinds of secrets can be powerful sources of shame for children. *The first is the secrets that are kept from the children by their parents.* Perhaps Mom became pregnant before she and Dad were married, and they have lied about wedding and birth dates ever since. Or perhaps Dad was dishonorably discharged from the military. Or maybe Mom had an abortion when she was a teenager. The nature of the secret isn't important. What matters is that something dark and mysterious was withheld from the children. They know it, and they carry around a burden of shame because of it.

A second kind of secret that causes shame is the secret that the whole family keeps from the outside world. The classic example is alcoholism. All members of the family work together to cover up Mom's "little problem." They pass it off as an illness; they make excuses for her slurred speech by blaming her migraine headache medication; and if she seems unsteady when she walks, her inner ear infection is the culprit. They hide her car keys, cancel her appointments, and live in fear that someone someday will find out the truth.

A third type of shame-inducing secret is the kind that children keep from their parents. For example, if Dad is a rageaholic, his daughter may decide not to show him her algebra examination with the failing grade on it. Withholding the test results seems more logical than enduring the horror of one of his tantrums.

During our counseling with Luci Stewart she was able to uncover a secret so painful that not only had she kept it from her parents, but also she had succeeded in blotting it from her own memory for many years. The secret came to the surface as she completed her relationship inventory, described in chapter 5. We noticed that when she jotted down thoughts about each of her family members, she became obviously troubled as she recalled a certain uncle. Then, when she did an exercise in which she imagined herself as a young girl returning home after a long absence, she became agitated.

"Tell us which family members you most want to see at your reunion," we prodded her.

"I want to see Mom, Dad, and my sisters," she replied.

"Is there anyone you don't want to see?" we asked. "Anyone you hope won't be at your family reunion?"

"Not Uncle Ted. I don't want to see Uncle Ted."

"Why not?"

She started to tremble and shook her head. "Not Uncle Ted," she repeated.

The memories came back in fragments, and she had difficulty putting together the pieces. She had been very young, perhaps six or seven years old, when Uncle Ted had briefly ducked in and out of her life. He was her father's younger brother. He was in the Navy and only had visited their home when he was stationed nearby at the Great Lakes Training Center. The extent of his abusiveness was unclear, but she remembered his touching her in ways that she didn't like. She never told her parents because Uncle Ted made her promise that she wouldn't; he said that her parents wouldn't understand and that they would spank her for lying. She kept her promise and her secret, first from her mother and father and then from herself. Although it was hidden under layers of denial, it was a major contributor to her shame base.

At our treatment centers we tell patients that secrets can create or contribute to a general sense of shame. For that reason, we say, "You're only as sick as your secrets."

_____ *Shame of Personal Addictions* Most of the sources of shame that we've listed up to this point have been traced to the family of origin. They've been someone else's shame imposed on the child.

It's also possible for a person to make his or her own contributions to the personal, ever-expanding shame base. For instance, a workaholic, such as Barbara Ryan, may be addicted to her job as a way of compensating for the shame she felt at having an alcoholic father. But that same addiction to perfectionism and work has caused her shame to expand. She's truly ashamed that her husband and her baby are suffering because of her compulsion to be a high achiever.

Michael Potter's shame base can be traced to his family of origin, and particularly to his raging, demanding father. But Michael also made personal deposits into his shame base when he became drawn to pornography. He hated the addiction and hated himself for falling victim to it. As his appetite for the material expanded, so did his shame.

How to Reduce Your Shame Base

Locating the source of shame is a giant step toward recovering from an addiction. The next step is to combat the shame head on. If you followed our suggestion and envisioned the shame base as a large holding pond fed by springs that trickle down from the past, you now must imagine yourself stopping the flow of shame and draining the pond forever.

How is this done? In our work at the clinic we encourage patients to complete several exercises and tasks that we've designed specifically to help them reduce their shame bases. You can do the exercises, too. One way to begin is by composing what we refer to as a "last will and testament."

Last Will and Testament

Pretend for a moment that you are your parents and that you are writing your last will and testament. However, unlike most wills, which deal with property and money, this document centers on the emotional and spiritual legacy that your parents left to you.

For instance, if you were Michael Potter's father you might leave all of your unfinished business to young Michael. You might pass on a heritage of frustration, dissatisfaction, and unmet ambitions. You would also mention your sense of shame and inadequacy about not having fulfilled your ambitions. As a part of the will, you must include instructions as to how it will be executed. You should instruct Michael that to carry out your will he must become very compulsive and overachieving. He must put his family dead last on his priority list and concentrate on building the family business and his personal image in the community.

As you put yourself in your parents' place, try to focus on their unmet goals. These, most likely, are what they have passed on to you, the next generation. Assume that you are your mother or your father and ask yourself: Am I a success? Have I made peace with the opposite sex and found ways to achieve intimacy with my mate? Have I grieved out any setbacks or major disappointments in my life? If any of these questions brings a negative response, you can be assured that the issues have resurfaced as a part of your legacy.

The purpose of this exercise is not to stir up feelings of anger toward your mom and dad, but rather to understand where your drivenness originated.

You will never be able to deplete that pool of shame if you don't take a careful look at the guilt you feel. How much of it is warranted? How much is unwarranted?

Inventory False Guilt and Authentic Guilt

Many of our patients follow our advice and become a part of therapy groups, such as Emotions Anonymous, Workaholics Anonymous, Alcoholics Anonymous, or Al-Anon. Central to these helpful organizations are Twelve Step recovery programs. Since our patients are familiar with each of the twelve steps, we ask them to focus on Step 4, which states that they have "made a searching and fearless moral inventory of ourselves."

"We want you to start to separate your authentic guilt from your false guilt," we told Luci Stewart shortly after she uncovered the painful memory of her sexual abuse by her uncle. "We want you to make two lists. The first is an inventory of those areas of your compulsion, addictions, and drivenness that you feel guilty about and that you are responsible for."

She winced. "You mean my perfectionism?"

"Yes, and perhaps your unwillingness to go with Richard on business trips."

She started to argue the point, but decided against it. She was still trying to sort out her feelings about travel. Her hesitation to leave home and accompany her husband on out-of-town trips had become more of a problem in the past two years. On several occasions she had promised Richard that she would attend sales conferences and conventions but had backed out at the last minute. Sometimes her excuse was the need to babysit for Bud's new baby, Robbie. ("After all, a baby with a spastic colon can't be left with just anyone.") Or it might be a touch of the flu or a head cold or any other minor illness that she could invent.

In our therapy sessions we had been trying to help her see that her increasing dislike of travel was directly linked to her compulsivity. When she was away from the familiarity of her home she felt out of control. Her routine was upset, and she was vulnerable to missed flights, late meals, and lost luggage. It was difficult for her to perform to perfection when she was forced into an imperfect world.

"You said I have to make two lists," she reminded us. "What's the second?"

"We also want you to inventory the areas of shame that were *not* your fault and that you should feel no responsibility for," we replied. "We call this false guilt, and it's totally different from the authentic guilt you feel about your perfectionism or the disappointment you cause Richard when you cancel a trip."

Twelve Suggested Steps of Emotions Anonymous

1. We admitted we were powerless over our emotions—that our lives had become unmanageable.
2. Came to believe that a Power greater than ourselves could restore us to sanity.
3. Made a decision to turn our will and our lives over to the care of God as we understood him.
4. Made a searching and fearless moral inventory of ourselves.
5. Admitted to God, to ourselves and to another human being the exact nature of our wrongs.
6. Were entirely ready to have God remove all these defects of character.
7. Humbly asked Him to remove our shortcomings.
8. Made a list of all persons we had harmed, and became willing to make amends to them all.
9. Made direct amends to such people wherever possible, except when to do so would injure them or others.
10. Continued to take personal inventory and when we were wrong promptly admitted it.
11. Sought through prayer and meditation to improve our conscious contact with God as we understood Him, praying only for knowledge of His will for us and the power to carry that out.
12. Having had a spiritual awakening as the result of these steps, we tried to carry this message, and to practice these principles in all our affairs.

Note: Emotions Anonymous reprinted this through the permission of A.A. (Alcoholics Anonymous) World Services, Inc. The Twelve Steps are reprinted and adapted with permission of Alcoholics Anonymous World Services, Inc. Permission to reprint and adapt the Twelve Steps does not mean that AA has reviewed or approved the content of this publication, nor that AA agrees with the views expressed herein. AA is a program of recovery from alcoholism. Use of the Twelve Steps in connection with programs and activities which are patterned after AA but which address other problems does not imply otherwise.

She nodded her understanding. "The incident with Uncle Ted would be false guilt, right? Even though it's part of my shame base, it wasn't my fault, and I shouldn't feel responsible for what happened."

She was learning quickly. The next exercise would be a natural offshoot from this one.

Journaling Your Shame

After Luci had completed her two inventories, we asked her to concentrate on the second, her areas of false guilt.

"It's time to write a letter," we told her. "Address it to your parents or anyone else who might have been responsible for specific incidents of false guilt."

"Such as Uncle Ted?"

We nodded. "In this letter, we want you to acknowledge what the false guilt was all about, and then we want you to hand over the responsibility for the guilt to its rightful 'owner.' "

This letter would never be read by the person to whom it was addressed. The purpose is not to blame the previous generation, but it is to give the adult child the opportunity to step out from under the false responsibility that he or she has carried for so long. Luci would have the chance to confirm that Uncle Ted was to blame for the sexual violation that had occurred when she was six. She might state that as a young child she was not responsible for setting the sexual boundaries in the family. That was an adult responsibility. She would no longer carry any shame for what had happened. That shame belonged to her uncle.

This exercise not only lightens the shame base of the driven person, but also helps to give a sense of direction. For example, Michael Potter wrote to his father that he could no longer try to be the super businessman that his dad had expected him to be. Michael gave back to his dad the feelings of drivenness and ambition. He stated that from that point onward he would set his own goals for achievement, and some of those goals might not be related to building a real estate empire but to building a stronger bond between himself and his wife.

We often tell our patients, "If you don't hand your shame back (to your dad or your uncle), you'll hand it down."

This is an informal slogan of the Adult Children of Alcoholics, which was derived from the A.A. slogan, "Pass it on." The A.A. slogan was positive: "You are to pass on recovery and the twelve steps to others." ACOA took this slogan and varied it to say, "If you don't pass it (the shame) back (to previous generations), you'll pass it on."

Unless you can mentally and emotionally and symbolically hand back that false shame or guilt, inherited from your family of origin, to that previous generation where it belongs, you're at risk of passing it on in two ways. First, you will pass it on to yourself. You will inflict shame and damage on yourself and reinforce your own addiction cycle. Second, you will probably pass it down to the next generation as well.

Hand it back. Don't hand it down.

Your Bill of Rights

People who have struggled for years under a heavy burden of shame often don't think they deserve equal rights because they don't see themselves as being equal.

"Put it in writing," we tell them. "Itemize all of your basic rights—things such as your right to express your anger within reason; your right to enjoy a healthy relationship with your spouse; your right to feel happy and satisfied; your right to take credit for the good work you are able to accomplish in an eight-hour day, and your right to say yes or no."

As fundamental as these rights may seem, they often are foreign concepts to the shame-based person. Many times as we review the lists with patients, they shake their heads in disagreement. "You may have a right to all those good things, but I don't," they emphasize. "I'm not entitled to them." Our assurance that all people have these basic rights is more readily accepted if the message is echoed by a circle of friends.

Build a Network of Friends

Another effective antidote to the shame base is encouragement from a group of friends. As a rule, persons who suffer from shame tend to isolate themselves. Just as a child buries his or her head or goes off to a corner after being publicly scolded, so also an adult will retreat to the sidelines. This is especially true of traditional Christians who are convinced that their shame makes them unworthy of being part of a church family. They deprive themselves of that meaningful connection as a way of punishment. The more isolated they become, the more heavily the burden of shame weighs on them. They have too much solitary time, and they use it to agonize about their shame. They don't have the benefit of hearing good friends balance the negative inner voices with affirmations of their positive characteristics.

Particularly in the cases of persons who have suffered from applauded addictions, their addictions may have occupied so much of their days that the addicts didn't have the opportunity to cultivate relationships. Encouraging these people to plug into good fellowship is vital. An entire new support circle may have to be found if the old relationships are destructive. For example, a recovering shopaholic may have to see less of her best friend, who also was her favorite shopping companion. Or a workaholic may have to stop spending off-hours with pals from the office who share the compulsion to climb the corporate ladder.

Say Goodbye to the Past

Finally, if the shame base is to diminish, it is essential that the shame-based person say an emotional goodbye to his or her family of origin. Most people who are addiction prone are either overly connected with their families, or they have broken all ties. The goal is to achieve some kind of healthy middle ground. We're not suggesting that communication be cut off or relationships severed. Instead, we're saying that boundaries must be established if the family ties are too binding. For example, since Michael Potter's shame base was

175

fed by his father's negative messages and his embarrassment about his dad's drinking, it becomes essential in recovery for Michael to loosen the tight family bond.

By the same token, driven persons who have been alienated from their families for years may need to reestablish contact long enough to make amends. We're not suggesting that the person who was so damaged by a dysfunctional family jump back into the negative situation for another harmful dose of pain and shame. Instead, we're encouraging the person who once angrily ran away from the past to now turn around, walk back and face that past, shake hands with it, and then walk away from it. This way, the shame is acknowledged, grieved, and released.

In this chapter we have reviewed a number of techniques for relieving the burden of false shame. As imperfect humans, we are also confronted with a degree of authentic guilt for the damage we have inflicted on others by the practice of our compulsions. One of the central messages of the Christian faith is that we do not have to carry the weight of that guilt by our own human power. As an aspect of God's spiritual union with us, the price for that guilt has already been paid at a cosmic level. The good news about healing our shame base is that we do not have to shoulder the responsibility for a previous generation's shame issues. God has provided a divine means of shouldering the guilt for which we do bear direct responsibility. We do not have to become our own codependent saviors. We do not have to engage in the self-sacrifice of compulsive overachievement. God's union is available for the asking. Atonement does not have to be purchased through addictive accomplishment.

After the shame base has been located and confronted, the journey around the addiction cycle can continue. At the next step we'll deal with low self-esteem, the natural offshoot of shame.

Chapter Eight

Driven to Be More to Keep from Being Less
Point 4: Low Self-esteem

"Sometimes, not often, but sometimes, less is more," Donald Trump said in his best-seller *The Art of the Deal*. Trump might have said that—he might even have thought it at times—but he certainly didn't seem to live this philosophy.

To the average American observer Trump's philosophy was just the opposite: "More and more and then some more is always best." Extravagance. Opulence. Any superlative seemed to accurately describe the man. . . .

Until 1990, when Trump's kingdom became so top-heavy with debt that it began to crumble.

What drove Donald Trump, one can only guess. We've counseled quite a few millionaires in our practices in Dallas, and the pattern seems to be much the same. The lower the self-esteem, the more grandiose the achievement—and the drivenness. These multi-millionaires are <u>continually driven to be more, to keep from being less.</u>

In Trump's case, his treasure chest includes Trump Tower, Trump Plaza, Trump Parc, Trump Palace, Trump Castle,

Trump Taj Mahal Casino, and the Trump Airlines. The impulse to imprint one's name on human institutions is often a manifestation of the spiritual need to be remembered by posterity. It is a quest for immortality.

One person who knows Trump well said recently in *People* magazine, "There is in Donald a genuine need to self-destruct. In order to feel real and whole, he had to exceed himself constantly, make more money, build bigger buildings. Underneath there's despair: *Nothing I do is enough, and it never will be.* And you can't outdo yourself forever, so you have to . . . start over."[1]

If anything is left, that is. A survey by Kenneth Leventhal & Company estimated Trump's debt as of April 30, 1990, at $3.2 billion. Leventhal projected Trump's net worth at anywhere from a negative balance of $295 million to a positive balance of $282 million, depending upon the market value of his real estate, which is continually fluctuating.[2]

We wonder if Trump isn't driven by that age-old desire to please his dad—or beat him! While most of us will never know the negative messages that might echo through his mind, Trump himself once said, "If I ever wanted to be known as more than Fred Trump's son, I was eventually going to have to go out and make my own mark."[3]

Except for the size of their businesses, Donald Trump sounds very similar to Michael Potter. Both men's low self-esteem (Point 4 on the addiction cycle) seems to be rooted in their desire to please—or beat!—dad. Both men's addictive agents are money, power, and control. Both men may be driven to transcend human vulnerability by the illusion of superhuman achievement. As Trump once said, "Money was never much of a motivation for me, except as a way to keep score."[4]

The Craving to Be #1

Certainly the craving to be #1 drove Michael Potter, and he was finally ready to admit this to us. At first, we were surprised when he called our office, scheduled an appointment, and explained to our receptionist that he wanted to talk about himself, not Virginia. Until this time Mike had only participated in discussions and exercises that related to Virginia. He had dodged all of our efforts to reach out directly to him, although he had begun talking about his father's legacy of unfinished business—the desire for Michael to accomplish things that papa couldn't—and how this had contributed to his shame base and feelings of guilt. When Michael entered Dr. Hemfelt's office for his appointment he looked obviously troubled.

"There's more," he said quietly. "My dad isn't the only reason I have such low self-esteem. I can't blame it all on the past. There are a couple of other items going on that even Virginia doesn't know about. That's why I thought I needed to talk with you alone."

We knew about both of the "other items," since Virginia had told us about her husband's generous loans to friends and business associates (and how she suspected that the family's real estate company was beginning to sag under the burden of the bad debts), and she also had talked about the discovery of pornographic magazines in Michael's desk. Since she had shared the information with us in confidence, we didn't let on to Michael that we already knew what he was going to tell us. We hoped that later, however, he would feel comfortable talking openly with his wife about the problems.

"I'm in some hot water financially," he began. "I think Virginia and Dad might suspect that I've made some bad business decisions, but they don't know the extent of it. The truth is, our company may have to file for Chapter 11 protection if the shopping mall project falls through. It's all my fault, too. Watching your family business go belly up is tough enough, Doc, but knowing that you're responsible for it happening is incredibly hard to accept."

The whole story came tumbling out—his inability to turn down requests for money, particularly from high school and college friends who were down on their luck; his failure to draw up legal documents to be signed by the borrowers; and his failure to ask for any collateral against the loans. Even pals who hadn't paid their old debts found an open credit line for new ones. Rather than losing Michael's friendship because of their inability to settle accounts, these borrowers had an open invitation to all college reunion events at the C.C.C., and they were always on the guest list for the annual football team steak fry.

"Which is another story," Michael said sheepishly. "The cost of the steak fry has gone through the roof. Every year it gets bigger and fancier. Ginny keeps telling me to either cut it out or scale it back. I can't seem to do either. Even though I feel guilty about spending money that I don't have, I can't imagine going to the coaching staff and telling them that I can't afford to do it."

"What would the coaches say to you if you told them there wasn't going to be a steak fry this year?" Robert Hemfelt asked.

"It's not what they'd *say*," Mike replied. "It's what they'd think." He shook his head. "No, I could never call it off. I'd be too embarrassed. Somehow I'll come up with the money. I always have in the past. I just can't say no. I guess it's what Ginny and the doctors call my 'codependency.' I have to please others."

Michael Potter looked down at his hands as he spoke, purposely avoiding Dr. Hemfelt's eyes. When Michael finally glanced up, he shrugged his shoulders. "You don't seem very surprised by any of this. Does Ginny know more than I think?"

The doctor smiled. "Your wife has talked about the family's money squeeze, but even if she hadn't, what you've told me wouldn't have come as a surprise."

The Unflinching Testimony of the Checkbook

At the Minirth-Meier Clinic we often say, "If we had a choice between two sets of data for the diagnosis of a new patient—one set being a battery of sophisticated psychological tests and the second set being a few minutes to review the checkbook and financial records of the recovering person—we would choose the financial records."

Why? Because the way people manage and use money is an exquisitely sensitive barometer of how they nurture themselves and those people around them. Most patients, such as Michael Potter, are poly-addicted, as we've mentioned before. Money management or money mismanagement is nearly always one of them. Sadly, even when a person recovers from the primary addiction—work, perfectionism, even alcohol or drugs—the money problems usually remain in place. The guilt, shame, fear, pain, anger, and loneliness that a compulsive spender or debtor experiences are still present.

How About You?

Most victims of applauded addictions have one primary addiction and several secondary compulsions. Money mismanagement is nearly always among them. Check the statements below that apply to your own situation.

1.____ *"I have given inaccurate data in order to obtain credit."*
2.____ *"My debts make my home life unhappy."*
3.____ *"When I am faced with a difficult financial situation, the opportunity to borrow funds gives me a feeling of relief."*
4.__✓__ *"The pressure of my debts distracts me from my work."*
5.__✓__ *"I have worked out a strict plan for paying my debts, but then broken it under pressure."*
6.__✓__ *"My debts cause me to think less of myself."*
7.____ *"I'm afraid that my boss or my family or friends will learn the extent of my total indebtedness."*
8.____ *"I have borrowed cash without considering the rate of interest that I will be paying, because I had to have the money."*

181

9.____*"I feel superior to other people when I loan them money."*

10.____*"As soon as I get my 'big break' I'll be instantly out of debt."*

If you checked three or more of these statements, money mismanagement is probably one of your primary or secondary compulsions.

After Michael Potter had completed this diagnostic questionnaire, which clearly indicated his compulsion to overspend, he half-jokingly said, "I guess I can't blame this one on Dad, right, Doc? It would be a real cop-out to think my growing-up years or my parents had anything to do with my being a lousy money manager."

He was wrong. The roots of most money addictions can be traced directly to the family of origin and the formative years when the child was sent negative messages that contributed to his or her shame base. Low self-esteem and poor self-image resulted. As adults, heavily shame-based persons, such as Michael, can use money to nurture themselves, get even with dad, dull the pain, and boost their confidence level. They are driven to spend more—or lend more—to keep from being less. The abuse of money becomes a counterfeit way of addressing this deeper, unresolved emotional need. That's what makes a checkbook such a good clue to the patient's emotional well-being.

Money is a symbol of power, authority, and control. If there are doubts about one's emotional, physical, or spiritual strength, the abuse of money and credit become false means of shoring up those human frailties. Vulnerability and imperfection are universal aspects of the human condition. If we have not made spiritual peace with that condition, we are at high risk of trying to buy, spend, or owe our way around our humanness. The only meaningful path beyond our human limitations is not an open line of credit, but an open heart—a heart open to grieve the pains of the past and a heart open to spiritual growth.

Once we suspect that a patient has a money addiction we

confirm it, not by how much the person spends or how often, but by another benchmark: the reason *why* the person is running up bills. If he or she is spending money to express anger, hold off boredom, shore up a fragile ego, or strengthen a weak personal identity, then he or she is a compulsive spender, which usually leads to deficit spending (that old minus sign before the checkbook balance and those over-drawn notices from the bank).

"Compulsive deficit spending is a kissing cousin to com-pulsive spending," we explained to Mike. "But it goes a dan-gerous step beyond. Not only is the debtor spending money to shore up his or her identity or medicate personal pain, but the person is doing it beyond his or her means to pay for it. The fact that the person knows he or she can't afford the spree only makes the person feel more guilty. The shame base grows wider and deeper."

"I don't see the connection," said Mike, shaking his head. "I understand about the shame base, and I know that my dad laid a heavy guilt trip on me to accomplish things that he could never accomplish himself. That's where the 'unfin-ished business' comes in. But one of the best lessons he ever taught me was never to spend more than I had. Unfortu-nately, I wasn't a very good student when it came to money matters. I did just the opposite."

"You may have been a better student than you think," we said.

Dr. Hemfelt explained to Michael that because his father put a great deal of emphasis on careful money management, one way to "get even" with dad for all of his abuse was secretly to squander dad's money. This could be done con-sciously or subconsciously. Mike might never have actually said, "Hmmm, I think I'll equal the score with Dad by loan-ing company funds to people who will never pay them back." And he had not consciously thought, *I've never had a way to express my anger toward Dad, but now that I have access to the corporate books I can cause his company to fail. That surely will get even for all the times he put his job before me!* Whether or not he was aware of his motives, his actions were the same.

"Any time a person goes into deficit spending, at some level he is rebelling against and expressing anger about the limits around him," Dr. Hemfelt explained. "For example, you may be able to dip into your company's petty cash fund and loan an old friend a hundred dollars without doing the company any harm. On the other hand, you may not be able to afford the loan of a thousand dollars. If you give your buddy the thousand anyway, you're going out of bounds and defying your father's rules and limitations. You're doing it not as an act of friendship for an old acquaintance, but as an act of rebellion and anger toward your father."

The Link with Self-esteem

We suspected that there were other reasons why Michael Potter had gotten himself into a financial crunch. Probably the number one reason a person abuses money is to boost his or her fragile self-esteem. Low self-image is a natural result of shame, and people who suffer from the compulsions America applauds also suffer from poor self-image. Their addictions are a way of shoring up their sagging self-concepts. They spend more to keep from being less.

On the surface, Michael Potter's confidence level seemed to be high enough. He was handsome, physically healthy, had all the material trappings of wealth, and he was success-ful. He had a cheerful wife, three children, and was a leader in his hometown and in his church. He hardly appeared to be a person whose self-worth needed a boost. But, as the cliché says, "Looks can be deceiving." Who would expect a swaggering personality like Donald Trump to feel, "Nothing I do is enough, and it never will be"?

Like most driven people with low self-esteem, Michael was groping for control. This is typical of people who grow up in homes that are either overcontrolled, such as his had been, or homes that are out of control, such as Barbara Ryan's had been. As adults, these people see control as a way of setting things right at last. Their addictions become their means of seizing control.

"Money has always been a symbol of control, authority,

security, and power," Dr. Hemfelt reminded Michael. "Having money gives the driven person a false illusion of control. He feels secure and powerful, and that feeling boosts his self-esteem, at least for a little while."

The doctor recalled for him the story that John Bradshaw, author of *The Shame That Binds* and *Bradshaw on the Family*, tells about his early years of recovery from alcoholism. Although Bradshaw had successfully kicked his compulsion to drink and was building a legitimate career as a counselor and teacher, his self-esteem still was very low. He had little money; yet, he felt driven to buy expensive clothes, a luxury car, and flashy jewelry. Often as he drove around town he would amuse himself by tallying his dollars and cents value for the day. He would add up the cost of the suit he was wearing, his watch, his leather briefcase, his pricy cologne, and, of course, his automobile. This was his way of bolstering his confidence as he faced another eight hours of work. In the course of his workday he would lecture convincingly about self-worth, his own low self-esteem a well-hidden secret. He had to act superior in order to feel equal.

The Bradshaw anecdote helped Dr. Hemfelt to make the point. Michael nodded his understanding. "Let me make sure I've got this straight," he said. "Making money is a way for me to feel important. That's one reason why I work so hard, right?"

"Right."

"And loaning money to friends who are in jams is my way of settling an old score with Dad. He wouldn't approve of the loans, so I do it out of anger, as a way to get back at him," continued Mike. "Right?"

"Right again."

Michael seemed to mull these explanations over in his mind, testing them to see if all the pieces fit together. One didn't. "I still don't understand why I throw money away on loans that I know will never be repaid. I could speculate—take risks that Dad wouldn't approve of—but still have a shot at a big payoff. In that way, I'd be satisfying my need to get even with my father and my need to make a lot of money. So why do I always issue blank checks to my old college pals when I'm sure they'll never make good on their IOUs?''

Again, the answer was linked to control and self-esteem. By loaning money to people he knew well, Michael Potter was able to boost his image. It made him feel important among his former fraternity brothers and football team members. They looked up to him as the one who had succeeded in the world. They were a rung or two below him because they had to ask for his help in the most tangible, universally understood way: cash. By extending them loans, he wielded a certain degree of control over them. They were beholden to him. They were indebted to him. In a sense, he was "better" than they were. He was number one.

"By giving money to people who are unlikely to pay you back, you are assured that this feeling of indebtedness will go on and on," Dr. Hemfelt explained. "The more they owe you, the wider the gap between you and them. You become more, and they become less. Whereas most creditors wouldn't welcome the people who repeatedly default on their loans into their homes, you invite your debtors to all your reunions. You enjoy their company because they remind you of your importance and your increasing value."

"It's not a very pretty picture," said Michael. "I see what you mean about money creating a false illusion of control. It doesn't work. I still feel lousy about myself."

"That's the paradox about addictions," the doctor explained. "On one level they seem to increase self-esteem, but on a deeper level they tear us down. Giving away money pumps you up; yet, going deeper and deeper into debt only adds to your shame base. The greater the shame, the more you reach for your addictive agent. You give more, and you hurt more. The cycle goes around and around."

Healthy Remedies for Low Self-esteem

Too often people make assumptions about self-esteem on the basis of appearances. They think that a married duo as attractive as Michael and Virginia Potter must feel good about themselves; a man who looks like a million bucks, such as John Bradshaw, surely must ooze self-worth; and a man who owns Trump Tower, Trump Plaza, Trump Parc, Trump Palace, and Trump Shuttle must see himself as sitting on top of the world. So go the assumptions.

But it doesn't always work that way. If it did, actors, actresses, and other performers would enjoy incredibly healthy self-images. Yet, if you've read many celebrity autobiographies or watched the slew of television talk shows that feature heart-to-heart interviews with entertainers, you know this isn't always the case.

"It's true," confessed TV star Valerie Bertinelli in a recent interview. "I just don't feel secure about myself. I always wanted to be more than I am, I always wanted to be better. I'm an incredibly judgmental person—I judge people all the time, especially myself. For instance, I know I'm not gorgeous. I know I'll never make anyone's list of the 'Top Ten Most Beautiful Women.' "[5]

Like many people who struggle with low self-esteem, Bertinelli admits to an addiction, one that easily could be labeled as applaudable. "Some people are addicted to alcohol. Some people are addicted to food. I'm addicted to my husband," she says. Unfortunately, her husband, rock star Eddie Van Halen, is addicted to alcohol and has been in and out of treatment centers for years. Yet, Valerie has finally found help for her sagging self-esteem through Al-Anon and its Twelve Step recovery program.

"Al-Anon made me feel stronger," she explains. "I saw that I was worth a lot more than just seeing myself through someone else's eyes. I learned I can't wait for someone to say, 'Gee, you're terrific!' I had to say that to myself. Still, it's a struggle every day."

Believe in a Greater Power

The second step in the recovery programs of Al-Anon, Emotions Anonymous, Workaholics Anonymous, Alcoholics Anonymous, and other groups can be helpful in boosting low self-esteem: "Came to believe that a Power greater than ourselves could restore us to sanity."

We often use Step 2 in our counseling to address self-esteem issues. At first many of our patients balk at those words and say, "Hey, I'm not suffering from insanity. That's not my problem."

"That's not what we're saying," we assure them. "Our definition of insanity is much broader than yours." We remind them that a major definition of sanity is to restore wholeness to the mind and the emotions. "Insanity in our definition means that we are divided inside of ourselves. In other words, we are out of touch with or split off from our own feelings. When we ask God to restore us to sanity, we're praying that our body, mind, and soul be put back into a state of harmony. This would include elevating our self-esteem to its proper position—putting it in balance."

Step 2 is also important for recovering persons, because they recognize that they don't have to restore their self-esteem under their own power. Patients learn in therapy what events or messages shattered their self-image and they learn to rely on God to rebuild it during their recovery. This concept is encouraging because it assures patients that if they will do their parts, God will assume the burden that seems insurmountable. He will do the final healing, reshaping, and remolding of self-esteem.

Some of our patients doubt that this is possible. They see God as some distant policeman in the sky or some general force, some "Creative Intelligence," as Bill Wilson, the man who founded Alcoholics Anonymous over fifty years ago, did. We often tell them how Bill W. changed his mind.

Bill Wilson's Experience In 1934 doctors gave up on Bill Wilson, who had been a hopeless alcoholic since the beginning of the Great Depression in 1929, when he and many of his stock broker friends went bankrupt. The doctors told Bill's wife: Bill will either develop a wet brain within the next year or so and have to be committed to an asylum, or he will die of heart failure during delirium tremens.

In November of that year Ebby Thatcher, an old school

friend whose alcoholism had reached such proportions he supposedly had been committed to an insane asylum, visited Bill. The minute Bill saw Ebby he knew something was different. His complexion was ruddy, his eyes alive. Minutes later, when Bill offered Ebby a drink, the old drunk refused. "I've got religion," he stated simply.

Bill braced himself for some long tyrannical sermon. Instead, Ebby Thatcher simply told Bill how two men had appeared in court, rescued him from commitment to the asylum, and then told him of a simple religious idea and a practical program of action.

"I have come," Ebby said, "to pass my experience on to you. God has done for me what I could not do for myself."

Bill Wilson could not ignore what had happened to his friend, who had been raised from the dead. "Here was something at work in a human heart which had done the impossible. My ideas about miracles were drastically revised right then," Bill W. says in the "Big Book" of *Alcoholics Anonymous.* "Here sat a miracle directly across the kitchen table."[6]

Still Bill's old prejudices against God held him back, just as they hold our patients back. Often our patients are as angry at God as they are at their parents, particularly their dads. Parents are, in fact, our earliest representation of God. They are "gods" in the lives of the wee people who depend upon them for their every need. What if that "god" turns against them? Rejects them? Or abuses them?

The hurt, the pain, and the unbearable sorrow can never be described. No wonder these patients also reject or hate God. Often we ask our clients to inventory their relationship with God, just as they inventoried their relationships with their parents and other people in their lives. Then we ask them to go over that same list of statements and think about their mothers and fathers or another person who raised them.

How About You?

Take a moment now to consider your own relationship to God and how it might have been influenced by one of your parents. We offer you a shortened version of the inventory we give at the Minirth-Meier Clinics. Check the statements below that reflect your vision of God and then substitute the name of a parent or someone who raised you for God's name.

1.____"I see God as someone who cares personally and intimately for me and my welfare."

"I see____ as someone who cares personally and intimately for me and my welfare."

2.____"I view God as a source of nonjudgmental and unconditional love."

"I view____ as a source of nonjudgmental and unconditional love."

3.✓__"God is someone with whom I can dialogue openly and freely about my problems and my needs."

"____ is someone with whom I can dialogue openly and freely about my problems and my needs."

4.✓__"I trust that God hears and responds to my deepest needs and concerns."

"I trust that____ hears and responds to my deepest needs and concerns.

5.____"I question whether or not God genuinely loves me and accepts me."

"I question whether or not____ genuinely loves me and accepts me."

6.____"I see God as a harsh, stern disciplinarian, and I fear His punishment and wrath."

"I see____ as a harsh, stern disciplinarian, and I fear____ 's punishment and wrath."

7.____"I am angry and bitter at God about past failures or illnesses or disappointments. I wonder why God has not spared me from these."

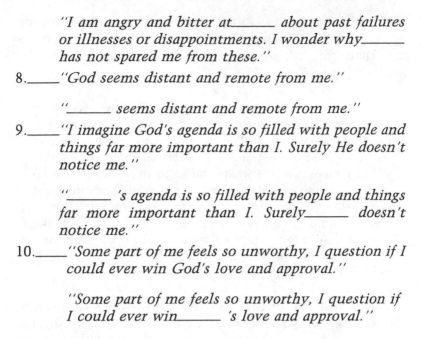

"I am angry and bitter at_____ about past failures or illnesses or disappointments. I wonder why_____ has not spared me from these."

8.____*"God seems distant and remote from me."*

"_____ seems distant and remote from me."

9.____*"I imagine God's agenda is so filled with people and things far more important than I. Surely He doesn't notice me."*

"_____ 's agenda is so filled with people and things far more important than I. Surely_____ doesn't notice me."

10.____*"Some part of me feels so unworthy, I question if I could ever win God's love and approval."*

"Some part of me feels so unworthy, I question if I could ever win_____ 's love and approval."

Our patients who are angry with God check few of the first statements, which obviously describe a loving, caring God. Instead they see the God described in the last six statements. And quite often they see their fathers or mothers or other caregivers in that same light.

How about you? If you checked some of the last six statements, your vision of God has been colored by one of your parents. It's almost as if you are seeing God through a distorted set of glasses. In fact, a major recovery writer, Chuck C., wrote a book called *A New Pair of Glasses,* in which he said his own spiritual conversion and rebirth was like taking off one old pair of glasses, through which he had been seeing God, and putting on a different set. God had not changed. This man's perspective of God had changed, however, during his Twelve Step recovery process.

At the clinic we challenge our patients to take off their old distorted glasses and to be open to another view of God, one that is more closely related to the God portrayed in the Bible. We ask them to turn to that book and look at a few descriptions of God's relationship to us.

It's difficult to see God as remote and uncaring, someone whose agenda is filled with people and things more important than you, when you read Psalm 139, particularly the following verses:

> O Lord, you have examined my heart and know everything about me. You know when I sit or stand. When far away you know my every thought. You chart the path ahead of me, and tell me where to stop and rest. Every moment, you know where I am. You know what I am going to say before I even say it. You both precede and follow me, and place your hand of blessing on my head. . . . I can *never* be lost to your Spirit! I can *never* get away from my God! . . . If I ride the morning winds to the farthest oceans, even there your hand will guide me, your strength will support me. (vv. 1–6, 7, 9–10 TLB)

This is just one of the many Scripture verses that refute the six negative statements about God. We usually suggest that our patients read other passages, like Psalm 37:23–24 and Isaiah 41:10–13. The psalms are particularly comforting to people who are driven by low self-esteem, particularly Psalm 27:10: "When my father and my mother forsake me, then the LORD will take care of me."

Bill Wilson says, "It was only a matter of being willing to believe in a Power greater than myself. Nothing more was required of me to make my beginning. I saw that growth could start from that point. . . . Thus was I convinced that God is concerned with us humans when we want Him enough. At long last, I saw, I felt, I believed."[7]

Bill Wilson's experience has been repeated by millions of other people since the 1930s. One person who recently turned to help from a personal God was Dennis Hopper.

Help from Your Personal God

Actor Dennis Hopper, star of such Hollywood classics as *Rebel Without a Cause* and *Easy Rider*, was once so powerless over his drug and alcohol addictions that the state of

California determined he was not responsible for his life. Two years in a psychiatric ward were prescribed, and even his family decided not to fight for his release. He lapsed in and out of consciousness, claimed he heard voices, and had violent reactions to the antipsychotic drugs he was given as part of his treatment. Although he was an agnostic, he became involved in the Alcoholics Anonymous Twelve Step program and now credits its spiritual aspects with his recovery.

"You've got to have a higher power," said Hopper after three years of sobriety. "You can't get yourself sober, and no other human being can get you sober. The only thing that can get you straight is a higher power, a belief in a higher power than yourself."[8]

These are strong words, especially coming from someone whose wild life-style was legendary even according to Hollywood's standards. The concept that helped Hopper recover is spelled out in Step 3 of the AA program: "We made a decision to turn our will and our lives over to the care of God as we understood Him."

This step has the same application for driven people as it does for drug or alcohol addicts. What it means is that if driven persons hope to have real success in overcoming their compulsivities, they must fully surrender their lives to the care of God. This is no easy job because the very nature of compulsivity pushes the driven person to try and manipulate the world around him or her. The compulsions themselves become false gods or mini-deities. But in recovery, the person is told to let go of the material aspects of life—dogged pursuit of money, work, success, power, flawless appearance— that have absorbed him or her for so long. In recovery, the person has to concentrate on the emotional and spiritual needs inside. As his or her goals are overhauled, new priorities are set.

Often, after reading those Scripture passages and hearing about people like Dennis Hopper, patients say to us, "Okay, maybe I do need to grow closer to God, but how do I do that? What are the mechanics of it?"

We answer, "Willingness. If you can just crack the door a little bit, then God will begin to direct you in that process."

Once you realize how much God loves you, you will truly realize how valuable you are. You will be ready to find real self-esteem.

Looking for Real Self-esteem

Before Michael Potter left Dr. Hemfelt's office at the conclusion of their first one-on-one counseling session, the doctor asked Michael to complete a "homework" assignment. You can do it too. Just follow the simple directions that the doctor gave to Michael.

"Make two lists of your sources of self-esteem," said Dr. Hemfelt. "The first list should be the counterfeit sources—the false ways that you derive your self-worth. For instance, you might write: 'I get my personal esteem from the approval of my father.' Or you might say: 'The major source of my self-image is my bank book. As the numbers increase, so does my esteem.' Or 'My self-esteem comes from the round of thank-you letters I receive after the annual steak fry.' As a rule, counterfeit sources are based on things outside of yourself, and they often include self-sacrifice. If the major source of your esteem is the feedback that you get from the coaches and players of your college football team, you may be willing to sacrifice your savings account and your wife's anger to pick up the tab for the steak fry."

Michael scribbled down the assignment. "And the second list?" he asked.

"The second list should be the more authentic, interior sources of your self-esteem," replied the doctor. "Consider your personal characteristics—things like your good sense of humor, your optimistic attitude, and your genuine love for people. Concentrate on those attributes that you really feel good about. For instance, you might feel obligated to say that an authentic source of your self-esteem is the Realtor of the Year award you won last year. Yet, you may take a lot more pride in the cedar chest that you and Chip built in your basement workshop a couple of weeks ago, which showed your natural talent to create a beautiful piece of furniture. The Realtor award could be a counterfeit source of esteem, the talent to build the cedar chest may be the real thing."

If a patient has difficulty coming up with authentic sources of self-esteem, we sometimes suggest that she or he construct a list of affirmations about herself or himself—personal traits the person likes and is proud of. The patient might also ask a close friend or family member to jot down several positive characteristics of the driven person. This is similar to the paper heart exercise that Virginia Potter did with the help of her therapy group. Often the patient is surprised by the response that he or she gets. If the patient has a heavy shame base, she or he might even discount or downplay the nice comments and observations that friends heap on her or him. That's why we add another suggestion to this exercise.

Look for the Good

The driven person needs to befriend himself or herself. There's an axiom that says, depending on a person's point of view, a glass is either half empty or half full. The joke in counseling circles is that an emotionally healthy person sees the glass as half full, the neurotic person sees it as half empty, and the person whose self-esteem is low sees it as two-thirds gone and leaking fast!

An appropriate slogan that Emotions Anonymous uses is "Look for the good." Just as the healthy person views the glass as half full, the recovering addict needs to view himself in a positive light and focus on the positive aspects of her or his own personality. When Barbara Ryan downplayed the comments of her friends, we suggested that she try to look for the good in herself. She reminded herself that she had super sales skills, was an excellent organizer, and was liked by the staff she supervised. She focused on her attributes rather than on her doubts.

The Ever-Present Danger of Backsliding

One of the most difficult parts of working through the addiction cycle is the ever-present danger of backsliding. This is similar to the Texas two-step that we talked about earlier. Driven persons can make great strides in locating the sources of their shame base, uncover all sorts of negative messages from the past, and even begin to rebuild their faltering self-esteem. Just when they seem well on their way to a Stage II recovery, a painful memory resurfaces, an old message is replayed, and they sustain another blow to their confidence. It's back to point one. Emotional pain, point 5 on the addiction cycle, seems to be a way of life.

In the next chapter we'll look at ways not only to get rid of unnecessary emotional pain, but also how to endure the day-to-day pains that inevitably come from living in an imperfect world.

Chapter Nine

The Devastating Boomerang
Point 5: The "Ouch!" of Emotional Pain

Luci Stewart's sobs nearly drowned out the clink of the coins as she dropped the necessary change into the slot of the pay telephone.

"Go ahead," said the long-distance operator.

"Dr. Minirth? Oh, thank *goodness* you're still there," Luci began, her voice full of emotion. "I was so afraid you might be gone for the day. I'm all confused about the time. It was so early when we left Hawaii, but now we're in Los Angeles on a stopover, and. . . ."

"Luci, what's wrong?" asked Dr. Minirth. "Did something happen to Richard?"

She started to cry again. "No, it's not Richard. He's okay. It's me, Dr. Minirth. It was awful, so demeaning . . . the worst thing that's ever happened. I . . . I knew I shouldn't have taken this trip. You *know* how much I didn't want to come! But you and Richard said it would be so good for me. Now I feel as if I've been violated. Why would anyone do such a thing to me? I'm so scared."

Her words were punctuated by sobs, and Dr. Minirth feared the worst. Luci Stewart sounded very much like someone who had been assaulted. He had counseled dozens of rape victims, and they often used the same terms that Luci was using to describe her feelings: *violated, demeaning, scared.*

"Slow down and tell me what happened, Luci," began Dr. Minirth, kindly. "Has someone hurt you? Maybe you should let me talk with Richard for a moment."

Luci took several deep breaths to calm herself. When she spoke again, she was more in control. "No, I'm okay; I'm physically all right," she assured the doctor. "But it was so awful!" Her voice began to catch. "Someone stole my purse . . . and . . . my briefcase with all my jewelry in it!"

Dr. Minirth hoped that Luci couldn't hear his sigh of relief. "I'm so glad that you're all right," he said.

"But I'm not!" Luci cried. "It happened right before take-off in Honolulu. I was waiting for the call to board our plane to Los Angeles, and I walked over to one of those vending machines. I wanted to buy a newspaper to read on the way home." She sounded breathless as she recounted the story. "I was only five or six steps from the chair where I left my purse and my briefcase. I turned my back on them for only a few seconds. But when I walked back to my seat, they were gone. Gone! I couldn't believe it. At first I thought Richard must have picked them up when he got in line to board. But, no, he had his own things. Mine had been s-s-stolen!"

The sobs took over, and Richard Stewart rescued the phone from his wife and continued the conversation. "Dr. Minirth? I'm sorry to bother you with all of this," he said. "I told Luci that you two could talk about it when she sees you next Thursday, but she insisted on calling." He lowered his voice to a whisper. "I've never seen her this upset, Doctor. She cried all the way from Honolulu to Los Angeles. Do you know how *long* that flight is? Passengers kept coming up and offering condolences; they thought someone had died! I didn't bother to correct them. I figured that no one would understand how a lost purse and briefcase could cause this much misery. For that matter, I'm not sure *I* understand." Richard paused. "Do you suppose that you could switch appointments and see her earlier in the week, Doctor Minirth?

I don't think I can handle much more of this. Every time she retells the story it seems to get worse—the tears and the trauma."

Richard wasn't exaggerating. On Monday morning when Luci entered Dr. Minirth's office, her eyes were swollen and her lower lip was quivering. It had been a long weekend for her and Richard. The fact that she was already having problems with her insurance carrier didn't help matters.

"He doesn't believe me," she said indignantly. "The claims adjuster asked me to put together a list of everything that was in my purse and briefcase. Of course, that wasn't a problem since I always make a record of whatever I take on a trip. I stopped by his office and gave him the list this morning, and he actually questioned me about some of the items. He acted as if he didn't believe that I had packed all of my good jewelry and my dad's antique coin collection in my briefcase. As if I'd leave them home where they might be stolen!"

Luci laughed in spite of herself. How could we tell her that most people weren't so obsessed by their possessions that they had to carry them around on their backs, like a turtle, to feel that their valuables were safe? Luci wasn't ready to accept the blame for any part of the theft. That responsibility was to be shared by her husband and her psychiatrist, both of whom had encouraged her to take the trip in the first place. And the thief. Dr. Minirth could tell from the accusing look Lucy gave him that she thought he belonged behind bars with the purse snatcher.

"If I had stayed home where I belong, this never would have happened," she said between sniffles. "I was right all along. I will never, *never* travel again."

Instead of helping Lucy to overcome some of her fears, the trip to Hawaii, which we had encouraged her to take as part of her new decision to be less rigid and controlling, had reinforced her old belief that if she ventured out of the controlled environment of her home, she would be vulnerable to all sorts of dangers. Just as a child learning to ride a horse must get back in the saddle after falling off, Luci needed to travel again as soon as an opportunity presented itself. But she was determined never to take another risk. If anything, she would be more rigid in the future. Her world would become smaller instead of larger, and there was a chance that she might develop agoraphobia, the fear of leaving home, even for the most routine errands.

This unplanned event—minor, by most people's standards —represented a setback in Luci's recovery, but setbacks are common on the addiction cycle. Often the ouch of emotional pain on the cycle will cause persons who are making real progress in their recovery to revert to an earlier point on the cycle, pause there to regroup, and then continue toward their healthy goals.

Suddenly Luci was grappling with old issues from her childhood, throwing her back to point one on the cycle. Her feelings of insecurity and low self-esteem, linked to her student days when she had felt so inferior to her classmates, had been revived. She had timidly stepped out of her comfort zone and into the unknown. She had attempted a new boundary: to travel with her husband. Unfortunately, the adventure that could have boosted her esteem by proving she could survive in a world she didn't control had failed. Her rigidity and perfectionism had always caused her pain, but now our remedy for her controlling personality also was causing her pain. Instead of her recovery taking one step forward, it took four steps back to point one on the cycle, the pain of her childhood, which had developed the negative messages (Point 2) that led to her shame base (Point 3) and her low self-esteem (Point 4). We were "back to ground zero," as the old saying goes.

Where Do You Send *Your* Emotional Pain?

We don't pull any punches when we talk with our patients about emotional pain. We tell them honestly that emotional pain, like physical pain, is inevitable. And pain is always a part of recovery from addiction.

This recovery pain comes from at least five sources: first, the old pain of childhood memories that must be grieved;

second, the new withdrawal pain that accompanies the surrender of our compulsions; third, the daily pain of confronting normal human stresses without the buffer of our addictions; fourth, the inventory pain that arises from an honest assessment of the damage our applauded addictions have inflicted on ourselves and others; and finally, the self-image pain generated by the bombardment of countless negative messages originating from our low self-esteem.

Our goal is not to teach patients how to enjoy pain-free lives; that would be unrealistic. Instead, our goal is to give patients the tools they need to face and discharge their emotional pain. We tell them that there are three directions that pain can take as it works its way out of us: (1) Pain can boomerang right back and go inside us; (2) pain can take an about-face and hit others; or (3) pain can release itself and be grieved out. As we describe each option, try and picture it, and then decide which one of the three paths your pain usually takes.

The Boomerang

Here, the pain shoots up and out of you, then makes a 180-degree U-turn and zings right back at you. With this option the pain burrows into you and becomes depression or other self-punishing or self-destructive behaviors.

The About-face

Think of a marching platoon when the commanding officer orders an about-face. Suddenly the unit, going one way at one moment, is going in another direction at the next moment. Pain can execute this same fancy maneuver. It comes up and out, but then twists at a 90-degree right angle. It discharges away from you and toward the people around you. It takes the form of anger, blame, criticism, and rage.

The Grief Process

Here's the healthy direction. The pain works its way up through the grief process and is dispersed, never to return or to harm anyone else.

Often we suggest that our patients think of emotional pain as toxic waste. If they bury it, they may succeed in getting it out of sight for a while, but eventually it comes back to harm the emotional environment of their family. It never really goes away until it is disposed of properly.

A good example of this was given in Suzanne Somers's book *Keeping Secrets.* The family "secret" was the alcoholism suffered for thirty-five years by Suzanne's father, Ducky Mahoney. Night after night during the work week, Ducky would return intoxicated from his job loading cartons of beer into trucks at the local brewery. Suzanne could hardly sleep at night because of her father's shouting or his intrusion into her and her sister's bedroom, flicking their lights on at 1:00 or 2:00 A.M., chatting and teasing if he was playfully drunk or shouting and abusing them if he was falling-down drunk.

Suzanne says, "I grew up watching my dad behave so horribly, I hoped he'd pass out, while my mother prayed and covered up for him, hoping one day it would all just go away.

"I watched my parents argue and abuse one another. Eventually all of us children joined in the violence. I listened to my parents yell and scream at each other long into the night. I never knew what would happen next. I didn't know what was real. The house was filled with violence, anger and fear."[1]

Every member of the Mahoney family endured horrible emotional pain because of the disease, but they tried to bury it like toxic waste. Their little house in northern California gave no indication of the pain inside. It was picture perfect, right down to the carefully manicured yard and flowerbeds. The children looked like innocent blond models in the spotless uniforms of their Catholic school. Mom was a wonderful cook and seamstress, and Dad annually coached the local softball team to the league championship.

Yet, the pain that each family member suffered eventually

surfaced in ugly, horrible ways, just like toxic waste. As a child, Suzanne wet her bed every night, hid in her closet for hours, was a poor student (Who can study over yelling and arguing or the paralyzing fear of what will happen next?), had few friends, and was finally expelled from Catholic high school for writing passionate notes to a neighborhood boyfriend. A couple of months later, she became pregnant and had to marry yet another boy.

"Once I left home, I retreated into a fantasy life," Suzanne says. "My new life was a lie. I was so ashamed of who I was, I tried to become someone I was not. My old life didn't exist. My fantasy became my reality. Being unrealistic threatened my mental health; it threatened my freedom. It was impossible to get close to any other human being. I became lonely. I lacked self-esteem. I lived in constant crisis. I was suicidal. But I didn't drink, so I thought I was 'okay.' "[2] No wonder Suzanne became a compulsive debtor and even was jailed for writing bad checks. No wonder she sought love from other young adults and even older men. Suzanne wasn't an alcoholic, but she was driven by the compulsive behaviors America applauds.

Her sister, Maureen, and her brother Danny became alcoholics. Her younger brother, Michael, developed an addiction to alcohol and cocaine. Her mother developed psoriasis and was so psychologically battered by her codependent marriage relationship that the children worried for her life.

Each member of the Mahoney family carried an incredible amount of emotional pain. Rather than venting this pain in a healthy way, they let it boomerang back inside themselves as depression, and they let it make an about-face and explode in anger and hate at Dad—who just kept drinking—and at one another. In part, emotional pain flows from points three and four on the cycle of addiction, from the person's shame base and low self-esteem. If I am feeling deep shame about who and what I am, if I suffer from chronic low self-esteem, even though I've covered that up with a mask of Donald Trump bravado and grandiosity, I ultimately feel that shame and low self-esteem as emotional pain—a deep sense of fear and insecurity, chronic depression, sustained levels of anxiety, and chronic sadness and unhappiness.

Luci Stewart's pain after the loss of her valuables took the form of anger and blame. Dr. Minirth's challenge was to try to redirect Luci's pain up and out through therapy and to help her continue the progress that she had made prior to the trip. She had to understand that emotional pain is inevitable in life, and that no one, not even Luci Stewart, can control all the events that can cause pain. Her valuables might as easily have been stolen from her home while she was poring over her husband's financial books or while she and Richard were sleeping in the next room. Instead of trying to control the events in her world, Luci needed to learn to release the pain caused by events beyond her control.

The Serenity Prayer

The Serenity Prayer of Alcoholics Anonymous is a roadmap for the journey people like Luci Stewart need to make: "God, grant us the serenity to accept the things we cannot change, courage to change things we can, and wisdom to know the difference."

Luci Stewart, Suzanne Somers, and all of us who are driven by obsessive-compulsive behaviors need to *"accept the things I cannot change, to change the things I can, and the wisdom to know the difference."*

Dr. Minirth had to help Luci understand the importance of the grief process and the role it plays in helping us to accept the things we cannot change. Only then could she hope to disperse her current hurt and get on with her long-term healing.

Grieving So We Can Accept the Things We Cannot Change

Learning how to cleanse ourselves of emotional pain is a skill that every human being needs to master, since, whether we like it or not, every human being is subjected to emotional pain throughout life. Emotional pain attacks us at three levels.

Old Buried Pain

The wounds and hurts that we carry from our childhood days contribute to our shame base and to our low self-esteem. The old buried pain for the Mahoney family was Ducky's alcoholism. For Luci Stewart, the old pain was her Uncle Ted's sexual abuse of her. We warn our patients that the deep emotional scars and scabs of childhood pain should never be underestimated. Way back, when we walked Luci through points one and two of the addiction cycle, she had explored this childhood pain and grieved about her uncle's violation of her sexual boundaries.

Now, at point five, she assumed, "I've acknowledged that. It's behind me." Yet, denial is often layered; even after we have removed the top layers, we may be protecting ourselves from a full awareness of how great that old childhood pain is. Like many people who have suffered significant childhood abuse, Luci had to go back frequently and recycle through the grief process. The wound was deep and was similar to a persistent infection that has to be lanced several times before the pus is completely drained from it.

Fallout Pain

We feel pain when we stop denying our addictions and start counting the losses that they have cost us. It hurts us to see the damage that our compulsions have caused.

Dr. Minirth had to help Luci face the losses that her compulsivity had cost her in more recent years:

- She had allowed herself little time to relax and enjoy her family.
- She had deprived her husband and son of her company on vacations.
- She had heaped incredible responsibility on her shoulders by managing Richard's home office.

- There had been little spontaneity in her life; everything had always been planned and controlled.

When Luci broke through denial and recognized the negative effects of her workaholism and her perfectionism she
felt overwhelmed with grief. She had agreed to take the Ha-
waiian trip as she set some new directions and new boundaries. The fact that the plan had faltered gave her the unique
opportunity to test her strength and her ability to work
through the pain that had resulted.

Contemporary Pain

This is the normal, predictable pain that comes with sickness, business setbacks, and daily disappointments. It is the
grin-and-bear-it kind of hurt, which is the pain we can sometimes change.

Luci Stewart struggled with the "garden variety," everyday
kind of emotional pain that plagues all of us. Her grandson's
spastic colon worried her, Bud's financial dilemma was a
source of anxiety, and the state of her marriage to Richard
was an ongoing concern. Dr. Minirth warned Luci that if she
buried all of this pain it eventually would surface and poison
her world just as surely as toxic waste poisons the environment where it is hidden. Her only healthy choice was to
grieve it out. She had learned the importance of the grief
process when she had tried to rid herself of the negative
messages of her past (Point 2 on the addiction cycle). Now
she must repeat the same three-step grieving process: Grieve
her pain out by expressing the pain to herself, to God, and to
others.

Grieve Out the Pain by Thoroughly Airing It to Yourself

In our years of counseling driven people, we've designed
dozens of exercises to help heal our patients' emotional pain.
Here are the two exercises that we feel are a necessary part of
learning to accept the things we cannot change.

Have a Heart-to-Heart Talk with the "Child" in You

The poet William Wordsworth once wrote that "the child is father of the man." It's an interesting twist of words and means that adults are formed and shaped by their childhood experiences. In other words, what we are depends on what we were and what happened to us. Many therapists today believe that not only do we adults evolve from what we were as children, but also that the "child" is always present inside of us.

Author Jeremiah Abrams puts it this way: "We all carry within us an eternal child, a young being of innocence and wonder. And that symbolic child also carries us, who we have been, the record of our formative experiences, our pleasures and pains." [3]

Often we suggest that a patient have a heart-to-heart talk with the child inside.

Meditation Exercise

Put your paper and pen away for a few minutes, close your eyes, and relax. Try to imagine yourself as a child attending a very important childhood gathering. Perhaps it's the final game of the season for your Little League team. Or maybe it's your sixth-grade class play, and you have the leading role. Or it could be a Scout picnic where badges will be awarded, and you are scheduled to receive several. Unannounced and unexpected, your dominant or difficult parent arrives on the scene. Describe how you feel the moment you realize he or she is there. Are you proud that Dad has joined the group? Frightened at what his behavior might be? Ashamed by how he looks or acts? Is there a lump in your throat or a knot in your tummy? What is your response at this critical moment from the past?

Often our patients will begin to cry as they remember such events. One patient, Jeannette, told us of a time when her dad offered to take her and her friends to the opening game of the Pittsburgh Pirates as a special tenth birthday celebration.

"Somehow," she said, "I didn't realize what would happen. Maybe my dad just hadn't been an alcoholic that long, maybe he'd been dry for a while and I thought he'd reformed.

"At any rate, my dad began drinking during the first inning and, of course, by the end of the game he was drunk. He could still walk, but his condition was quite obvious. I will never forget how upset I was—how ashamed and how scared. Now the secret was out, and my best friends knew it!" Jeannette's voice broke; she could no longer hold her tears. The anger, the frustration, the disappointment, and the shame that the ten-year-old Jeannette felt were still buried deep inside her.

To help Jeannette reduce her pain and shame, Dr. Meier told her to imagine that she, the adult Jeannette, was sitting down with the child Jeannette to comfort her.

"You need to explain to the child, 'Daddy is sick. That's not your fault; you didn't cause it.' It's important for the adult to tell the child that," Dr. Meier said. "You also need to acknowledge the pain and empathize with the pain the child is feeling. Imagine yourself saying, 'I know you are scared, embarrassed, and maybe angry at Daddy. I hear your pain. I'm sensitive to it. My heart is with you.'

"Finally you need to remind Little Jeannette that Big Jeannette is here now, and that Big Jeannette is a mature, competent adult. Big Jeannette can set boundaries that could not be set by Little Jeannette, who was ten."

Jeannette interrupted the doctor. "What do you mean, 'set boundaries'?"

"Well, for example, if you went to a ballgame tomorrow with a friend, and the friend got drunk, you might just get up and excuse yourself. You certainly wouldn't ride home. You'd take a taxi. You could take care of Jeannette and take her out of the situation. The ten year old couldn't do that. The adult Jeannette needs to tell the little girl Jeannette, 'I'm here with you now. I will always be with you. I will take care of you in all future situations.'

"You already know that intellectually, but the little girl in Jeannette may not know that emotionally. Even right now, if you went to a ballgame and the stranger right next to you started getting drunk, you might start having queasy feelings in your stomach and not even know what that's about."

"Oh!" Jeannette's cry seemed involuntary, almost a cry from the child within. Dr. Meier knew he had touched upon a painful incident in her adult life, one she had never understood before.

The doctor paused a moment and then continued softly, "That little girl in you is getting scared. So the adult in you has to remind that little girl, 'I'm with you now. I can take care of you. I can set boundaries. You will never have to be exposed to that kind of vulnerability again.'"

How About You?

As you work to release your old emotional pain, it's helpful to get in touch with the child inside of you and to communicate with him or her. To help you do this, we suggest that you try this exercise: Place two chairs front to front. Sit in one of the chairs and try to imagine yourself, as a child, sitting in the other chair. Although you may feel silly at first, begin to talk earnestly with the child, just as our patient, Jeannette, talked to Little Jeannette. Acknowledge any abuse that you know the child within you has endured.

Luci Stewart used these words to apologize to her inner child for the physical abuse the little girl suffered because of her Uncle Ted: "What happened to you was wrong, and it caused you a lot of pain. I'm so sorry that you had to be hurt that way, and I'm sorry that you were afraid to talk about it with anyone."

As a final part of this exercise, you should assure the child sitting opposite you that in the future you will set boundaries to take better care of the two of you. You will remember that we told Jeannette, "You need to remind Little Jeannette that Big Jeannette is here now, and that Big Jeannette is a mature, competent adult."

Be sure to tell that little child within you—and yourself—

that if someone in your life is abusive, you will not let that person inside your boundaries. You also should pledge to the child—and to yourself—that you will find and nurture healthy friendships that will meet the needs of the child and the adult who co-exist in you.

The next part of the grieving process is to share the contemporary pain of your everyday life with God, since it is often too heavy for you to carry by yourself. This is the best way to dispel the pain you encounter every day.

Grieve Out the Pain By Sharing It with God in Prayer

We urge our patients—and you—to set aside a special time or an event to express the emotional pain that they have identified when they talked with the child sitting in the chair opposite them. The key to this activity is being specific. We don't want them to casually brush off the assignment by saying, "Yeah, I'll work through some of these things the next time I have a few spare minutes." That isn't good enough. We recommend that they find some time in the next week to be by themselves. They might take a walk in a secluded area, like a woods or along the beach; they might sit under a big oak tree or on a rock by the shore. "Allow yourself to grieve," we tell them. "Talk to God about your pain. Cry if you feel like it. Or shout out your anger to God."

We also recommend that our patients set aside a specific time each day to dialogue with God about their past and present emotional pain.

Applying the Twelve Step Process

We often use one of the Twelve Steps of such groups as Emotions Anonymous, Alcoholics Anonymous, and Al-Anon to help patients overcome particular points on the addiction cycle. However, we do not necessarily take the steps in order. For instance, two later steps are particularly helpful in dealing with emotional pain and preventing its buildup—

Steps 10 and 11, sometimes referred to as the daily inventory or the daily maintenance steps.

Step 10 reads this way: "We continued to take personal inventory and when we were wrong, promptly admitted it." We often use a housecleaning analogy to explain the purpose of this step to patients. Once or twice a year the homemaker may initiate a thorough cleaning effort in which furniture is moved, walls are washed, and closets are emptied and re-arranged. Step 4—"We made a searching and fearless moral inventory of ourselves"—is similar to a grand, all-out cleaning effort. Between those monumental scrubbing efforts is the day-to-day maintenance that keeps everything in order. Step 10 is similar to the routine tidying that a homemaker does each day.

By conducting a *daily* inventory of what's wrong and what's right in our lives, and by determining the order of our priorities, we quickly recognize whether our addictions are starting to resurface, or whether our emotional pain is building. For example, if workaholism is our problem and we're tempted by the old compulsion to bend the limits of time and stretch our workday beyond eight hours, we will see that problem recurring as we review our day, and we will be able to pull back and hand the problem over to God immediately. In this way we address the problem in its earliest stage and prevent it from expanding. Step 10 is the daily maintenance work that keeps our lives humming in good order.

In close conjunction with Step 10's inventory is Step 11: "We sought through prayer and meditation to improve our conscious contact with God, as we understood Him, praying only for knowledge of His will for us and the power to carry that out."

The two steps work in tandem. As we go about our daily tidying effort, we need to be in constant contact with God so that we can turn over to Him any problems or pain that we uncover as we clean our emotional and spiritual houses. We also need to feel comfortable in asking for His will, guidance, and direction as we do our important maintenance work. We often recommend that our patients use daily devotionals, like the Serenity Meditation Series, which is written by the doctors in the various Minirth-Meier Clinics throughout the country. The combination of these two Steps should lead to a regular surrendering of our pain to God. Ultimately, it will translate into a life-style that generates less interior and exterior pain.

Most driven people, even those who are active in their religious faith do not have a daily devotional time. When these people ask us, "Why am I a workaholic or an overeater when I believe in God?" we always answer their question with another question: "Do you find time each day for prayer and reflection?" The averted eyes or the silence that follows our question tell us that this key to overcoming drivenness is missing.

The final step (and perhaps the most difficult) is sharing your pain with someone else.

We Grieve Out the Pain by Talking to Others

Talk to some other person or group of persons, such as a self-help therapy group, about your pain. This was an important element in the recovery of Suzanne Somers's family.

All members of her family are healthy today thanks to individual therapy and the Twelve Step programs of Al-Anon and Alcoholics Anonymous, and Suzanne herself is honorary national spokesperson for the National Association for Children of Alcoholics. But it was a hard road back. If Suzanne's father had merely stopped drinking, the family would have experienced relief, but not recovery. The pain, like toxic waste, would have remained hidden, only to surface in other destructive addictions, like Suzanne's compulsive deficit spending. Instead, each family member dispersed his or her pain by talking openly about it to each other and to the members of their various support groups. They recovered from their addictions when they diminished their shame bases, boosted their self-esteem, and learned the value of directing their emotional pain through appropriate grieving processes.

A piece written in Suzanne's mother's diary on December

21, 1976, shows how valuable Al-Anon was to Ducky Mahoney's wife:

> My mind is filled with gratitude to my higher power and the people in Al-Anon who are responsible for bringing this about. I do not question. I do not expect too much; but everything is happening to bring about this peace. I . . . had just about given up but decided to try Al-Anon as a last-ditch stand. I had been looking at condominiums and apartments with the idea of moving out, and then this happened. Because of my nature I know I should be worrying about things, but his inner peace surrounds me.[4]

Finding the right person to serve as your listening post often takes some thought. A special friend, pastor, or counselor would be a logical choice. Many recovering persons who attend Twelve Step group meetings rely on one of the members to act as a sympathetic listener; often two people meet separately for coffee after group meetings or at some other special time. Support groups play an important part in dispersing emotional pain since they allow for regular opportunities to vent pain.

Honesty is essential at all three steps of the grief process. When we're confronting emotional pain head on, we shouldn't deny it and pretend it doesn't exist. Neither should we minimize it and pass it off as a minor setback that we'll soon forget. And we certainly don't want to medicate it by reaching for our addictive agent again—work, exercise, shopping, organizing—in an effort to distract ourselves from the pain of abstinence.

Luci Stewart's effort to break her addiction to perfectionism caused her new pain. Like withdrawing from drugs or alcohol, workaholics who attempt to curb their compulsions suffer waves of uneasiness, insecurity, and fear. The temptation is to throw themselves into a project to medicate their pain and push it down again. As Luci battled her emotional pain she repeated the slogan from Emotions Anonymous that promises, "This too shall pass." The premise is that God never gives us more than we can handle, and if Luci could

213

just hold tight and bear the discomfort, eventually it would go away. Sooner or later, her pain would crest and then diminish.

Without having a vent in place to dispose properly of emotional pain—like the daily inventory—the driven person risks buildup and an ultimate return to destructive ways. Pain that isn't dispersed has a habit of making a U-turn and coming back to hurt us again and again. When that happens, the compulsive person reaches for relief, the addictive agent, which is the topic of Chapter 10.

Chapter Ten

Our False Gods
Point 6: The Addictive Agent

One of the toughest cases we ever encountered at the Minirth-Meier Clinics involved a university mathematics professor who trusted only what he could reduce to an equation. If he couldn't touch, prove, or dissect something, it didn't exist for him. This man was so detached and rational that "Star Trek's" Mr. Spock seemed passionate by comparison. In fact, his students jokingly referred to him as Professor Spock. He took it as a compliment.

Spock came to us as a last resort. His marriage was failing, and his wife had issued an ultimatum: "Counseling *or else!*" It was the "or else" that convinced him to faithfully keep his 4:00 appointment with us every Friday afternoon for several months. Still, progress was slow. For exactly one hour each week he dutifully would submit to our questions, hear our words of advice, and then discount everything that didn't seem logical to him.

In a way, the professor's intelligence was a blessing. He listened carefully as we explained the addiction cycle and nodded as we presented evidence to indicate he was a compulsive worker. "Yes, that makes sense to me," he said. "Yes, I can see from your exercises, inventories, and pie charts that I am spending far too much time at work and in front of my home computer." He went on to commend us for building a good case, said he finally understood his wife's unhappiness, and agreed to embark upon a recovery program.

The distinguished professor even recognized the pitfalls that he might face as he tried to harness his addictive agent. "After all," he said, "a law of physics says that nature hates a vacuum, and I know that if I succeed in curbing my out-of-control work addiction, I will create a vacuum in my life. That's called transfer of addictions," he informed us knowledgeably.

We nodded and smiled. In addition to being a good math professor, Spock was a good student of behavioral science. He had learned his lesson well—at least part of it.

As he proceeded into his stages of recovery, however, we discovered that his insistence on logic was a stumbling block. He frowned when we explained that at the heart of every driven person's recovery program is the belief that only God can meet one's deepest needs. This, we stressed, is the cornerstone of healing. Spock shook his head when we pointed out that his universal human needs to stop time, feel invincible, achieve immortality, transcend to a higher plane, and find a perfect union could be met only on a spiritual level. The secrets of the human heart cannot be unlocked by a mathematical formula. We emphasized that an addictive agent can *seem* to fill these needs, but the fulfillment is false, short-term, and ultimately destructive.

As the professor reviewed our words of advice and counsel, his intellectual side acknowledged that his work had met his deepest needs for many years. "When I'm in my office working on my new textbook, hours can pass without my realizing it," he admitted. "My addiction allows me to suspend time. It also pumps me up to a higher level. I feel totally in control as I manipulate words and numbers into lessons and chapters. That must be the feelings of transcendence and invincibility that you doctors talk about." We nodded as the learned professor applied our words of guidance to himself.

"And as I create a book that someday will be used by thousands of students whom I'll never meet face to face, I suppose I'm flirting with immortality," Spock continued.

"In my own way, I'm trying to leave my mark on the world. As I fulfill this destiny, my work and I merge into a sort of mystical oneness; and it's a great fit. A perfect union, as you call it."

All this made sense to the rational professor, but that was as far as he could go with it. He couldn't take the next step and accept that God could meet these same needs in a more valid and personal way. Heal him from his work addiction, and the result would be that his need for transcendence, invincibility, and immortality would go unsatisfied, he concluded. God was an unknown quantity, as far as he was concerned—something that might be believed but could never be proven, an enigma whose presence might be felt, but could never be seen.

Filling the Gap

Some of our patients and readers are agnostics. Like Professor Spock, they're acquainted with God on a historic or academic level, but not on a personal plane. They may have attended Sunday school when they were children, but later became indifferent or embittered toward God. (That's why we suggest that they look at their relationship with God in earlier counseling sessions; we want them to understand how their relationship with their parents, for instance, has twisted their view of God.) As these people stray further and further away from their early beliefs they substitute false gods—such as work, money, and achievement—for the God they knew in their youth. Like Spock, they come to depend on their counterfeit gods to satisfy their deepest needs. They trust their gods because they are tangible. The god of work can be measured. The god of achievement can be seen. The god of money can be counted. These gods control the person, rather than the person controlling them.

Recognizing a false god for what it is—an addiction—is an important step toward recovering from its control. Removing the addiction is the obvious next step, but filling the gap that is left by the addiction may be the most important step of all.

If a healthy replacement for the addiction isn't found to fill the recovering person's deepest needs, the former addict often slips back into the old compulsion or picks up a new one.

Valid Alternatives to Addictions

The replacements, which legitimately can fulfill the same anesthesia function as a compulsion, are (1) giving control of your life to the real God rather than to the false gods of drivenness; and (2) building higher quality relationships with people both in and out of the family (and thereby allowing God to nurture us through the means of human fellowship).

Often when we counsel persons who describe themselves as agnostics, we suggest that they do a simple exercise. If you count yourself among this group, follow the directions we gave to our friend Professor Spock.

"Design your own god," Dr. Hemfelt said, giving Spock much the same challenge Ebby Thatcher gave to Bill W. so long ago. "Instead of getting bogged down in what you fear God might be or what someone once told you that God was, create your own version. Take your old picture of God, put it on hold, and start with a clean slate. List God's attributes. Is He kind? Sensitive? Interested in your needs and concerns? Is He a good listener? Does God forgive you without holding a grudge? Does He love you when no one else loves you? When you're in God's presence, talking with him, do you feel relaxed and at peace? Is God so strong and so powerful that when you sense that He's with you, you feel as if nothing can go wrong?

After persons have designed their perfect God on paper, we ask them to tell us about their creations. They often begin by assuring us once again that they don't believe in God, but if a perfect being existed, here is what it would be like. The exercise isn't heresy. Nearly always the perfect God that agnostics design is a mirror image of the living God in the Bible.

Spock's God was kind. So is the God of the Bible. No one knew this better than King David, whom God forgave for his sins of adultery with Bathsheba and the indirect murder of her husband. David says in Psalm 145,

> The LORD is gracious and full of compassion.
> Slow to anger and great in mercy.
> The LORD *is* good to all,
> And His tender mercies *are* over all His works.
>   (Ps. 145:8–9)

Spock's God was interested in his needs and concerns. Again King David, that man who was so tempted by the things of this world, said in the Psalms:

> The steps of a *good* man are ordered
>   by the LORD,
> And He delights in his way.
> Though he fall, he shall not be
>   utterly cast down;
> For the LORD upholds *him with* His hand.
>   (Ps. 37:23–24)

Spock's God loved him when no one else did. The apostle Paul, who admits to being driven to do the things he did not want to do, frequently reminded the early Christians (and probably himself also), "But God demonstrates His own love toward us, in that while we were still sinners, Christ died for us" (Rom. 5:8).

Professor Spock admitted that his version of God strongly resembled the Christian God; he conceded that there might be a personal Being somewhere in the universe that could have some concern about him. He would consider our premise, he said. He also agreed to attend weekly meetings of Emotions Anonymous so he could enjoy the support of people like himself who were working through recovery. And he kept looking for factual proof of God's existence.

"I keep waiting for a spiritual awakening, Dr. Hemfelt," Spock admitted during one of his Friday afternoon sessions.

"I don't know what to expect—a vision? A voice? Some kind of dramatic sign? Whatever it is, it hasn't happened yet."

Robert Hemfelt nodded thoughtfully and began to explain that a spiritual awakening can take many forms. Books have been written about the thunderbolt, burning-bush kind of conversion that sends chills down readers' spines. Many believers remember slower, more subtle experiences that occur over months or even years after much prayer, meditation, and study. Many believers remember the moment they trusted Christ as Savior. But for many others, their spiritual awakening was more gradual. They don't remember a specific moment of conversion. They just know that at the beginning, they didn't trust Him, but at the end they did. Whatever form the awakening takes, the goal of a spiritual experience for a person in recovery is the same: to find a quiet but profound way to satisfy the deepest hungers behind the drivenness. Through this experience the recovering person can live a balanced, healthy, and productive life.

Professor Spock's eventual conversion fell somewhere in between thunder bolts and subtlety. As he became more and more active in his Emotions Anonymous group, he began to read selected devotional literature, like our Serenity Meditation Series and the Serenity Bible. And he finally decided to make a definite commitment to the God of the Bible.

Yet, Spock still had to take the important step of giving control of his life to God. He now believed in God, but he was stalled at the same place as some people who attend church weekly. His false gods—money, work, success—still controlled him.

The Love of People and Things

Author/therapist John Bradshaw warns driven persons not to pursue necrophilia (the love of dead people and things). He equates a love of bank accounts, clothes, work, power, and other nonliving things with necrophilia. Persons who are addicted to getting their emotional and spiritual needs met through inanimate objects and activities suffer from a unique form of necrophilia, according to Bradshaw, which can be very destructive to themselves.

The Man Who Would Be King

One man who seemed to be addicted to getting his emotional and spiritual needs met through inanimate objects and activities was actor Yul Brynner. His addiction to tobacco was made famous by an anti-smoking commercial that was aired several months after his death from lung cancer in 1985. The clip was taken from an interview he did with a reporter from "Sixty Minutes," during which he publicly declared that he had beaten cancer. He said that if he hadn't whipped the dreaded disease he would look straight at the camera and declare, "The only reason I am dead now is because I was a heavy smoker." That snippet of tape later became his now-famous anti-cancer commercial. It will always be remembered for its drama.

Cigarettes weren't Brynner's only addictive agent. He had a long history of multiple compulsions that began with opium abuse as a teenager. Throughout his life he traded one addiction for another, including an obsession with his most famous role—the king in *The King and I*—that allowed him to suspend time, experience invincibility, and achieve immortality for more than 4,500 performances spread over three decades.

Some of Brynner's compulsions were short-lived and harmless; within six months of discovering the hobby of stamp collecting he assembled albums worth hundreds of thousands of dollars. Some of his compulsions were lethal; he smoked three to five packs of cigarettes a day for more than thirty years. He was so driven by money and success that shortly before his death he insisted on performing eight times a week in a revival of *The King and I.* His pain was overwhelming. He gulped oxygen between acts and waited an hour to leave the theater each evening so his fans wouldn't see his bodyguards carrying him to the car.

It was Brynner's addiction to his famous royal role that seemed to fulfill his deepest needs. He revived the Broadway musical again and again, each time coming closer to merging himself and his character into some kind of perfect union.

Toward the end of his life Brynner admitted that the only time he was happy was when he was on stage. When he performed as the King of Siam he felt time was suspended. His son wrote in *Yul: The Man Who Would Be King*, "He appeared to have conquered time itself. How was it possible? It was as if Yul had found the key to agelessness." A New York critic echoed the observation: "Mr. Brynner says he is fifty-six years old, but appears to be in a state of eternally lean, trim fitness."[1]

Brynner came to see himself just as invincible off stage as the King was on stage. He made incredible demands of everyone around him, and he could fly into a frenzy if his wishes weren't granted at the snap of his fingers. When he took his King on the road, his contract specified that his dressing room be freshly painted and carpeted in chocolate brown and be equipped with a special hammock, and that his limousine be bullet-proof. (Assassins generally don't shoot actors, but they do kill kings; another clue that Brynner saw himself as less an actor and more a king.)

Although he had been brought up as a Christian, Brynner had long since strayed from the church. He depended on his assortment of addictions to catapult him to a higher level and allow him to experience a feeling of all-powerfulness. His son, a recovering alcoholic who is active in A.A., explains in his book:

> The central teachings of Christianity held no attraction to Yul, and he never pretended differently. Having spent a lifetime imposing his will on the world about him, he had no patience for those who prayed, "thy will be done." Or the Serenity Prayer of Alcoholics Anonymous. . . . This was Greek to Yul; he had no patience with serenity. Ego unbridled, Yul was willfulness run amok. His rationale was the "The King and I" was some sort of holy crusade that took care of all the moral obligations he had: if he just kept performing eight shows a week, he was justified in doing anything to anyone, anywhere. He now espoused social Darwin-

ism with zeal, promulgating a dog-eat-dog view of the world with little or no empathy for the fallen—only the fittest survived, and so it was meant to be.[2]

At the end of his life Yul Brynner seemed to have moved beyond regal stature and ascended to his own unique version of immortality. His final professional honor came at the Tony Awards presentation in New York City. Other recipients used their moments at the microphone to thank their families for their support or their colleagues for their recognition or their God for their talents. Yul took the statuette, smiled, and simply said, "I just want to thank Yul Brynner."

If readers are to believe his son's written account, the actor refused to consider the most valid alternative to any addiction. Part of any driven person's recovery goal from necrophilia (or whatever you choose to call it) is to learn how to give control of these things to God. That's what finally happened to our distinguished professor.

One day Spock received some devastating news. After nine years of dedicated service at a local university, he was passed up for promotion to the rank of full professor. With his new textbook scheduled for release in a few weeks, he had felt that professional advancement was as good as done. The new rank and a raise were "givens"; the only question was how soon and how much.

The decision was not subject to review for another year. The announcement sent Spock reeling. His first temptation was to scold himself for slacking off his previous pace and to blame us for advising him to curb his drivenness. He failed to keep his next three appointments at the clinic and didn't return our calls of concern. Then, on the fourth Friday of the month, he appeared at our office, hardly looking like a man who had failed to achieve one of his life's major goals.

"I feel wonderful," the professor said in reply to our obvious first question. "I know now that my not getting promoted was one of the best things that ever happened to me. Hitting the bottom was a turning point, Dr. Hemfelt. It hurt so much that it forced me to really look at myself in a very critical way. I started to question my value as a teacher, a writer, and even as a man. My self-esteem was so deflated that I couldn't talk to anyone about what had happened. I was embarrassed and felt I didn't have a friend in the world. That's when the emotional pain got so bad that I turned to God. I gave all those ambitions to Him. 'If it's Your will, then let it happen. If not, that's okay,' I said, 'Just help me live with that decision.'

"I prayed when I first woke up in the morning for the strength to get out of bed and face another day. I prayed as I drove to work for help in getting into the elevator, walking into my office, and greeting all of my colleagues. They all knew I hadn't gotten the promotion. I prayed before each of my classes for the concentration to get through my lectures and to answer the students' questions."

It worked—for Spock and for many of our other patients, even those who already have a relationship with God. Christians sometimes come to us and wonder why they are so driven. "I accepted Christ as Savior long ago, I go to church each Sunday, I. . . ." The list goes on and on, but one step is noticeably missing. They haven't given control of their lives to God. They are still worshiping a false god or gods.

Bill Wilson knew how important this step was when he devised Step 3 of the Twelve Step program: "We made a decision to turn our will and our lives over to the care of God as we understood Him." Too often Christians omit this step from the salvation process. We often find that people hold back areas of their lives. They deny. They rationalize ("I'm working hard so we will have enough money to send the kids to college.") They lock the door to these "sacred" areas of their lives and keep God out.

Why? Because they are unwilling to trust God in areas they consider important. Often this lack of trust goes back to their childhood; the parent whose actions colored their image of God let them down in these same areas. Other times they're stumbling on the natural difficulty of trusting Someone they cannot see. Yet, that's what faith must be, as singer Michael Card says in his song of the same name. His definition of faith goes like this:

To hear with my heart,
To see with my soul,
To be guided by a hand I cannot hold,
To trust in a way that I cannot see,
That's what faith must be.

Our friend Professor Spock had taken another step in the process of faith. He'd given God control of his addiction to success and work in one instance: his failure to obtain the goal of professorship. The outcome had been good, as the apostle Paul promised when he said, "We know that all things work together for good to those who love God" (Rom. 8:28). Spock had failed; yet, Spock was happy. That peace and happiness was within, rather than dependent upon external circumstances, such as promotions.

If Spock continued to walk with God, he would slowly build a history of God's guidance through the many problems and disappointments of life. We often call these events "markers" along the way. The next time Spock needed to give control of an event or problem to God, he would look back over these markers and be willing to trust God more quickly and more completely because of them.

If driven persons hope to have real success in overcoming their compulsivities, they must give control of their lives to God each day of their lives. This is no easy job because the very nature of compulsivity pushes the driven person to try and manipulate the world—to become his or her own god. But in recovery, the person is told that she or he has to let go of the material aspects of life—the dogged pursuit of money, work, success, power, flawless appearance—that have absorbed him or her for so long. In recovery, the person has to concentrate on the emotional and spiritual needs inside.

Building Better Relationships

A new relationship with God is the first and most important replacement for an addiction. The second replacement

—building more satisfying human relationships—works hand-in-hand with the spiritual awakening.

As we talk with our patients about the value of relating to people on a deeper, more satisfying level, we generally add a note of caution. Driven persons sometimes turn to friends in driven and addictive ways. By their nature, they give 200 percent to everything, even to friendships. However, the goal in recovery is to nurture healthy, *noncompulsive* relationships.

Four main channels are available to persons attempting to build relationships with people who will love them for who they are, not for how they perform. These channels are:

1. Recovery groups, such as Alcoholics Anonymous, Al-Anon, Emotions Anonymous
2. Special friends who have reparenting skills
3. Intimate relationships (marriage, dating)
4. An extended support network

Recovery Groups

Throughout this book we have mentioned recovery groups. We mention them again because we see these groups as a necessary companion to one-on-one therapy. Without the interaction among group members, only limited results can be accomplished by individual counseling. The dilemma is not whether or not to join a group, but rather, which kind of program to join. (If you wish to make that decision, turn to page 315 in the appendix where we list the various recovery groups. As you choose a group, remember that a group such as Adult Children of Alcoholics is just as viable for the child of a rageaholic or controlling parent as it is for the child of an alcoholic.) Most churches have Bible study groups, fellowship groups, and even church-sponsored recovery groups, which also fill this need for sharing and accountability. We recommend lifelong participation in a "mini-church" or growth group at your local, Bible-believing church. Your spiritual progress should be a top priority.

Fellowship is a major component of all organizations, and members discuss in detail the spiritual dimension of recovery. The peer support that is available at these meetings is so valuable that many treatment centers ask patients to commit to attending ninety meetings in ninety days after they are dismissed. This means that the recovering person agrees to sit in on a meeting a day, seven days a week, for the next three months. Such a plan often is called "ninety in ninety."

Special Friends Who Have Reparenting Skills

Since many driven people were deprived of healthy, balanced relationships with parents during childhood, they need friends who are willing to provide what was missing in the past. The goal here is to find a trusted confidante skilled at offering good advice and strong support to her recovering friend. Reparenting doesn't mean that the confidante makes decisions, fixes problems, and acts as some sort of puppetmaster. To the contrary, the confidante listens, coaches, guides, and applauds. She or he functions much the way a parent functions for a child.

Most Twelve Step recovery groups, such as Emotions Anonymous, encourage more experienced members to take new members under their wings in an informal system of "sponsorship." A recovery group sponsor can be an excellent source of reparenting.

It's important to choose the right person for the reparenting job. Your confidante should be someone you admire, someone who is successfully implementing her or his own recovery program in a way that you would like to duplicate or someone whom you see as particularly mature, both emotionally and spiritually. Your confidante definitely shouldn't have a controlling nature, but should be one who is willing to firmly confront you if you begin to stray beyond the boundaries you have set.

This person is only a temporary parent, someone to walk beside you as you deal with the last three points on the addiction cycle and set and try to keep your recovery goals. The goal of this relationship is the same as that of any parenting process: to give support until the person can begin to parent herself or himself. That's your goal too. This person will gradually become less of a parent and more of a close friend and confidante until the final reversal takes place, just as it ultimately does in the parent-child relationship.

Intimate Relationships

Every relationship with key family members, living or dead, needs to be scrutinized. Unfinished business must be completed so you aren't in bondage to an earlier generation. Barbara Ryan, for instance, needs to take an honest look at her relationship with her dad. She needs to accept the fact that he may be a "dry" drunk for the rest of his life. Just as she isn't responsible for his alcoholism, so also she's not responsible for his recovery. That's God's business.

A person who has truly given control of his or her life to God can accept the imperfect world, be content with relationships that may be flawed.

Also, you have to make sure you are free from your family of origin in that you are not financially, residentially, or over-emotionally dependent on your parents. Such a dependency would contaminate the quality of your current relationships. For instance, Michael Potter needed to break the personal and professional ties that kept him on his father's leash. He needed to move away from the family compound and possibly from the family business.

Finally, you need to consider the quality of your relationship with either your spouse or dating partner. Chances are that if you have been compulsive in other areas of your life, you also have been compuslive in this relationship. You may need to read a book on codependency, such as our *Love Is a Choice.* Then each of you needs to acknowledge areas of personal dysfunction and share the details of your shortcomings. During this purging process, the listener shouldn't chime in with comments on the faults. A simple way to carry out this exercise is to set a time limit—perhaps ten minutes

—and use the time to tell your partner what problems you see in yourself. When your ten minutes are up, it's your partner's turn. Now you both need to agree to halt the blame cycle. This cycle never ends if the warring parties don't agree to suspend the compulsion to trade darts.

After you've thoroughly aired your areas of compulsivity, choose the ones you are going to concentrate on conquering. Write them down in the form of an inventory. After both parties have suspended the impulse to blame the other, and both have acknowledged dysfunctions they bring to the relationship, then it is possible to lovingly confront each other about personal needs that are not being met in the relationship. What's missing in your relationship? What do you need that you are not getting? Be willing to ask for what you need. Be willing to hear your partner's needs. Be willing to compromise; no one can change overnight, but everyone can change.

Extended Friendship Network

As our driven patients try to slow the pace of their lives and reconnect with people around them, we suggest five guidelines for building a strong friendship network.

First, we suggest that they choose friends of the same gender. Couple friendships are great, but for one-on-one relationships, you stick to your own kind. Beware of romantic entanglements during the vulnerable period of recovery.

Second, look for quality not quantity. A network of two, three, or four is better than fifty or seventy-five. Let the large number be your Christmas card list, not your intimate circle.

Third, find people who will offer unconditional love. Steer away from colleagues at work, who might be in competition with you; don't select pals who might be in awe of you and, therefore, won't give you honest feedback; and avoid people who are financially linked to you and have something to gain by winning your favor.

Fourth, pick a peer relationship rather than one obviously above or beneath your social or economic level. You may idolize your boss, but you might also feel uncomfortable sharing your weaknesses with him or her out of fear that your boss will think less of you. You want friends with whom you can be totally honest.

Finally, seek a healthy balance. Look for relationships that offer the opportunity for you to give and to receive. Codependent people often build networks that are strikingly out of balance. They may repeatedly choose friends who are crying to be rescued.

If you are willing to say to God, "Thy will be done, not my will," you have taken a step toward overcoming your necrophilia, your worship of non-living things, activities, and accomplishments. Close spiritual communion with the living God and warm, vibrant friendships offer satisfying resolution to that universal human hunger for union. Once you consider three more areas of the addiction cycle—the fallout of your addiction, the violation of your values, and the natural guilt that follows this self-inflicted damage—you will be ready to set your recovery goals.

Chapter Eleven

The Billion-Dollar Price Tag
Point 7: Fallout

Putting a price tag on addiction is nothing new. When Elvis Presley died in 1977 after consuming fourteen different drugs in a twenty-four-hour period, the losses tallied by his addictions were staggering. His obsessions included food; money; success; relationships; and over-the-counter, prescription, and illegal drugs. The fallout?

Once lean and physically fit, at the end of his life the "King" weighed more than 250 pounds. Once famous for his prowess with beautiful showgirls, he had been reduced to sexual impotency. Once the fantasy of female fans around the world, he was so unattractive that one girlfriend frequently sneaked out of Presley's Graceland mansion as soon as the former heartthrob lapsed into his nightly stupor. Once renowned for his bottomless bank account, he took out a $1.3 million loan against his home to underwrite the shaky business venture of a prescription-writing doctor.[1]

Calculating the costs of compulsions is common, and the terms are usually cash. Dollars make sense to us. Every time a drug bust is reported by the media, a "street value" is given for the confiscated goods. Addicts' daily needs are routinely translated into the price of supporting their habits. Even the high cost of applauded addictions is hinted at when we read that Americans spend more than $1.5 billion on skin-care products each year (addiction: staying young); we buy $200 million worth of diet pills annually (addiction: physical beauty); and we pay about $1 billion to have fat removed from our thighs and buttocks through liposuction, the most common cosmetic procedure today (addiction: perfectionism).

But the losses incurred by addiction can go far beyond money. The painful and dramatic demise of Elvis Presley proves that compulsions can claim the quality of a person's life-style long before they claim his life. Why else would the "King of Rock and Roll" frequently comment to his bodyguard, "I'd rather be unconscious than miserable"?[2]

Unfortunately, it's usually easier to see the fallout from negative addictions like Elvis Presley's than from the addictions America applauds. Negative addictions generate tears; applauded addictions generate cheers. For this reason, our driven patients often have to work through another round of denial before they can face the fallout.

Working Through Another Round of Denial

"I've drawn a blank," said Virginia Potter one afternoon toward the end of her hospital stay. She was sitting in the cafeteria, drinking coffee, and pondering a piece of lined notebook paper. It was blank. "I know I'm supposed to compile a list of the negative consequences of my drivenness, but I can only think of one or two. Can you give me a nudge to get me started, Dr. Hemfelt?"

We had explained to Virginia that every addiction carries a price tag. It's a trade-off, we had said. In order for a person to practice an addiction she or he has to be willing to sacrifice something in return. Occasionally patients say up front that they are willing to pay the price. Workaholics might come into counseling not with the goal of abstaining from their work addictions, but rather with the goal of setting a few boundaries and scaling back their compulsions to what they consider to be a tolerable level. It's our obligation as therapists to help these patients understand their options. Exactly what do they risk losing in exchange for this compulsion? Are they willing to pay the price?

This was the point we were trying to make with Virginia when we asked her to complete the fallout exercise. She needed to understand the exact cost of each of her addictions. Only then could she make the decision whether or not to abstain from them.

"The key to this exercise is in being specific," Dr. Hemfelt said. "We want you to isolate each one of your addictions, the serious ones and the not so serious ones. Then, as you start to list the consequences of each addiction, remember that fallout can spill over into five dimensions. Every addiction may not have fallout in all five of the categories, but you need to explore the possibility before you decide one way or another."

Dr. Hemfelt watched Virginia as she carefully listed her handful of compulsions on the left side of the paper, then partitioned the rest of the sheet into five columns. Each column was labeled with one of the categories of fallout we had given her:

- Physical fallout
- Material fallout
- Emotional fallout
- Relational fallout
- Spiritual fallout

Rather than beginning with one of her more obvious addictions—her constant busyness or her need to rescue everyone—we suggested that she start with a less troublesome compulsion that she only recently had recognized. Actually, it had been Michael who had mentioned during a conjoint counseling session that Virginia seemed to have an escalating drive to spend money. He objected to her sprees not because of what they cost him but because of the clutter that resulted. She rarely brought home big-ticket items, but preferred knick-knacks that he categorized as "dust catchers." The uselessness of little figurines on tabletops, plastic fruit in bowls, magnets on the refrigerator, and ceramic ashtrays (no one smoked) grated on his nuts-and-bolts personality. They were silly, he insisted.

"Okay," Virginia said, accepting our challenge and circling the spending addiction that was listed at the bottom of her notebook paper. "I'll see what I can come up with."

The assignment took her two days of sporadic work to complete, but when we sat down together to discuss her response, we noticed that each of the five columns on her paper was filled with scribbled notes. After much thought, she had been able to come up with damaging fallout in all of the categories. She seemed sobered by the exercise because it had proven to her that even a lesser compulsion could cause her and her family serious harm.

"The physical fallout was easy to see," Virginia began. "I usually shop in the middle of the day when Mike is at work and when I'm starting to feel a little restless and fragmented. I get in the car, fight the traffic and sometimes the weather, and head for one of the malls. I wander from store to store, get jostled by the crowds, pour over the racks, try things on, stand in lines at cash registers, and finally call it quits just in time for the commuter traffic at 5:00. It's no wonder I used to feel so tired at night! I'd wasted all my energy on my addiction. What a loss!"

Another consequence that was easy to identify was the financial fallout. Although Virginia rarely splurged on expensive items, her monthly charge card invoices reflected line after line of smaller purchases. She browsed through the avalanche of catalogs that arrived in the mail every day and often placed orders via the toll-free numbers. She liked the anticipation of packages—there was a certain element of mystery about ordering a gift for herself sight unseen. If the "surprise" proved to be a disappointment, she would merely pass it on to her daughter-in-law or to a friend rather than go through the hassle of returning it. Such a freewheeling philosophy resulted in sizeable monthly bills at a time when the family's financial footing was not particularly secure.

"The emotional fallout took some thought," Virginia admitted. "I had to concentrate on the feelings that I get as I schlepp around from mall to mall in search of bargains." She frowned as she tried to put her thoughts into words. "But I think I've figured it out. Buying trinkets gives me a little kick, an emotional high. When I order through catalogs, I'm able to suspend the 'high' because I have to wait for the delivery. Of course, the feeling is temporary. As soon as the package arrives and the knick-knack is in place, I come crashing back to earth. Like Mike says, 'It's just another dust catcher.' "

Virginia correctly identified the emotional need her shopaholism filled—that natural desire to feel better, to feel euphoric and transcendent. She talked about feeling the same high the drug addicts had expressed to Dr. Hemfelt during his years at the opiate addiction center in Houston. Now the doctor had to help her fill this need through her relationship with God and other people.

Dr. Hemfelt also pointed out to Virginia that her shopping expeditions were ways to distract herself from the real emotional needs that she preferred not to confront. When she was maneuvering through 5:00 rush hour traffic or elbowing her way through a crowded department store, stopping here and there to buy a temporary "fix," she couldn't think about the areas of emptiness in her marriage. In a similar, but not as destructive, manner, she used shopping just as a drug addict uses a narcotic: to dull her pain and to distract her from the real source of her pain. Her seemingly harmless shopping activity made her unconscious to the out-of-control world that awaited her at the C.C.C. That world confused and frustrated her. She wanted to blot it out and be unconscious to it for a little while. Much like Elvis Presley, she preferred being unconscious to being miserable.

Virginia looked at her piece of notebook paper and tapped her pencil on the column marked "Relational Fallout." She shook her head. "I'm ashamed about how I've used shopping as a way to hurt Michael," she said. "You've always told us, Dr. Hemfelt, that anger doesn't go away. It has to be expressed in one way or another. Well, I think I've practiced that old adage, 'Don't get mad, get even.' I've expressed my anger and resentment by shopping nonstop. Rather than telling Mike that I'm tired of his marathon work sessions and his constant stream of meetings, I've tried to get even by doing something that I know irritates him. I shop for clutter."

Dr. Hemfelt nodded. "It's called passive-aggressive anger," he reminded her.

"I call it sneaky," she replied with a grin.

Virginia moved down her fallout list. "At first I couldn't think of any other relational losses," she said, "but then I remembered how it used to be when the kids were young. My girlfriends and I would plan a whole day around a shopping trip downtown. We usually shared the cost of a babysitter and then carpooled into the city. We'd have coffee, split up and shop for a couple of hours, and then get together for lunch and show and tell. We had a lot of fun displaying our treasures. It was a real event, even if no one bought anything."

"And now," Dr. Hemfelt asked.

"Now the lunch part and all the chatter turns me off," Virginia admitted. "I don't want anyone teasing me about what I buy; I don't want to have to justify it. Also, when you travel in a group, you have to follow a plan. You agree to shop for a certain amount of time, then to break at such-and-such hour, and have lunch at a place that meets with everyone's approval. I like the faster pace of going alone." Virginia shrugged her shoulders. "Pretty antisocial, huh? And addicted?"

Virginia had saved the toughest for last—the spiritual fallout that her compulsion had caused her and her family.

"This is a little off-the-wall, but here goes," Virginia warned us with a laugh. She picked up the sheet of paper and refreshed herself on her scribbled notations. "In a counterfeit sort of way, my trips to the shopping malls helped me to shut out the world—and all my problems with it. I felt free and exhilarated as I concentrated on what little trophies I wanted to reward myself with that day. My purchases became like false gods to me. They comforted me and lifted me up."

The fallout exercise was a revelation for Virginia. It helped her see the potential danger in what she always had considered to be a harmless preoccupation. If she could generate such a list of negative consequences for her shopping compulsion, we knew she would have no trouble facing the fallout of her busyness and rescuing.

Moving Beyond Fallout

The grieving process is put in motion at several points around the addiction cycle, and the fallout stopover is one of them. Just as we grieve about the trauma of our family of origin, and as we grieve out our emotional pain, so must we also grieve the consequences that our compulsions have caused ourselves and the people around us.

We will never forget Tony, a workaholic patient who realized, very dramatically, that one of his losses was time spent with his wife and children. Midway through his recovery, he and his wife sat down to look at videotapes she had made of their children's earlier years. As Tony watched his children's "firsts"—their first steps, their first bike rides, their first dates—he realized he was literally seeing these events for the first time! He had not been there! He had missed these moments in his children's early years and could never regain them. As he told us about this revelation, he cried out with the pain of his irreplaceable losses.

What Has My Drivenness Cost Me?

Take a moment now to think about your own drivenness. Ask yourself: What is the negative fallout of my drivenness? Physically? Materially? Emotionally? Relationally? Spiritually?

Now give yourself the opportunity to grieve for those losses by checking the statements below that apply to you.

Physically?

1. ✓ *"I grieve the loss of my good health. I seem to be spending more and more time in a doctor's office, complaining of fatigue or headaches or a pain in my stomach."*

2. ✓ *"I grieve the loss of a good night's sleep. It seems impossible to turn my mind off at night."*

3. ___ *"I grieve the loss of having time to relax, 'to stop and smell the roses.' "*

4. ___ *"I grieve the loss of a moderate pace. I always feel rushed, as if I never have time to do everything that needs to be done."*

5. ✓ *"I grieve the loss of feeling good about the way I look. Whenever I look in the mirror, I'm not at peace with what I see."*

Materially?

1. ✓ *"I grieve the loss of money in the bank. This year I made more money than ever before, but I don't have enough left to pay my taxes."*

2. ? *"I grieve the loss of spontaneity in life. I'm never able to drop everything to go to a show or out to dinner or on a weekend getaway."*

3. ___ *"I grieve the loss of knowing who I am. I know all the things I own, but I can't tell you my own identity."*

4. ___ *"I grieve the loss of <u>fun</u> in my life. I am so busy pursuing goals that I never have time for recreation."*

5. ___ *"I grieve the fact that everything I own seems to own me. My life is consumed with trying to acquire things, <u>pay for things</u>, service things, and hold onto things."*

Emotionally?

1.____ *"I grieve the loss of my emotional health. Most of the time I feel emotionally drained or bankrupt, as if I'm watching myself go through the motions."*

2.✓___ *"I grieve the loss of feeling happy. Every year I seem to feel less happy than the year before despite my accomplishments."*

3.✓___ *"I grieve the lack of a feeling of stability and security in my life. I never seem to feel as if I have enough money or whatever to be okay."*

4.✓___ *"Even though I have more than ever before, on the inside I feel as if I'm running on empty."*

Relationally?

1.____ *"I grieve the time lost with my family. I feel as if I don't know my spouse or children any more (or my parents and my brothers and sisters)."*

2.____ *"I grieve the loss of genuine friendships and the fun my friends and I used to have together. When we do get together now, we are always talking about things that happened in the past, the 'good old days' that aren't here anymore."*

3.____ *"I grieve the loss of a romantic relationship in my life. My marriage isn't a marriage any longer (or my relationship with my dating partner has gone stale)."*

4.____ *"I grieve the loss of a sexual relationship. I don't seem to have time or energy for sex. I seem to be out of touch with my own body."*

5.____ *"I grieve the loss of my marriage. I wish my spouse hadn't decided on separation (or divorce)."*

Spiritually?

1.____ *"I grieve the lack of a spiritual dimension in my life. I have never allowed myself to slow down long enough to explore this dimension."*

239

2.____*"I grieve the lack of a feeling of wholeness or oneness in my life. I feel as if something is missing, as if there's a void. Part of me longs for the assurance that people who have a deep faith seem to have."*

3.____*"I grieve the lack of a close relationship with God. Even though I may practice the formal rituals of religious faith, I don't feel that personal connection with God."*

4.____*"I fear running out of time. I fear death. Will there ever be enough time to accomplish what I desire?"*

5.____*"I grieve the meaninglessness of life. Is there a grand purpose or plan to all of our efforts?"*

Although this exercise seems depressing, we often combine it with a "But for the grace of God" exercise. We remind our patients that as long as their loss lists may be, they could have been even longer—*but for the grace of God.*

But for the Grace of God

We tell our patients to repeat this statement and fill in the blank. For instance, they might say:

"But for the grace of God . . . I could have lost my husband through divorce, instead of just damaging my marriage through my perfectionism."

"But for the grace of God . . . I could have had a heart attack because of my workaholism."

"But for the grace of God . . . the bank could have foreclosed on our mortgage because of my compulsive get-rich-quick investments."

Now fill in a couple of "But for the grace of God" statements yourself to balance the losses you listed above:

"But for the grace of God I could have _____
_____."

"But for the grace of God I could have _____
_____."

You might also fill in a corollary statement: "If I don't stop my obsessive-compulsive behavior, I could lose _____ _____."

Sometimes patients' walls of denial aren't easily penetrated. Some are so thick that the fallout and grieving exercises aren't sufficient to break through them. When that happens, we sometimes suggest an intervention, a technique explained in depth on page 82 when we discussed the necessary step of learning to cry "Ouch!" before a positive pattern crosses that invisible line and becomes an addiction. We use intervention any time a patient's recovery is blocked by denial—in this case, the denial of the fallout of their addiction.

Intervening to Overcome the Denial of Fallout

When Dr. Hemfelt was an employee assistance program specialist (EAP) for a Fortune 500 corporation in Dallas, one of his duties was to train his staff to document the fallout of employees' addictions. The purpose of this documentation was not to build a case for dismissal of the employees, but rather to collect data for possible intervention and treatment. For example, he recalls the case of a gifted research scientist who suffered the dual addictions of perfectionism and rageaholism. No one in the product research department escaped the man's scrutiny—or his wrath.

"In his ten years with the company he had offended nearly everyone he had ever worked with," recalled Dr. Hemfelt. "When co-workers started to ask for transfers out of his area, we realized that we had to act. We contacted five of the people he had verbally attacked and asked them to help us stage an intervention. Each person documented an actual day and an event that had triggered the man's anger. Then they gathered as a group to face this man, and each one told him how they had felt when he attacked them. For an hour he listened to the firsthand fallout of his rage."

Extracting a promise from the driven person to "do better

in the future" isn't good enough. His chances of making good on his word are very slim. Instead, the goal of an intervention is to convince him to enter treatment voluntarily.

Often intervention is a last resort. That was the case with Barbara Ryan's husband, Hal. In the course of her own recovery Barbara had recognized that Hal struggled with two related addictions. He had a need to control everything around him, and he compulsively rebelled against all persons in authority. Both of these addictions were rooted in his childhood when he had grown up under the oppressive thumb of a dictatorial father.

Barbara had never put together the pieces of Hal's addictions until she was sensitized by her own therapy. Then the puzzle started to fit, and the picture wasn't pretty. She realized that if she was ever to trust a man to take care of her, it couldn't be a man who seemingly wanted to dominate her. As long as she had worked full-time she had handled her own income, but now that she had decided to decrease her hours to part-time, Hal expected to be the primary bookkeeper as well as breadwinner. An obsessive money manager, he controlled the household finances with scroogelike tactics. Every cent had to be accounted for, every purchase had to be budgeted, and he had the irritating habit of following her around the house and turning off "unnecessary" lights even if she needed them to see properly.

"My recovery is being hampered by my husband," Barbara Ryan complained to us. "I'm afraid Hal is going to suffocate me just as my father suffocated my mother with his addiction. It's hard enough for me to relax and let my guard down without feeling someone is waiting to gobble me up when I do."

The irony of Barbara's situation was that the therapy, designed partly to strengthen her marriage was driving a wedge between her and her husband. As she worked her way around the addiction cycle, identifying her sources of shame and low self-esteem, she also came face-to-face with Hal's needs. She realized that unless he was willing to improve his own emotional health, her chances of achieving a Stage II recovery were limited. To have an effective team, both partners had to be strong. She began to question the future of their marriage. Before she made any decision about separating from Hal, she wanted to explore every possible option.

Barbara invited Hal to attend meetings of Adult Children of Alcoholics with her. He declined, pointing out that for all of his father's shortcomings he hadn't been a drinker. She pointed out that the fallout from rage was often the same as from alcohol—embarrassment, low self-confidence, and shame. Still he refused. She explained that his need to control their marriage was propelling her work addiction. Success on the job was her means of maintaining her own identity. He brushed aside her pleas for change.

"What about an intervention to help Hal realize the fallout of his compulsions to control others and to rebel against those in authority?" Barbara asked us one afternoon during a counseling session. She ticked off the names of possible participants. There was Hal's supervisor at work, a woman who once had hinted to Barbara that Hal's attitude was thwarting his advancement in the company. And there was a friend who shared Hal's flying hobby. The reason she thought both persons would be logical participants was because Hal recently had turned against them and criticized them at home. Barbara said Hal's relationships seemed to follow that pattern. At first they flourished, and then they soured. Seldom did one last more than a few months.

On the day of the intervention Hal arrived, expecting to sit in on an hour-long couple's counseling session with Barbara and Dr. Hemfelt. Instead, he was confronted with an expanded circle that included his boss and flying partner. One by one, the key players explained the fallout of Hal's addiction that each had witnessed. His boss also predicted some negative future fallout if Hal didn't make some changes.

"You're a good salesman, Hal, but you'll never be promoted to a regional manager if you don't shake that chip off your shoulder. Frankly, I'm tired of apologizing for your moodiness. I've gone out on a limb for you more than once, but the men at headquarters are losing their patience. If things don't change, you may lose your job."

Hal's flying friend recounted a weekend trip that turned their formerly warm relationship into a cool association.

"We both had looked forward to a laid-back fishing trip to southern Florida, remember, Hal? But you had every minute planned right down to the restaurants where we'd eat, how much fishing we would do, and what we would spend on a motel room. When the weather turned bad and we were delayed at the airport, it was *my* fault because I had overslept half an hour. I had more fun in boot camp!"

Then it was Barbara's turn. "As part of my recovery it's important for me to build a network of friends. Yet, you criticize everyone I invite to the house. And it's gotten worse, Hal. The cookout I planned on the Fourth of July turned into a nightmare when you wouldn't even try to make conversation with anyone. For the next two days I had to listen to you complain about how much I had spent on the food."

The intervention was a success in that it convinced Hal that he needed to find help for his escalating addictions. Not only did the confrontation force him to listen to the past and present consequences of his compulsions, but also he picked up on future fallout. His boss had hinted that if he didn't change his attitude he might be out of a job. His wife had issued a warning: If he didn't go into treatment she might leave him. The intervention had gotten his attention; now the real work could begin.

Dodging Your Fallout

Nobody likes to be reminded of failures. Tuning in to the consequences of your addictions either through self-exploration (by completing the fallout exercises) or through the scrutiny of others (by being the target of an intervention) is like being Mike Tyson's punching bag on a day when the champ is in a bad mood. It's not a lot of fun. However, if recovery is to be complete, facing your fallout is a necessary part of working your way around the addiction cycle.

Three notes of caution:

Remember the power of denial. It's human nature for us

to go to great lengths to protect ourselves from facing the pain we've caused. In his more sober moments Elvis Presley would burst into tears when he was reminded of the fallout his only child, Lisa Marie, had suffered because of his addictions. She was nine when he died, and although she visited him often, he was too impaired to give her the fatherly attention that every child craves. As a way of denying the truth and compensating for his neglect, he lavished expensive gifts on his daughter. Seeing her smile as she opened her presents helped him to wriggle out from under his shame burden.

Tap into outside help. While Elvis's corps of yes-men was well paid to help the "King" deny the fallout from his addictions, most people can rely on honest friends for honest feedback. Often the people around you have sharper vision than you do when it comes to reading the price tag on your compulsion. Addicts tend to believe that no one is aware of their obsessions, but generally, an addiction is the secret that everyone knows. If you are having trouble identifying the consequences of your addictions, ask a friend. You'll probably find your answer.

Beware of the "Gifts of the Magi" syndrome. Everyone knows the famous O. Henry story about the poor newlyweds who struggled to come up with the necessary funds to buy each other a suitable Christmas gift. In the end, each gives the other something that can't be used. Jim sells his watch to buy Della the tortoise combs she has admired for so long, and Della sells her hair to buy a chain for Jim's watch. She can't wear the combs, and he can't use the chain. The gifts were given in love, but neither was what the person needed.

A Modern Example of the "Gifts of the Magi" Syndrome

A good example of how this syndrome works in a driven home comes from Dr. Meier, who for several months counseled an unhappy insurance executive and his depressed wife. The man had grown up in an impoverished family, and for him the greatest gift he could imagine giving to his wife and children was financial security. It had been missing from his childhood and had caused him low self-esteem, embarrassment, and shame. He was determined never to subject his family to the pain of poverty; therefore, he worked night and day to make sure they had everything that money could buy.

The executive's wife had grown up in a single-parent household that had no stability, no structure, and no control. She had been ashamed of the chaos at home, insecure about who was in charge, and confused about which of her battling parents deserved her allegiance. The gift that she brought to her own marriage was order in the house. Every room was beautifully decorated; every drawer was perfectly organized; nutritious meals were provided promptly at seven in the morning, noon, and six in the evening. Punctuality was stressed, and service came with a plastic smile.

Just as in the O. Henry story, each marriage partner was providing what the other didn't need. The wife desperately hungered for attention and emotional security; instead, she got an absent husband and a huge bank account. The husband craved the kind of warmth that would assure him that he had value as a person not just as a provider. Instead, he got a meticulously tidy sock drawer and dinners that always included items from the basic food groups. The fallout from their dual compulsions was pushing them apart, rather than pulling them together. They didn't deny the fallout; they simply were too busy to see it.

Often driven people are much better at giving than receiving. Although they may not give what is needed or wanted, they give what they *need* to give or what they *think* is wanted.

Are you giving your spouse or dating partner a watch chain when he or she no longer owns a watch? Instead we suggest that you discuss your needs openly with one another. Be flexible; and, above all, be honest. The most difficult kind of fallout that you will face is at point 8 of the addiction cycle: the violation of values. And that's our next stop.

Chapter Twelve

The Split Personality
Point 8: Violation of Values

In spite of his addiction to women, the late Richard Burton believed marriage was forever. "Monogamy is absolutely imperative," he once stressed to a journalist during an interview in his hotel room. At the same time that Burton was pledging total loyalty to his fourteen-year union with Sybil Burton, his girlfriend, Elizabeth Taylor, was floating in and out of the hotel suite in hot pink pajamas. Burton offered no explanation to the baffled journalist, who was hearing one message and seeing another.

From Burton's point of view, staying married didn't necessarily mean staying faithful. The ever-patient Sybil often had to look the other way as her roving mate romped through one affair after another.

"I can't hurt Syb" was one of Burton's most repeated phrases. "I'll never leave Syb" was another. The women who flocked to his side and to his bed understood that no matter how serious their encounters with the actor might be, he would never divorce his wife. He had a strict—though offbeat—code of values. Marriage was forever, he insisted, and he was married forever to Sybil. His dedication to the family was rooted in his Welsh childhood where he was the eleventh of thirteen children. His father was a gambling, alcoholic miner who couldn't pass a pub without stopping in for a pint. In spite of the hardship caused by too little money and too much alcohol, his long-suffering mother never considered divorce as an option. Marriage, after all, was forever.

Unfortunately, one of the characteristics of any addiction is that eventually it overpowers the addict and makes him violate his value system. When this happens, the shame base increases and prods him to reach more frequently for an addictive agent to dull the pain. Burton became so obsessed with Elizabeth Taylor that he did what he promised he never would do: He deserted Syb. He succumbed to his addiction and left his family, then he punished himself by giving most of his money to his ex-wife. Whatever was left was donated to charity rather than providing a nest egg for his new marriage. It was as if he were trying to atone for his sin by sacrificing his fortune. However, neither his generosity nor his escalating use of alcohol eased his guilt. When he tried to anesthetize his pain with alcohol (which was often), he unleashed his imagination and wondered aloud whether his infidelity was to blame for his youngest daughter's being autistic. This self-incriminating thought caused more pain, and the additional pain prompted him to reach for more alcohol. The cycle churned around and around until his death in 1984.

Consequences of Addiction

There are two consequences of addiction. The first is fallout, which we talked about in the last chapter, and the second is violation of values. They are closely linked, although the second is on a deeper level than the first. Fallout is usually visible and often measurable; violation of values is more profound and intensely private. Just as Virginia Potter was able to chart the fallout of her shopaholism, so also might Richard Burton have ticked off the damages caused by his multiple addictions to tobacco, alcohol, women, success, and rescuing others.

The physical fallout for Burton was obvious in his swollen face, raspy voice, and dramatic loss of weight. The relational fallout is a matter of record—five marriages and well-documented broken friendships attributed to his outbursts, insults, and unpredictable Jekyll-Hyde personality. His financial ups and downs were a result of his urge to lavish money on friends and to finance his extended family back in Wales. "You okay for cash?" was his frequent question, according to his biographer Melvyn Bragg.[1]

Violation of values is more difficult to track. It may not be evident on the surface, but when a person violates his or her personal code of ethics that person suffers nearly unbearable pain. The person is aware of his or her hypocrisy and hates himself or herself for it. Examples are evident in our files and in the daily news media. They include:

- The elected official who publicly fights drug abuse and is arrested for buying cocaine from an undercover police officer.
- The businessman who earns his community's "Father of the Year" citation but is too caught up with civic work to spend more than a few minutes a day with his love-hungry children.
- The Christian athlete who spiritually refers to her body as the temple of God but persistently abuses diet pills and laxatives as ways to control her weight for competition.
- The law-abiding citizen who causes a serious traffic accident when he races through a red light while driving under the influence of alcohol.

In all of these cases, the addict is powerless over addiction. The obsession with drugs, work, perfectionism, and alcohol causes the addict to turn his or her back on beliefs, thumb the nose at his or her code of ethics, and violate a long-held set of values.

Michael Potter violated his values in at least two ways. Having grown up with a neglectful and abusive father, he had promised himself that as an adult he would be loving and supportive of his family. Yet, his addictions to work and service kept him away from home and caused him to be preoccupied even when he was physically present in the C.C.C.

Also, if you asked Michael how he felt about fidelity and sexual morality he would espouse sincerely held beliefs. Yet, he was driven to secretly meet some of his deepest intimacy needs through pornography. Mentally he hated the cheap magazines that exploited women and reduced sexual relations to animalistic acts. However, he persistently bought and consumed such material. This was in direct contradiction to his value system. He knew he was a hypocrite—saying one thing and doing another—and he hated himself for it.

Michael struggled with guilt on two levels as well. He could see how he had injured Virginia and their children, and he knew that many of *their* problems were caused by *his* problems. His deeper, more burning sense of guilt resulted from his realization that he was no longer true to his own value system. He didn't know who he was. He talked a good line and passed himself off as a model husband and Christian businessman, but he felt he was living a lie. He could fool everyone around him, but he couldn't fool himself.

Positive vs. Negative

It is much easier to identify a violation of values when a person is addicted to a negative substance rather than to an activity America applauds. For instance, we once counseled an anesthesiologist whose personal and professional reputation had always been flawless. He was active in his church, didn't drink or smoke, and had served as president of his county's medical association.

Why was he in therapy? As out of character as it seems, the doctor had begun abusing the narcotics that he used in his practice. Dependence on these drugs didn't occur overnight, but gradually took hold of him over several years. When he was tired he would reach for a pick-me-up; when he was tense he'd swallow a fistful of downers. The addiction quietly sneaked up on him to the point that it controlled him. Disclosure to his colleagues happened in a dangerous and dramatic way. He was in surgery, administering a drug to a patient, when he felt the overwhelming need for a fix. He reached under the operating table and attempted to self-inject. Partly because he couldn't see what he was doing and partly because his hands were shaking, he nicked a vein and bled profusely. He could offer no excuse. News of his addiction instantly became public knowledge and spread to every corner of the hospital and the city where he lived. Still, people who knew him were amazed. Drug abuse violated everything this man stood for.

More difficult to pinpoint is when the violation of values involves an addiction America condones. For example, every world-class athlete knows the importance of following a carefully designed training schedule that includes a certain amount of exercise balanced with a certain amount of rest. Thanks to sports medicine experts and sports psychologists, even non-athletes know that too much exercise can lead to injury, exhaustion, and mental burnout. Yet Alberto Salazar, track and field star in the 1980s, ran 120 miles a week when he was in college, and in one week he ran 105 miles while nursing a stress fracture in his foot. Another time he ran so hard that he suffered heat prostration; his body temperature rose to a near-deadly 108 degrees, and doctors had to pack him in ice to prevent permanent damage to his health.

A tip-off that a positive pastime like running has become a negative addiction is when the athlete begins to schedule secret workouts despite warnings from a coach. Even injury doesn't curb the drive to push to exhaustion. The athlete may be aware that the excessive activity is having diminishing effects on his or her performance and is violating health and fitness values. Still, the athlete can't stop.

Have *You* Crossed Over?

Often when we tell patients about the concept of violation of values, we suggest that they envision a split movie screen. On one-half of the screen are characters engaged in some noble activity. Perhaps a young mother is explaining to her children about the importance of eating well-balanced meals, or maybe a husband and wife duo are instructing an adult Sunday school class about the value of honesty and faithfulness in a marriage.

On the other half of the screen our patients imagine the same characters involved in acts that seem to be in total contrast to their noble words. The young mother is binging on high-calorie processed foods, and when she reaches the saturation point she purges her body by inducing vomiting. The husband, who teaches the adult Sunday school class, is on the telephone with his wife and is telling her that his boss has asked him to work late at the office again. As soon as he hangs up he leaves to keep a date with a young secretary, the most recent in his string of girlfriends.

Just like the on-screen examples, driven people exhibit split behavior. Part of them knows better. Part of them understands what is right and what values should be embraced. But because of their shame bases, insecurity, low self-esteem, and emotional pain, they are driven to act in ways that are contrary to what they know to be correct. They have crossed over the line. Rather than being in control of their lives, they are controlled by the addictions in their lives. They become like Richard Burton when a film director offered him a large chunk of money to stop smoking for three months. Burton needed the money and knew his voice was being damaged by his addiction to cigarettes. He enthusiastically accepted the offer, but after two months of abstinence had to admit that he was powerless over his compulsion. Tobacco won. He had crossed over the line.

To bring the concept closer to home, we ask our patients to build on the exercise that we assigned them in Chapter 12. In that exercise they listed each of their addictions and then tried to isolate five types of fallout that had been caused by the various addictions—physical, material, emotional, relational, and spiritual fallout. We tell them to look at those addictions again, review the fallout, list the values that are at stake, and then figure out how those values had been violated.

As an example, Virginia Potter went back to her notes on shopaholism and concentrated on the relational fallout that had resulted from it. She had bought countless knick-knacks as a way of irritating Michael and getting even for his neglect of her.

"What value is at stake here?" we asked her.

"Communication in our marriage," she replied. "I've always been a very verbal person." She laughed and added, "Which is a nice way of saying that I talk too much. But people usually know where they stand with me. If I'm upset with someone, I like to air my feelings face-to-face. If I'm hurt, I cry. If I'm happy, I smile. Subtlety has never been my strong suit."

"What does that have to do with your addiction to shopping?" we probed.

"If I'm upset with Michael, I believe that I should look him squarely in the eyes and tell him what's on my mind," she said. "In this case, I should have explained that I felt neglected and that I wanted to spend more time with him. Instead, my addiction to shopping caused me to violate my belief in open communication. As I came to rely more and more on shopping as a means of indirectly expressing my anger at Mike, I withdrew from him. I didn't want to talk about my feelings; I preferred to shop instead."

How About You?

Has your compulsive behavior caused you to violate your values or beliefs? For instance, is there some area of your life, or some activity in your life, in which you've set a particular boundary, like a New Year's resolution, that you've repeatedly violated? Check the statements below that apply to you.

1. ✓ *"I believe in complete honesty; yet, I tend to withhold information from my family."*

2. ____ *"Someone close to me has told me that I am not 'practicing what I preach.'"*

3.____ *"I tend to add extra meals or travel expenses to my expense reports and 'fudge' on my income tax even though I see myself as an honest person."*

4.____ *"I do not want my children to become involved in drugs or alcohol, but I sometimes use these chemicals to relieve my own tension."*

5.____ *"I believe that marriage is a lifetime commitment, but I have become involved with some other person."*

6._✓_ *"Every once in a while I look in the mirror and realize that I'm not living as I'd like to live."*

7.____ *"I know the hurried pace of my life is taking its toll on me and my loved ones. But I can't seem to slow down."*

8._✓_ *"I tell myself that my relationship with God and with my family should be the highest priorities of my life. Yet, in reality, most of my energy is devoted to pursuing other goals, such as money, achievement, and activity."*

9._✓_ *"Often I feel like a hypocrite. The 'public me' others see doesn't match the 'private me' that I know."*

Each one of these statements shows some split between a person's values and actions. The more statements you checked the greater this split.

Recognizing what values have been violated is an important part of any addict's recovery process. But there is more to be looked at beyond the short-term consequences caused by fallout and the violation of values. There also is long-term damage to cope with: a change in personality.

Drifting Toward Self-centeredness

Some psychologists call it narcissism, a word derived from the Greek myth about a beautiful young boy named Narcissus who fell in love with his own reflection. More simply put, narcissism is a label for self-centeredness, or the over-abundance of love for oneself. For our purposes, it's not so much a matter of self-love as it is self-absorption. It comes into play in a driven person's life at two points and in two ways. Originally it can contribute to the formation of the addiction. Later, self-centeredness can propel the addict deeper and deeper into his or her drivenness.

Unlike fallout and the violation of values that might crop up soon after a person crosses the line into addiction, self-centeredness is a condition that is rooted in the past and gradually grows until it causes a negative transformation of character and personality.

"Whoa, back up," said Michael Potter during the conjoint therapy session devoted to discussing the link between self-centeredness and addiction. "You've lost me, Dr. Hemfelt. Up to this point you've told Ginny and me that we have to scale back our feeble attempts to save the world. I'm supposed to stop making loans to all of my friends who are in financial jams, and we're both supposed to ease off on our charity work. Now you're saying we're self-centered. I don't get it. I thought we were trying to think *more*, not *less*, about ourselves and each other. Since we've been in therapy we've come to recognize a lot of problems we didn't know we had, but selfishness sure hasn't been one of them."

Dr. Hemfelt nodded. Michael Potter had just hit on one of the baffling paradoxes connected to the addictions America applauds.

On the surface it doesn't seem to make sense. Many driven people truly hate the idea of self-centeredness. They have a real concern for others and want to show Christian charity toward the people around them. They don't consider themselves to be selfish; in fact, their actions smack of kindness and generosity. For instance, at the height of his addiction, Michael was donating enormous chunks of time to community organizations to help the elderly, the youth, the handicapped, and the poor in his hometown. No wonder it was difficult for him to accept the idea that part of his motivation was selfishness.

"Self-centeredness is something each one of us is born with," Dr. Hemfelt assured the Potters. "As babies we demand constant care, affection, and affirmation. Think about your own children for a moment. Remember how much attention they required when they were newborns. They wanted to eat as soon as they felt the first pangs of hunger; they howled if they experienced the discomfort of being wet; they let you know in no uncertain terms if they had the slightest tummy ache. They expected to be rocked, cuddled, and loved."

"I remember," said Virginia with a smile. "I enjoyed holding the kids; it made me feel as happy and secure as it made them feel."

"Exactly," the doctor agreed. "Most parents are delighted to dote on their babies' needs, and if the children receive all of the nurturing and attention that they demand, their natural self-centeredness gradually subsides as part of their maturing process."

"But if the needs aren't satisfied? What happens when the babies grow up?" asked Virginia.

"The self-centeredness remains intact, although buried, and becomes like a time bomb waiting to go off," Dr. Hemfelt answered. "Somewhere, later in adulthood, the person begins to slip into an addiction as a way of coping with the negative messages, shame base, and low self-esteem that were formed during childhood, when living with the family of origin. Then, in time, the self-centeredness, which also was part of childhood residue, resurfaces. The addict becomes totally absorbed in himself or herself and in the addiction. The addict's first priority is taking care of personal needs, whether those needs involve amassing money, acquiring success, accumulating honors, or achieving physical perfection. Since addiction is a progressive illness, it grows progressively worse as years go by."

Michael nodded his head in understanding. "I get it," he said. "I rescue people in order to boost my self-image and to ease my emotional pain. So I'm doing charity work to benefit me as well as to help others." He smiled as the puzzle started to make sense to him. "What looks like generosity is also selfishness, and this selfish motivation becomes another violation of my values," he continued. "I've always believed that self-absorption is wrong, and now I've violated that belief by becoming too caught up in myself. When I violate my values I feel more guilt, which causes me to do more charity work to ease the guilt. The cycle just keeps going around."

As addicts sink deeper and deeper into their addictive lifestyles, they become more and more self-centered. They think only of themselves and of feeding their addictions. Again, this is easiest to recognize when the addictive agent is a negative substance, such as alcohol or drugs. Given the choice of spending their paychecks on their families or on their addictions, addicts opt for the addiction. If his wife needs a dress and he needs a drink, he services his need for a drink.

Persons driven by a compulsion America applauds act in a similar way. Given a choice between spending a quiet evening with their children and working late at the office, workaholics opt for the office, where their reward might be a promotion. If their spouses are hungry for companionship and their egos are hungry for applause, they service their egos by donating time to a charity event that will reap a plaque and a picture in the local newspaper.

An Egomaniac with an Inferiority Complex?

The idea that most addicts eventually slip into a state of acute self-centeredness is nothing new. Bill Wilson, cofounder of Alcoholics Anonymous, recognized this concept many years ago. He likened addicts to actors who are so engrossed in themselves that they think they can control the whole show. These actors see themselves on center stage with all of the action revolving around them. They make the decisions, and they call the shots. Their wants and needs are top priority.

"Most people try to live by self-propulsion," wrote Wilson, in explanation of an addict's self-centeredness. "Each person is like an actor who wants to run the whole show; is forever trying to arrange the lights, the ballet, the scenery and the rest of the players in his own way. . . . What usually happens? The show doesn't come off very well."[2]

Because of an addict's tendency to become self-absorbed, Alcoholics Anonymous and other Twelve-Step recovery groups emphasize the importance of healing the overall character and personality flaws caused by addiction. In addition, the recovering addict must explore and understand the deepest roots of self-centeredness that laid the groundwork for the formation of the addiction. Usually the chain of events follows this sequence: First, the child's natural needs for nurturance were not satisfied in the dysfunctional family of origin; as a result, the child then suffers "love hunger," low self-esteem, and even self-hatred; third, the child grows into a narcissistic teenager or young adult who has an exaggerated, self-centered need for attention or accomplishment; fourth, this adult-child becomes addicted to the compulsions America applauds as a means of gaining the attention he or she needs; this then leads the addict to violate his or her most sacred values. The pain of this violation of values must be addressed through the process of moral inventory.

The Moral Inventory

In Chapter 9 we likened Step 4 of the Twelve Steps of Alcoholics Anonymous ("We made a searching and fearless moral inventory of ourselves") to a grand, all-out cleaning effort—"spring cleaning," some call it. At that time we were suggesting that driven people consider the daily version of this Step, the ongoing inventory of Steps 10 and 11. When we are helping driven people to see their self-centeredness, we often ask them to pause and reflect on the in-depth moral inventory of Step 4.

Sometimes people see the moral inventory as merely a confession list of all the things they've done wrong. Surely that can be a *part* of the written inventory suggested in Step 4. But more important is the attempt to determine what is wrong with the personality and to identify the deepest defects of character that have been the underpinning of the drivenness. Typically, four personality shortcomings are discovered: (1) self-centeredness, (2) aggressiveness, (3) anger and resentment, and (4) fear.

Self-centeredness

·Neither Michael nor Virginia Potter had had their narcis sistic needs totally filled in childhood. Now their self-centeredness had resurfaced and was being addressed by their driven life-style. They were the pivotal forces in the C.C.C, where they held court. Friends looked to them for answers, for encouragement, and, in Michael's case, for money.

How about you? Are some of your narcissistic needs from childhood resurfacing to drive your life-style? Is your addiction to work, for instance, really satisfying your self-centered need to be loved?

I realize that my (workaholism, for instance) _____
is not really driven by my desire to (provide for my family or benefit my company) _____,
but is a self-centered desire to fulfill my narcissistic need (to prove that I deserve to exist or to be loved by others)_____.

Aggressiveness

Driven people often are demanding people. They want what they want when they want it. The shopaholic is an excellent example of this. He or she is an adult version of the demanding child who goes into a dime store and walks up and down the aisles, saying, "I want this! I want that!" This aggressiveness is linked with self-centeredness. Not only does the driven person put his or her needs at the top of the priority list, but he or she will do anything to fulfill the needs.

One of our patients who is a corporate executive unconsciously transfers to his employees his anger at his dad for overly controlling him in his childhood. He uses a basketball metaphor to express his tyrannical standards in an acceptable way: "I do set high hoops for all my employees."

Dr. Meier recognized this man's aggressive personality and his need to control others the first time he arrived in Dr. Meier's office for a 2:00 appointment. Dr. Meier walked out of his office at 2:05 because the last appointment had taken a little longer than anticipated.

The executive looked up at the doctor with a parental scowl and then pointed to his watch. "What's wrong?" he asked.

At first Paul thought the executive meant that his watch was broken, so he looked back at the man with a puzzled look on his face.

"I thought my appointment was for 2:00," the sales manager retorted. "If we are going to start at 2:05, then make my appointment for 2:05."

Right away Paul Meier knew this man was using his punctual standards as a cover for his anger at someone, probably his parents.

How about you? Is your aggressiveness really driven by a selfish desire? Be realistic as you fill in the statement below.

My aggressiveness with (my spouse, my children, my colleagues, or my friends) _____
is really a self-centered expression of my narcissistic need (to be in control or to rebel against a parent) _____

_____.

Anger and Resentment

No matter how thoroughly driven persons practice their addictions, part of them feels as though their requirements are not being met. The shopaholic never makes enough purchases. The perfectionist is never satisfied with the imperfect world, wanting it to spin one way—her or his way—and it invariably turns in reverse. Anger and resentment result.

Bill Wilson said that resentment destroys more alcoholics than anything else. "From it stems all forms of spiritual disease, for we have been not only mentally and physically ill, we have been spiritually sick. When the spiritual malady is overcome, we straighten out mentally and physically."[3]

He suggested that persons addicted to alcohol should make a "grudge list" that details exactly whom the addicts are angry with, the action that caused the anger, and how the action affects the addict. Such an exercise works equally well for the driven person. For instance, Virginia Potter might jot down on her grudge list that she is angry at her husband, Michael. The cause? He prefers spending his time at work or in community service rather than with her. The effect? Her self-esteem suffers; she feels insecure about her marriage; and her pride is wounded.

How about you? Who is on your grudge list?

I realize that I am angry with the following persons (my mother, father, sister, brother, spouse):

1. _____
2. _____
3. _____

Now ask yourself, "Why did I put this person on my grudge list? What is the reason for my anger toward him or her?"

The reason for my anger toward this person is (My mother belittled me. My brother was my dad's favorite.):

1. _____
2. _____
3. _____

Finally think about how your anger toward this person affects you.

261

My resentment and anger toward this person affect me in this way (My self-esteem was hurt. My pride, my ambition, or my personal relationships were threatened.):

1. ___[handwritten]___
2. ___[handwritten]___
3. ___[handwritten]___

The most common emotion underlying resentment and anger is fear. Bill W. says, "The fabric of our existence was shot through with it. It set in motion trains of circumstances which brought us misfortune we felt we didn't deserve. But did not we, ourselves, set the ball rolling?"[4]

Fear

Behind most anger and resentment is a strong sense of fear. Virginia Potter's anger toward Michael, for instance, is driven by her fears:

- She is afraid she isn't attractive anymore.
- She doubts her sexuality.
- She fears that her marriage might fail.
- She worries that she can't keep up with her husband's fast pace.

In order to resolve our anger and resentment, we must deal with our fears. Again Bill Wilson suggests that alcoholics put these fears on paper.

We suggest that you do the same:

Behind my anger and resentment toward these three people is my fear that (I won't be loved by someone who is important to me, or I will lose control of my destiny or my control over others.):

1. ___[handwritten]___
2. ___[handwritten]___
3. ___[handwritten]___

Bill Wilson then suggests that alcoholics ask themselves,

> Why do I have them [the fears]? Wasn't it because self-reliance failed us?
>   Perhaps there is a better way—we think so. For we are now on a different basis; the basis of trusting and relying upon God. We trust infinite God rather than our finite selves. . . . We never apologize to anyone for depending upon our Creator. . . . Instead we let Him demonstrate, through us, what He can do. We ask Him to remove our fear and direct our attention to what He would have us be. At once, we commence to outgrow fear.[5]

Once our patients face their fears, the underlying emotions that drive their self-centeredness, they are able to begin to correct their character flaws and the self-absorption that drives their addiction.

Healing the Roots of Addiction

As driven persons complete the list of character flaws, they are working on their problems at a very deep level. Rather than praying that God will give him the strength to bow out of his community entanglements, Michael Potter prays that God will help him to grieve the self-centered needs that were not met in childhood. He asks for guidance in discovering new bases of self-esteem beyond money. Instead of asking God not to let her shop anymore, Virginia Potter asks Him to take away the resentment, fear, and insecurity that motivated her to shop excessively in the first place.

Our addictions are like an endless shell game. Our self-centeredness is a mask that covers our resentments. Our resentments disguise our deepest hurts and fears. The most profound human fear is the fear of abandonment. If we grew up in a dysfunctional home, that fear was more than just a fear—it was reality. We experienced abandonment, at least on an emotional level, on a firsthand basis. Now as adults, our drivenness and aggressiveness is a desperate effort to out-run that old nagging fear.

[The antidote to this fear is unconditional love.] The answer to our self-centeredness is *not* self-deprivation or self-con-demnation. The answer to our self-preoccupation and self-absorption is an undeniable encounter with God's uncondi-tional love for us. We experience that love through: a re-newed direct relationship with Him; His love expressed by other people in support relationships; and accepting His for-giveness for violating our values.

By getting to the roots of the addiction, the driven person experiences a welcome reduction in guilt. This ninth, and final, point of the addiction cycle will be explored in Chapter 13.

Chapter Thirteen

Verdict: Guilty!
Point 9: Guilt

Like most driven people, the late Christina Onassis was a master of the fine art of "awfulizing." This term isn't original with us—it was coined by psychologist Albert Ellis—but we use it often to describe the practice of inflating negative situations into world-class catastrophes. Here's how it works: When one of Christina's many love affairs ended unhappily, she couldn't merely shrug it off as experience. Instead, she "awfulized" the breakup, elevated it to a major trauma, and took an overdose of sleeping pills in an attempt to end her misery.

When her addiction to food caused her weight to balloon beyond two hundred pounds, she "awfulized" her appearance until she was convinced that the whole world was laughing at her and making jokes about "the Greek tank." In spite of her friends' pleas, she would refuse to come out of her room, preferring to hide, gobble diet pills, and binge on chocolate bars.

Christina is a perfect example of someone who struggled with multiple compulsions and spent most of her life being buffeted around and around the addiction cycle. Sadly, we can follow her odyssey from Point 1 to Point 9 of the cycle and recognize all of the negative indicators that hinted at her untimely death at age thirty-eight. An overview of her journey, with the signposts marked along the way, would look like this:

Family of Origin. Her father, Aristotle Onassis, didn't want a second child and was upset when his wife became pregnant with Christina. He gave the child little attention beyond calling her on her birthday and granting her permission to buy herself a gift from him. The Onassises divorced by the time Christina was twelve years old, with each parent embarking on a global life-style that had little room for a chubby preteen.

Negative Messages. Not an attractive child, Christina was told by her father that "all any man will ever want is your money." He often neglected to introduce her to his friends because her appearance embarrassed him.

Shame Base. Her parents clearly preferred her brother, Alexander. Christina was described as the ugly duckling, and her eyes were said to resemble a raccoon because of the dark circles around them. Like so many children with large shame bases, she seemed to be begging for an answer to the question, "What's wrong with me?"

Low Self-esteem. Christina was so insecure that she felt friends wouldn't want to spend time with her unless they were paid to do so. As an adult she found an ex-athlete and his girlfriend who were willing to be her companions for $1,000 a day.

Emotional Pain. Her mood swings were described as volatile. As much as she wanted to love someone, she was haunted by her father's warning that men would only be attracted by her money. Rather than venting her pain in a healthy way, she either directed it inward where it took the form of depression, or she aimed it outward toward the people closest to her. The newspaper tabloids tracked her famous feuds with her brother; her father's wife, Jacqueline Onassis; and her father's lover, Maria Callas.

Addictive Agent. Although Christina disapproved of illegal drugs, she popped tranquilizers and amphetamine-laced diet pills. When she was on a food binge she would wash down countless hamburgers with ten soft drinks in a row.

Her spending addiction gave her short-term relief from the fear that no one loved her. If a pal admired a trinket in a shop window, she bought it and offered it as a gift. The friend showed gratitude, and Christina felt loved. When she became acquainted with an affable dog that showed her affection, she did everything possible to claim the dog as her own. She became convinced that the pup would make her happy and offered its owner $100,000 for it.

Fallout. The results of her addictions were obvious in her overweight body, her inability to sustain a long-term relationship with a man, and her eventual death, brought on by drug abuse.

Violation of Values. In many ways, Christina held on to traditional values. Her greatest desire was to have children; yet, she knew her dependence on drugs reduced her chance for pregnancy and jeopardized the health of any baby she might conceive. Still, she couldn't stop taking her pills.

Guilt. She struggled with two kinds of guilt. There was the legitimate remorse she suffered because of her addictions to food and drugs. She knew her dependencies were wrong, and she was ashamed of them. There also was the false guilt about being unattractive to men. This was counterfeit because she actually had a dark kind of beauty; however, the guilt had been planted by her father when she was a child. She could never be free of it. The verdict she carried inside herself on all counts was Guilty![1]

Guilty as Charged

We often tell our patients that guilt is one of the most powerful emotions known to humans. Although we cite guilt as the ninth point on the addiction cycle, we certainly don't place it at the bottom of any priority list. As you can see from the diagrams before each chapter in this book, the addiction cycle comes full circle, with Point 9 positioned alongside Point 3. In reality as guilt builds up, it feeds and fuels the earlier points of the cycle. It spills into the shame base and, working like acid, begins to erode the self-esteem. The lower your self-esteem dips, the greater the emotional pain you experience; the greater your pain, the more frequently you will reach for an addictive agent. And so the cycle continues, around and around, with guilt providing much of the push. In Chapter 7 we had you inventory your false guilt and your authentic guilt, which is derived from past shame. Now we will look at the guilt you feel from the fallout of your negative addiction—the harmful affect on yourself, your family, and your friends—and from the violation of your values. Let's begin by taking a close up look at guilt, which can be both a positive and a negative factor.

How God Uses Guilt

Guilt can be an important safeguard to a healthy life-style, if it is used correctly. To drive home the positive aspects of guilt, we sometimes liken it to emotional acid.

"God can use guilt almost as an engraver uses acid in an etching," Dr. Minirth explained to Luci Stewart shortly after the incident at the airport when her purse and briefcase had been stolen. Luci had "awfulized" the theft to the point that her husband, Richard, feared she was becoming agoraphobic. Not only had she vowed never to take another extended trip, but also more recently she had hesitated to leave the house when Richard suggested dinner and a movie.

"An engraver uses tiny amounts of acid, applied in carefully measured doses, to clean and make perfect the designs," suggested Frank Minirth. "Rough edges are smoothed, and the fine lines are more clearly defined. The work of art becomes even more beautiful because of the acid."

He paused before making his key point to Luci. "In a similar way, God uses small amounts of guilt in our lives to cleanse us of our flaws and help us rid ourselves of our imperfections. The guilt serves as a warning signal, which alerts us that we are doing things we shouldn't be doing and that our lives are moving in directions that aren't good for us."

Luci shrugged her shoulders to indicate her confusion. "What on earth do acid and guilt have to do with me, Doctor? Exactly what are you trying to tell me?"

The doctor made a further attempt to explain. "Guilt, like acid, when used in small doses is a powerful but positive force that can make a godly work of art—a human being— even more beautiful than it was. Guilt can shape and even strengthen us. We suffer from it, but we're better off because of it. If we use guilt as we should, it will prevent us from making the same mistakes the next time."

Luci's eyes ignited. "There won't be a next time," she snapped. "Read my lips: I will never, *never* travel again."

As exasperating as Luci's reaction was, it also was predictable. Rather than using guilt in small doses as an artist uses acid, most driven people overreact and, figuratively, pick up the entire beaker and drench themselves with its contents. They bathe themselves in guilt and loathing and self-remorse. Rather than saying, "I have learned to be more careful when I travel," Luci awfulizes and asserts, "I will never, *never* travel again."

Dr. Minirth summarized to Luci: "Remember, Luci, all addictions are what we call 'shame-based.' That shame base consists of a massive residue of false guilt that we heap upon ourselves, not that God imposes on us. This shame base, this beaker of emotional acid, includes false guilt about dysfunctions in your family of origin over which you had no control, and unnecessary self-shaming about your current entrapment in the addiction cycle. This relentless self-blaming does not slow the addiction cycle. It only feeds and accelerates the cycle. Furthermore, this preoccupation with unnecessary guilt can obscure your recognition of legitimate sources of guilt—those dysfunctional aspects of your life which do need to be confessed and released through the process of recovery."

In retrospect, we can apply this acid-guilt concept to the tragic life of Christina Onassis. If she had been a less driven, less compulsive person, she might have used her guilt in a positive way to cleanse her life of its imperfections. The guilt she felt about her food binges might have nudged her to adopt a more healthy, moderate diet. Instead, she over-reacted, doused herself with a beaker of shame, and gobbled appetite suppressants to overtreat her bad eating habits. By the same token, the legitimate guilt she felt about her prescription-drug abuse might have served as a warning that she needed to seek treatment for her dependency. Instead, as her guilt escalated, so did the number of pills she required each night to assure her the welcome relief of sleep.

How Much Guilt Are You Carrying?

One of the ways you can gauge your recovery from drivenness is to look at how you use guilt in your life. As engravers use acid, non-driven persons employ guilt judiciously to remove their flaws. In contrast, driven persons present a strange paradox when it comes to guilt. On the one hand, they may douse themselves liberally in great showers of remorse concerning matters over which they have little control, such as growing up in an abusive home. Simultaneously, on the other hand, driven persons may categorically deny authentic guilt about the fallout and negative consequences of the practice of their addictions. For example the workaholic father may steadfastly deny the emotional injury his compulsivity has inflicted on his family.

This strange mixture of exaggerated false guilt and partially denied authentic guilt merge together to form a toxic shame base. One patient at the Minirth-Meier Clinic referred to this free-floating sense of universal guilt as "global guilt." This patient further elaborated: "Even though I work like crazy to justify my existence, I wake up each morning feeling guilty about the very fact of my existence."

To help you determine how much guilt you are carrying on your shoulders, put a checkmark by any of the following statements that describe you. As you work through this checklist, remember that denial may prevent you from recognizing your guilt. Many driven people claim that they know exactly what they are doing and that they feel no guilt about doing it. However, on a deeper level, they usually are aware that their drivenness is pushing them to violate their values, and guilt is starting to accumulate because of it. Their words may condone their drivenness, but their drivenness is controlling their words.

1.____*"I have a tendency to 'awfulize' situations. Gloom and doom are my specialty. I can out-worry anybody."*

2.____*"I apologize too often. I misread people's reactions to me and fear that I have angered or disappointed them. 'I'm sorry' is one of my favorite phrases. 'It's all my fault' is another."*

3.____*"I don't know how to respond to a compliment. Rather than say, 'Thank you,' when I am complimented, I usually try to invalidate the nice words by mentioning one of my shortcomings."*

4.____*"I feel fragmented. Because I overcommit myself by saying yes too often, I feel pulled in a dozen directions. The positive part of my overcommitment is that I'm so busy I don't have time to dwell on my guilt."*

5.____*"I worry that God is keeping score. Whereas some people count on God to love and forgive them no matter what, I see God as keeping score and planning appropriate punishment for all my wrongs."*

6.____*"I feel that I constantly have to justify my right to exist, and no matter how much I've done, I feel inadequate. I'm not sure I deserve to exist, but I'm certain I don't deserve lasting happiness."*

Each of these statements is typical of guilt-ridden people. If you checked two or more of them, you are carrying excessive guilt.

Six Techniques to Reduce Guilt

Because guilt is such a powerful emotion, all of us who have a tendency toward drivenness need to be familiar with ways to minimize guilt's impact. Guilt fuels our compulsivity and propels us around and around the addiction cycle. Anyone who is serious about recovering from drivenness must know how to reduce guilt. At the Minirth-Meier Clinics we suggest six ways for patients to combat their guilt.

1. Make a Confession

The Christian practice of confessing sins goes back thousands of years. What had value then still has application today. Members of Alcoholics Anonymous and other Twelve Step groups recognize this, and Step 5 of their recovery programs is based on the premise that confession is good for the soul. It also goes a long way toward curbing an addiction.

Step 5 affirms that the recovering addict has "admitted to God, to ourselves, and to another human being the exact nature of our wrongs."

Admitted to God Just as no one—compulsive or noncompulsive—is immune to guilt, so also no one is able to resolve guilt feelings without help from a Greater Power. This is a good-news/bad-news kind of concept. The bad news is that every human being battles guilt, and those of us who are compulsive struggle with an extra large measure of it. More bad news: No matter how hard we try, none of us can work through or resolve all of our guilt feelings. They are simply too powerful. If we try to conquer them singlehandedly, we are in for a hopeless defeat.

All of this bad news becomes good news in that it assures the driven person that he or she is not uniquely bad. In other words, compulsive people haven't been singled out and burdened with guilt while noncompulsive people dance merrily through life unencumbered. We're all in this together, and guilt is a universal emotion that plays a part in everyone's life.

As surely as we know we can't handle guilt on our own, we also can be assured that we don't have to try. Salvation through trusting Christ is the central message of Christianity. He died on the Cross to pay for all of our sins and guilt. It was His gift to us. We trust Him by depending on that gift to pay for all of our past, present, and future sins, just like we depend on a chair to hold our body off the ground. In Ephesians 2:8–9, the apostle Paul said, "For by grace you have been saved through faith, and that not of yourselves; it is the gift of God, not of works, lest anyone should boast." Just as we can hand back false guilt we may have carried for the dysfunctions of previous generations, so also can we hand over our authentic guilt to God. We don't have to bear our own crosses, because Jesus has already done that for us. We only have to confess our guilt to Him, and He will remove it from our shoulders.

We often suggest that our patients say a prayer that King David prayed as he confessed his sins of adultery and murder:

> Have mercy upon me, O God,
>   According to Your lovingkindness;
> According to the multitude of Your
>   tender mercies,
> Blot out my transgressions.
> Wash me thoroughly from my iniquity,
> And cleanse me from my sin.
>
> For I acknowledge my transgressions,
> And my sin is ever before me.
>   (Ps. 51:1–3)

"Surely you have not committed any sin worse than adultery and murder," we tell our patients. "God forgave David for these sins because David was truly repentant. God will forgive you. In fact, God promises, 'Though your sins are like scarlet, they shall be as white as snow.'"

A key way for driven people to diminish their shame and

guilt is to hear God's forgiveness. How? They can turn to the Bible and read God's Word; they can study recovery literature that emphasizes God's unconditional love; they can attend church and listen to pastors talk about God's acceptance; they can regularly attend a church growth group for fellowship and unconditional acceptance; they can join recovery groups that stress the spiritual aspects of healing and that extend an outstretched hand of nonjudgmental fellowship.

Admitted to Ourselves By the time our patients have worked their way through their denial of their addiction, inventoried their authentic guilt, and considered the fallout of their obsessive-compulsive behavior, they have admitted the exact nature of their wrongs to themselves. It is helpful to write out these self-acknowledgments. The process of committing these awarenesses to paper strengthens this effort toward self-honesty. We caution our patients that "if we cannot be fearlessly honest with ourselves, that internal dishonesty will paralyze our efforts to be candid with others." Building on this foundation of personal honesty, the next healing step is to make appropriate disclosure to another trusted human being.

Admitted to Another Human Being The key premise here is that when you acknowledge your wrongs, your true guilt is released. Typically, the "other human being" mentioned in the step is a psychologist, a pastor, or a sponsor in one of the recovery programs. He or she might also be a very close and trusted friend. The flaws, taken from your list of authentic guilt, are spoken as the driven person and the listener sit face-to-face. As each flaw is aired, the burden of guilt becomes lighter. There is a real sense of relief and release.

As positive as it is to know about God's forgiveness in the abstract, most of us also need to have some experience of it in the flesh. This can come from friends who love and accept us as we are. God's love can be expressed through the human beings we encounter at the office, at home, and at support group meetings.

2. Express Amends to People We've Hurt

Amends are an excellent second technique in easing the burden of guilt. Of course, words are empty if they are not accompanied by appropriate actions. If a driven workaholic continues to step on toes but now says, "I'm sorry," afterward, an apology is meaningless.

Sorting Through the "I'm Sorries" Knowing when to say "I'm sorry" is a risky business. While it may reduce the burden of guilt from the driven person, it might also generate new pain for the people who have been on the receiving end of the driven person's compulsions. The founders of Alcoholics Anonymous recognized this risk when they carefully worded Step 9 in the Twelve Step program: "[We] made direct amends to such people whenever possible, *except when to do so would injure them or others"* (our italics).

At this point, driven persons identify all the people they might have hurt through practicing their addictions. Then they begin to repair these damaged relationships with words like, "I realize I was living a destructive life-style and my drivenness hurt you. I'm truly sorry for that."

Many of our patients have taken great pains and invested hours and money to execute these steps. One workaholic not only made amends to his family members for the lack of time he spent with them, but he also tracked down the peers he had elbowed aside during his corporate climb. This was no easy task. Several of his former associates had long since left the company and were scattered across the country. Somehow he managed to find forwarding addresses, and he wrote letters of emotional apology to the people. The exercise had a purging effect on him and liberated him from some of his guilt.

Before any patient enthusiastically embarks on a mission to make amends, we issue a few words of caution. We always urge them to pray, meditate, and reflect on the lists of people they wish to contact with their apologies. Occasionally, saying "I'm sorry" can have backlash effects.

Dr. Hemfelt once counseled a man who had been involved in unscrupulous business practices for several years. As part of his recovery and in an effort to reduce his guilt, he wanted to "come clean" by telling his former partners about his indiscretions. However, he realized, after much reflection, that if he were to do this, he would implicate many other people. He couldn't take the responsibility of exposing other people's guilt. So, he made his confession only to God.

The "except when to do so would injure them or others" principle sometimes requires that we doctors step in and talk our patients out of expressing regrets to the victims of their compulsions. Dr. Meier found himself in this role several years ago when he was working with a recovering sex addict. The woman was making great strides toward reducing the guilt she felt for her former promiscuity. One day during a counseling session she presented Paul Meier with a long list of former boyfriends and announced her intention to visit each of them and apologize for her seduction of them. She knew that she had caused several of them to break their marriage vows and had even been responsible for one couple's divorce.

Although the woman's intentions were good, Dr. Meier convinced her that her plan of action would have negative fallout. Many of the men were happily married to spouses who wouldn't appreciate her sudden appearance, regardless of her noble motivation. Also, the woman risked reviving memories of her former life-style. Such memories could make her vulnerable to slipping back into her addiction.

3. Make Living Amends and Reparations

Living amends is a variation of the old "actions-speak-louder-than-words" expression. Instead of a workaholic boss going to his or her employees and saying, "Hey, I'm sorry if I've been too demanding about everyone keeping Saturday office hours," this boss posts a notice that announces, effective immediately, the work week is limited to Monday through Friday.

An example from our files: Michael and Virginia Potter traded apologies for neglecting each other's needs, and then they embarked on a plan to make living amends. Weekly dates, joint tennis lessons, and a second honeymoon were all part of the program. Not only were the Potters voicing their regrets for past mistakes, but also they were taking action that would improve their relationship in the future.

These living amends or *reparations* may involve financial compensation. The Alcoholics Anonymous "Big Book" recommends that sometimes the recovering addict needs to make financial and material amends for his or her mistakes. This advice works equally well for persons with compulsions other than alcohol.

Dr. Meier once counseled a spendaholic whose addiction to risky business ventures had forced him into bankruptcy. Not only had he lost his personal savings and his home, but he also had abused his role as overseer of his children's trust accounts and had spent those funds as well. His overwhelming remorse was reduced somewhat when he confessed his wrongs, apologized to his family, and changed his life-style. However, he knew that the only way he could completely free himself from his guilt was to pay back every cent he had lost. This was an enormous task and required years to complete. In the end, he not only made restitution but he did it with interest as well.

Note of caution: Sometimes guilt-driven people will use money to buy their way out from under their heavy burden of shame. For instance, parents who feel guilty about neglecting their children emotionally may continue to financially

277

subsidize the kids well into adulthood. Each time they write a check to a son or daughter, they feel they are making an installment payment on their guilt. They don't realize that the sacrifice of time or money alone can't pay off the shame base. It's important for the driven person to determine when reparation is an appropriate part of guilt reduction and when it isn't. Throwing money at a problem doesn't necessarily make the problem disappear.

Thus far we have reviewed the guilt-reduction tools of confession, expressed amends, and living amends. These spiritual tools hold far more potential and promise than just the obvious purpose of diminishing the shame burden. As these tools are used to cleanse the shame base, other miraculous emotional and spiritual transformations are set in motion. These long-term benefits are perhaps best described in a section of the "Big Book" of *Alcoholics Anonymous*, a section commonly referred to as "The Promises."

> If we are painstaking about this phase of our development [steps 8 and 9, the amends steps of the Twelve Steps], we will be amazed before we are halfway through. We are going to know a new freedom and a new happiness. We will not regret the past, nor wish to shut the door on it. We will comprehend the word *serenity* and we will know peace. No matter how far down the scale we have gone, we will see how our experience can benefit others. That feeling of uselessness and self-pity will disappear. We will lose interest in selfish things and gain interest in our fellows. Self-seeking will slip away. Our whole attitude and outlook upon life will change. Fear of people and of economic insecurity will leave us. We will intuitively know how to handle situations which used to baffle us. We will suddenly realize that God is doing for us what we could not do for ourselves.[2]

4. Continue to Inventory and Release Authentic and False Guilt

Just as confession is an ongoing process, so also is the disposal of real and false guilt. At least once a month the driven person should jot down her or his areas of guilt and divide them according to authenticity. For example, Luci Stewart might correctly identify her refusal to travel with her husband on business or pleasure trips as a source of real guilt. She needs to apologize to Richard and make real amends.

However, Luci's deeply imbedded guilt about being unworthy was put in place by her Uncle Ted and his sexual violations of her. This is false guilt that belongs to someone else. In counseling Luci had recognized it as counterfeit, and she handed it back to the person in her past who rightly deserved to carry it. Still she was tempted every once in a while to pick up that discarded bag of false guilt. At times like these she needed to play an imaginary game of "Hot Potato" and hand it back again.

Kitty Dukakis, wife of former presidential candidate Michael Dukakis, traces many of her addiction problems and low self-esteem to the false guilt she carried for most of her adult life.[3] When Kitty was eighteen she learned that her mother had been illegitimate and had been adopted by a couple Kitty had always believed to be her natural grandparents. Her biological grandmother had given up her daughter (Kitty's mother) on one condition: That she be allowed to live with the adoptive couple and function as her baby daughter's nurse.

When the truth finally was revealed by a cousin, Kitty confronted her mother with the obvious question, "Why did you keep this from me?" Her mother shrugged and answered, "Well, now you know."

Kitty recalls the moment of truth as being devastating. She felt she had been living a lie, that her mother was guilty of an enormous breach of trust, and that somehow the result was that she, Kitty, was less than she appeared to be. Her self-esteem plummeted. Within a year she began using amphetamine pills that she discovered in her mother's room. It was the beginning of an addiction that haunted her for twenty-six years.

Although much of Kitty's guilt was false—it belonged to another generation—she claimed it as her own and carried it for the previous generations. She became yet another example of the recovery slogan "We are only as sick as our secrets." Time and a successful marriage didn't ease the guilt; if anything, the guilt escalated, and her self-esteem eroded. Now, in recovery, she realizes that if her husband had been successful in his White House bid, the pressure of being First Lady might have sent her out of control.

"Michael was good enough to be president, for sure, but was I worthy to be his partner? In my despair, I turned to alcohol," she wrote in her autobiography, appropriately titled *Now You Know.* We can only hope that through her treatment program Kitty Dukakis has learned to hand back her false guilt to the generation that initiated it every time it reappears.

If you don't continue to inventory your guilt and deal with it immediately, you may become so convinced of your unworthiness that you will again believe that God would not want to reach out to you, assume your burden of shame, and love you unconditionally in spite of yourself.

Accumulated guilt can also cause you to believe that since God would never fulfill the needs of anyone as unworthy as you are, then you must act as your own god. In time, you believe this charade. Your driving internal message becomes, "If I don't take care of myself, no one will." You adopt the false illusion, "I can fulfill all of my needs. I don't need anyone else's help because I can do anything. I am invincible." To maintain this illusion you will reach again for your addictive agent: that obsessive-compulsive behavior.

Finally, guilt can lead you to try to compensate for your secret sense of lowliness through godly overachievement. The more pumped up you become with your accomplishments, the more attainable immortality seems. Intellectually you may know you can't live forever, but emotionally you are convinced that through your accomplishments your spirit will live on. You're back on the addiction cycle again, driven by that internal need for God and the attributes of God, driven to compress more activity into a finite human life, driven to cover insecurity with a fixed layer of inflated invincibility.

Perhaps the most powerful antidote to this addiction cycle

is ongoing prevention. That prevention requires a change in lifestyle.

5. Embrace a New Life-style That Avoids the Creation of Future Fallout

The obvious question here is "What kind of 'new life-style' must you create?" The answer depends on what kind of fallout you are trying to avoid.

As an example, let's look back at Christina Onassis's addiction to food. The fallout from this addiction was her excessive body weight. She felt guilty when she saw pictures of herself in the tabloids, and her obesity brought to mind all the guilt her father had instilled in her when he insisted that no man would find her attractive. Any change in life-style for Christina would have had to include carefully supervised menus and a disciplined exercise program. This new life-style would prevent future fallout (more weight gain) and would reduce guilt caused by the fallout. She would also have had to give herself new permissions to make new decisions and to create new boundaries, which would make a change of course possible. This is the advice we gave to Michael Potter.

New Permissions, New Decisions, and New Boundaries It's very common for driven people to have difficulty setting boundaries for themselves. Sometimes their self-esteem is so low that they don't believe they are entitled to set limits. For example, we've worked with women who were sexually abused as children and later, as adults, were unable to say no to a man. They felt they had no right to refuse.

Sometimes the opposite occurs. A woman who was sexually violated in her youth builds a concrete wall around herself when she grows into adulthood. She lets no man past the barrier.

One way we help patients move into recovery is to urge that they give themselves permission to set appropriate boundaries. They learn that they have the right to say both yes and no. For instance, a woman may say yes or no to a romantic relationship. Or she can say yes or no to demands on her time. She can speak up and she can speak out.

The words *permissions, decisions,* and *boundaries* sound very much alike. However, these terms refer to three distinct stages in the boundary setting process. First, I must grant myself internal permission to take care of me, nurture me, and suspend self-destructive patterns. Second, I must formulate these permissions into realistic new decisions concerning the conduct of my life. Third, I must translate these decisions into specific enforceable boundaries that will govern my lifestyle, and on a daily basis I must be willing to implement these boundaries, honor them, and insist that others honor them as well. Put in the simplest terms, Boundaries are the vitally important yes's and no's that govern my life.

Michael Potter, like many of our patients who are workaholics, blurred these three progressive steps into one step. He skipped immediately to the action level, the boundaries, bypassing new permissions and new decisions. Mike nodded his head in agreement and said, "Okay, I overwork. I can deal with that. I'll devote Sunday exclusively to my family; I'll make sure I'm home by 6:00 a couple of nights a week; and I'll cut back on my community service [specific items on his action plan]."

This approach carries a guarantee of failure. Michael Potter, like all workaholics, has again overlooked the forces that drive him to overwork. Instead he must begin by giving the child within himself permission to change.

New Permissions Dr. Hemfelt suggested that Michael needed to become his own parent and reevaluate his view of himself. "You need to tell yourself, 'I deserve to exist and live without having to prove myself twenty-four hours a day.' Once that permission becomes a part of your self-image, you can be more specific as to how that will happen by making some new decisions."

It didn't take Michael more than a few minutes to assert,

"I'm ready to give myself that permission. I don't want to have to prove myself twenty-four hours a day."

New Decisions Dr. Hemfelt encouraged Michael to think about some decisions in the week between their appointments. During his next appointment he gave the doctor the following list:

- "I will balance my work and play."
- "I will cultivate nonbusiness relationships."
- "I will set aside time for rest and rejuvenation."
- "I will make family relationships and a spiritual relationship with God high priorities in my life."

Michael was now ready to implement his new permissions and new decisions with action—new boundaries.

New Boundaries Michael set five very specific boundaries from the overall goal of balancing work and play:

- "I will limit myself to forty-five hours per week in office work time. I will inform my dad and my subordinates of this new time boundary."
- "I will not take my briefcase home with me on weekends."
- "I will not conduct business calls at home in the evening."
- "I will devote at least one-half day per week to a sport or recreation."
- "I will reserve time each day for meditation on the Bible and solitude."

Michael Potter repeated this exercise in other areas of his obsessive-compulsive behavior, like his perfectionism. He recognized that his dad had been angry, unhappy, and depressed for some fifty years and would probably always be that way, so there was no reason for Michael to try to earn his father's approval. With that in mind, he gave himself *new permission* to boost his self-esteem from the inside rather than from the outside. His *new decision* was to stop trying to please his father. No longer would he scramble to serve on every committee or board in his community. Instead, he would concentrate on reacquainting himself with his children and his wife and enjoy his woodworking hobby. He set a *new boundary* to cut his volunteer efforts in half and devote a couple of hours on the weekend to making a blanket chest for his wife.

Following are a few other examples from our files that will show you how this exercise works.

A woman who was rejected by her father during childhood grows up feeling inferior to men. Consequently, she maintains a distance from all members of the opposite sex. After counseling with us she gives herself *permission* to have intimacy in her life. She then makes a *new decision* to date and interact with men whose company she enjoys. Finally, she sets a *new boundary*, which allows her to join a singles group in order to expose herself to singles' activities and to the possibility of dating.

Another example: A young woman who could never please her perfectionistic father now is an overpleaser in her own marriage. She does everything that her husband asks her to do. Her *new permission* is to be more assertive in her marriage relationship. Her *new decision* is that she doesn't have to agree with her husband on every issue. Her *new boundary* is to insist on having a fifty-fifty vote in all major financial decisions that affect the family.

How About You?

What new permission do you need to give yourself? If you are a workaholic, do you need to tell yourself: "I deserve to exist without having to prove myself twenty-four hours a day"? Give yourself that permission by filling in the statement below:

I give myself permission to _____
_____.

What new decision do you need to make? If you are a workaholic, for instance, you may need to decide, "I will balance my work and play" or "I will cultivate nonbusiness relationships." Make that decision by filling in the statement below.

I decide to _____

_____.

What boundaries will be necessary to make this new decision a reality? For instance, "I will not conduct business calls at home in the evening."

I will set the following boundaries:

_____

_____

_____

_____

The final step in this process of combating guilt is to uniformly treat others, even strangers, as we would like to be treated.

6. Treat Others as You Would Like to Be Treated

Too often our driven patients, bent on recovery, focus so tightly on trying to improve relations with a key figure, such as a spouse, boss, or friend, that they ignore the nameless faces they encounter daily.

As we embark on a healthy new life-style that won't generate excessive guilt, we need to discover ways to be kind, gentle, and loving to all of the people we meet. These might include the checker in the grocery store, the motorists we pass in our cars, the paper deliverer, and the telephone solicitor. Driven people have a tendency to make great strides in improving important relationships and, simultaneously, shift their anger, sharp words, and impatience to people they don't know.

Dr. Minirth once worked with a prominent businessman who was well into recovery from his compulsive perfectionism. His family relationships were warmed and his office associates complimented him on his kinder, less tense demeanor.

However, as this executive continued to take regular inventory of himself and his faults, he discovered that he was compensating for his new calmness in a very unhealthy way. He was becoming more demanding and controlling in his passing relationships with anonymous service people. On business trips he was short-tempered with hotel clerks, flight attendants, and taxi drivers. He realized that he had merely shifted his tension onto people he didn't have to be accountable to on a regular basis. As part of his recovery he decided that he had to change his style of interaction with everyone —even those persons he dealt with in small ways. And he needed to endorse himself as he pursued his new decisions.

We often find that our clients need some help in making their new decisions a part of their everyday lives, so we suggest a Recovery, Inc., practice called "Endorsing yourself."

Endorse Yourself

Change is always frightening, especially when, like Michael Potter, you set new boundaries for yourself, break old addictions, and make decisions to live differently from the way you've lived for years. Recovery, Inc., has a slogan that applies in cases like this: "Endorse yourself."

Here's how it works: When Mike Potter locked his office promptly at 5:00 P.M. on Friday afternoon and got into his car without his briefcase for the first time in more than three decades, he felt guilty and insecure. He hesitated, had second thoughts, then remembered the advice from Recovery, Inc.

"I've made a good decision," said Mike out loud. "I'm taking care of myself, and I'm giving time to my family. I endorse myself for my commitment to lead a better balanced life."

Until his new schedule becomes comfortable, he may have to feed himself morsels of positive feedback minute by minute and hour by hour. He may need to encourage himself, praise himself, and gradually rebuild his faltering self-esteem. The old tendency will tug at him and try to shame him back into familiar ways. But through interior dialogue, he can stave off the temptation to revert to his workaholism.

The Potters, the Stewarts, the Ryans, and you, the reader, have taken a careful look at that dizzily spinning wheel called the addiction cycle. You've applied the points on that wheel to your own life and your own family of origin and your own emotional pain. You've been honest with yourself about the destructive fallout from your addiction—and the guilt that results from it.

You've stopped the cycle by understanding it and relieving the drivers that push it to such terrifying speeds. Now you're ready to look at recovery and how to maintain that recovery. We'll do that in the final section of this book.

PART THREE

Recovery

Chapter Fourteen

Touchstones for Living a Balanced Life

"Guess where we're going," teased Virginia Potter as she settled into the familiar chair that she had occupied so many times during our weeks of therapy. We already knew the answer—Michael had explained his plan when he had called for an appointment—but we played along. We didn't want to deprive Ginny of her surprise. She leaned forward as if to impart a secret.

"Hawaii," she said almost in a whisper, "without the kids!" she added exuberantly. "Can you believe it?" She reached for one of her husband's hands and gave it a squeeze. "It was all Mike's idea. But when I heard we could catch the connecting flight either in Chicago or Dallas, I suggested Dallas so we could see you before we took off. Thanks for making time for us. It's been an age."

Five months was more like it, and by looking at the Potters, we could tell that the weeks had been well spent. The couple appeared relaxed and happy.

"This trip to Hawaii," Dr. Hemfelt asked, "is it business or pleasure?"

"About an eighty-twenty split," answered Michael.

"Eighty percent pleasure and twenty percent business. Our company is looking at a joint venture on Maui. Someone from our office needed to check out the site—tough job, but *someone* had to do it, Dr. Hemfelt!" He winked. "Our plan eventually is to build a hotel and convention complex."

" 'Potter's Paradise'?" joked Robert Hemfelt. "Or 'The Potter Plaza'?"

Mike Potter laughed. "No, we decided to scratch our name from all future projects. After all, there will always be a bigger, taller, glitzier hotel going up on the next beach. We're in it to make a living, not to make a living legend of ourselves. My father wasn't entirely convinced by my argument, but he finally agreed."

Robert Hemfelt's next question was obvious; he'd been waiting to ask it: "How are you doing with your recovery goals?" From what the Potters had told him so far, they seemed to be right on track, but the doctor knew the answer to this question would tell the tale. During the last weeks of counseling we work with our patients to establish recovery goals and to give them the tools to maintain this recovery. This had been done before Virginia left Dallas. Dr. Hemfelt knew she was seeing a therapist in her hometown so she could make the transition between the hospital setting and home, and both she and Michael were attending an ACOA group in their church. Still he wanted to assess the Potters' recovery progress himself.

To Quit or Not to Quit

Recovery is a choice. It's also a decision.

At some point in the counseling process we tell patients that they no longer need to schedule weekly counseling sessions with us. They've walked around the addiction cycle, have broken through denial, have come to terms with their compulsivity, and have acknowledged the changes they must make in their lives if they are to experience healing. Whether or not they make the changes is their choice; how many changes they make is their decision. Unlike some addictions where only two options are available—to quit or not to quit—a lot of gray area exists with the compulsions America applauds.

Drivenness may call for abstinence in some cases and balance in other instances. The determining factor is the addictive agent. If a person is addicted to sexual relationships outside of marriage or to pornography, abstinence is essential to recovery. The necessary recovery goal in these cases is the complete cessation of the compulsive behavior. On the other hand, if a person is driven by work or perfectionism or exercise or voluntarism, some kind of balance may be the goal. For example, the recovery goal for the workaholic is not unemployment. The goal is to maintain the delicate balance between work and play, activity and rest.

Occasionally, as we help patients to design their personal recovery programs we recommend a combination of abstinence and balance, depending upon the type of obsessive-compulsive behavior the patient displays. To see how this works, let's look at a couple of the case studies that we have been following throughout this book and review the recovery goals set by the patients.

Luci and Richard Stewart

Luci decided early in her recovery to abstain from continuing as her husband's Girl Friday. She realized that working for Richard was unhealthy because it doubled as a way to run his life. She weighed the option of trimming back and limiting the number of hours that she spent in her home office, but she knew the power of controlling Richard's business was too intoxicating to her. She had always felt insecure about her femininity, and had subconsciously decided that if she could make herself invaluable to Richard in a business sense, he would never end their personal relationship. She was working not for pleasure and not even for accomplishment. She was working to earn the right to be in her marriage. In recovery she recognized how unhealthy such an outlook was. Working for her husband was one addictive agent that required abstinence.

Luci was educated enough in the ways of addiction to know that cutting out her office hours would create a void in her life, and that she might be tempted to substitute a new compulsion for the old one. Always a meticulous house-keeper, she feared she might transfer her energy to scrubbing and organizing her home. She decided to set several limitations on her cleaning chores, so she blocked out a certain number of hours on her daily planner to devote to house-keeping. She pledged that once she reached her limit she would shift her attention to something else. Housekeeping was a potential addictive agent that she would carefully balance as she worked her way through recovery.

Another area of balance that she set for herself involved the control of the household finances. Since she was a book-keeper by profession, it had always made sense to her that she would take care of the family accounts as well. Again, during therapy she realized that she had used her knack for numbers as an excuse to seize control over an area that she and Richard should share. Through discussion, they worked out a plan in which they would jointly approve of any financial decision that involved more than $500. This arrangement not only assured shared responsibility, but it also opened up another area of dialogue between the couple.

Interestingly, an activity that Luci decided to abstain from was one that she hadn't yet engaged in. For about five years she had been considering the idea of having a facelift and liposuction on her hips. While she was in Dr. Minirth's care she began to fantasize more and more about the positive results that such surgery might accomplish. Dr. Minirth confronted her about her plans and urged her to postpone her decision, not because cosmetic surgery is wrong, but because the timing might be inappropriate.

"Right now you're trying to look inside yourself and sort out the characteristics that you value and esteem," Frank Minirth reminded Luci. "It seems more than coincidental that suddenly you have the urge to 'improve' yourself in a cosmetic way. It could be that you have uncovered old feelings of insecurity and fears of unworthiness. Your knee-jerk reaction is to improve yourself in a quick, but superficial, way—by changing your appearance. Wouldn't it be better to abstain from the surgery for a year, then, after you've made more progress with your recovery, consider it again?''

Luci agreed. During several subsequent conjoint sessions with the Stewarts, Dr. Minirth gave Richard the opportunity to speak to Luci about his feelings toward her. Richard assured his wife that he considered her to be very attractive and that cosmetic surgery was certainly her decision, but he loved her as she was.

Finally, Richard and Luci jointly set as one of their recovery goals abstaining from bailing out their financially troubled son, Bud. They had been underwriting his losses for years, and the practice had led to a codependent relationship. Cutting off the stream of loans and gifts was a difficult decision for the Stewarts because they knew Bud was facing personal bankruptcy. Their willingness to make good on several outstanding bills would save their only son from the embarrassment of having his car repossessed and having to move to a less expensive home. However, they realized that a total bailout would merely enable Bud to continue his disastrous practice of investing in pie-in-the-sky schemes.

Barbara Ryan

We always stress to our patients that they have to set their own recovery goals, that we as therapists can't do it for them. Sometimes it requires a great deal of time for driven persons to commit to a specific list of recovery objectives. By their nature, compulsive people are intense, and they pull out all the stops when it comes to making good on their goals. They don't take obligations lightly.

In addition to Barbara Ryan's earlier goal of achieving a balanced work-home life by reducing her schedule to part-time, Barbara identified three areas of addiction where only abstinence would be appropriate. First was her old tendency to purge food from her body by self-induced vomiting. She had always worried about her weight, and the concern had prompted her binge-and-purge behavior during college. Now that her part-time work schedule allowed her more time at home, she realized that she might be tempted to snack. This would lead to guilt and possibly a revival of her purging habit. She vowed to abstain from that dangerous compulsion and to adhere to a carefully balanced exercise program instead.

A second area of abstinence involved her compulsion to argue with her husband, Hal. Often her old insecurities, caused by growing up in an alcoholic home, prompted her to erupt like a volcano. Her emotions took the shape of criticism, and her anger generally was aimed at Hal. Not only did such extreme conflict weaken their marriage relationship, but now there was the baby to consider as well. Barbara knew as well as anyone that tension in the home can have devastating effects on children. Therefore, her recovery goal called for a moratorium on explosive fighting, but it allowed for plenty of discussion. Her feelings needed to be aired, and she learned that she could express her feelings without resorting to addictive rage.

Finally, Barbara decided to take a cue from Luci Stewart and abstain from making an important decision for one year. The question didn't involve cosmetic surgery, but rather the idea of enrolling at a local university to pursue another degree. On the surface, her taking an evening class seemed to be a worthwhile activity. However, as Dr. Hemfelt cautioned, going back to school might be Barbara's way of trading one addictive agent for another. She could be swapping the tension of a full-time job for the tension of a classroom. There would be similar pressures, demands, and opportunities to excel. In the end, she might be busier than she was when she was working. Putting the decision on hold seemed to be a wise compromise.

What Are Your Recovery Goals?

To help patients design their recovery goals, we often suggest that they complete a simple exercise. As you think about your own recovery, you also need to determine what you are going to do with the addictive agents in your life.

Are you going to abstain from their use, or can you carefully balance their influence?

Compulsions That Require Abstinence

Which addictive agents must you abstain from?

During the last weeks before Virginia Potter was scheduled to be released from our inpatient therapy unit, Michael gave the doctor his list of abstinence boundaries. He put his practice of viewing soft pornography at the top of this list. He also clearly recognized his addiction to entering into shaky business arrangements with friends, by listing that obsessive-compulsive behavior second.

Virginia also decided on two abstinence goals. First, she recognized that her relationship with her friend Ray was a threat to her marriage and had to end immediately and completely. There would be no attempt to "balance" their friendship by spending only limited time with each other. They would no longer see each other or even talk on the telephone.

Finally, she pledged that she would not shop for anything other than food and basic household supplies for six months. If she needed a specific item outside these boundaries, she would tell Mike what that item was, and he would hold her accountable for coming home with only that purchase. Mail-order knickknacks were strictly off limits. The intensity of her long-standing shopaholism required this period of complete abstinence as a stepping stone to the eventual recovery goal of a balanced approach to shopping and spending.

If you need to abstain from some of your addictions, list them below (remember, be specific and comprehensive; no addiction is too minor to be included):

1. _____
2. _____
3. _____

A Plan of Action Once Michael Potter had listed his areas of abstinence, he needed to devise a plan to make those changes possible. So determined was he to recover from his addiction to pornography that he even decided to halt what he recognized to be subtle triggers of the addiction. Certain magazines, cable television shows, and popular films, available on tape, played to his vulnerability. He pledged that he would cancel his subscriptions to these magazines, refuse to watch any cable television shows that contained intimate scenes, and decline to view films rated R or X.

Since his position in the family's real estate company required him to participate in ongoing buy-and-sell transactions, he couldn't permanently abstain from that practice. However, with his family's blessing, he decided to abstain for six months from inking any new financial agreements. He would use the time to organize and manage his current accounts and projects, and his brother and father would handle whatever prospective transactions came across his desk.

How about you? What actions do you need to take and what specific boundaries do you need to set in order to abstain from the addictions you noted above? List them below.

1. _____
2. _____
3. _____

The Necessity of "Accountants" The final area Dr. Hemfelt had asked Michael and Virginia Potter to consider had been accountability. Who would hold them accountable for maintaining their recovery goals?

We tell patients, "Call these people your watchdogs or your accountants, whatever you feel most comfortable with. They must agree to meet with you on a regular basis and review what is happening in your life, specifically as it relates to the abstinence/balance boundary areas. They have your permission to confront you if you start to drift toward your old addictive ways. We encourage you to have different accountability people for your different compulsions."

Virginia Potter had asked her sponsor in her Al-Anon group to take on watchdog duties in the delicate matter of her relationship with Ray. Virginia's resolve was so strong about abstaining from any involvement with him that she and her accountant only had to touch base by phone a few times each month. The sponsor could tell by Virginia's earnest assurances that she was adhering to her recovery goals.

To help Michael abide by his decision to abstain from inking any new financial agreements, he had asked a member of his A.C.O.A. support group to act as his accountability person. Once a week the two men had met for coffee and to review Mike's business dealings. In the course of their discussions, if the friend picked up on any indication that Michael was drifting back into his old patterns, he confronted Mike.

Of course, sometimes a watchdog does more than merely listen. We once counseled a shopaholic who asked a certified public accountant to act as her accountability person, and the CPA actually put the shopaholic on a weekly allowance and audited her expenditures.

Who can be your accountant? List below the people you want to hold you accountable for each of your addictions.

1. _____

2. _____

3. _____

Now that you've looked at the compulsions that are "off limits," consider those behaviors that need to be balanced.

Compulsions That Need to Be Balanced

In addition to abstaining from certain addictive agents, Michael Potter had decided to balance his use of other agents. One area of compulsivity that needed to be controlled was his rigorous exercising. His jogging had gotten out of hand and had to be contained by his setting some strict boundaries. He knew that running six days a week not only was addictive, but also it was abusive to his body. He used the draining regimen as a way of anesthetizing the emotional pain caused by his job, his marriage, and his financial predicament. By better balancing his exercise program, his awareness of emotional pain might be increased, and this awareness could now function as a warning signal—that flashing red light we discussed earlier—and sensitize him to the changes he needed to make in his lifestyle.

How about you? What compulsions do you need to balance more responsibly?

1. _____
2. _____
3. _____

Dr. Hemfelt had offered Michael two options for achieving balance in his exercising program. First, he had suggested that Michael might make a contract with himself that stipulated that he would not jog more than three miles three times a week. The second choice had been to abstain from jogging in order to break the addiction pattern and to halt the aerobic "high" that resulted. In place of running, Michael could schedule long daily walks that would guarantee the benefit of exercise without the intensity of pounding the pavement. The choice had been Michael's, and he eventually opted for a schedule of jogging on Monday, Wednesday, and Saturday. Dr. Hemfelt favored the second option, but, as always, it was the patient's decision.

How about you? What actions do you need to take to achieve balance in the areas you listed above?

1. _____
2. _____
3. _____

Just as Michael and Virginia Potter had designated "accountants" for their areas of abstinence, they also selected specific "accountants" for the activities they wished to balance. For example, Virginia Potter asked a member of her Bible study group to act as her watchdog in the area of community service. They agreed to meet on Friday mornings for breakfast to talk about Virginia's six-month hiatus from volunteer projects. Whenever Ginny was tempted to take on a small task—"for a good cause"—the friend reminded her of her recovery goal.

Another patient, a workaholic, recruited his boss as his watchdog. The boss valued the man's talents enough to realize that if the employee didn't balance his work life with some outside interests, he might burn out. The boss-turned-watchdog used his supervisory position to order the workaholic to leave the office by six in the evening, and he made sure that the employee took every vacation day that he had earned.

We always caution patients to choose persons other than their spouses as their watchdogs because objectivity comes with distance. An outsider can firmly say, "Mike, you're starting to work too many hours again," whereas a wife might offer the same observation and get an argument in return. "I'm just trying to take advantage of overtime pay," the husband might cajole. "School starts next week, and the kids are going to need books, supplies, new clothes, and lunch money." The wife gives in, allows the limits of the boundaries to be stretched, and control of the addictive agent begins to erode.

Another suggestion that we make is that the watchdog should be of the same sex as the driven person. Sharing vulnerabilities and goals can closely bond people. The last thing you want to risk is getting yourself entangled in an inappropriate romantic relationship. As unlikely as it may seem, it can happen.

How about you? List the people who can be watchdogs for the areas you intend to balance.

1. _____
2. _____
3. _____

Often a recovery plan looks workable on paper but fails in practice. Addictive agents wield tremendous power, and persons who are struggling to stay on their recovery courses sometimes need encouragement along the way.

Learning to Honor Your Recovery Goals

We suggest a two-pronged plan to patients as they look toward the years ahead. The first prong of that plan consists of two slogans and concepts, borrowed from Recovery, Inc: "The will to bear discomfort" and "Make muscles move." These slogans will help patients whenever they feel themselves slipping back into their addictions. The second prong of our recovery plan is a monthly or yearly inventory of relationships and recovery goals, which helps patients maintain their recovery for the rest of their lives. We suggest that patients ask themselves ten critical questions as they do this mental inventory.

Let's begin by looking at the slogans.

The Will to Bear Discomfort

New boundaries always bring a certain amount of discomfort. Virginia Potter's decision to abstain from seeing her friend Ray resulted in genuine pain. She missed him; she ached to sit across from him at their favorite coffee shop and talk about harmless topics, such as good books, current events, and even religion. Several times she punched his number into the telephone, and then hung up before the first ring. Once she even waited until he answered, just so she could hear his voice. Still, she hadn't revived the relationship. She knew she had to simply dig in and bear the pain. If she didn't act on her feelings and slip back into her addiction, eventually the hurt would subside.

Make Muscles Move

One of the techniques that Recovery, Inc., endorses is that "even if you are emotionally craving your addictive agent, you still have control over your physical being."

Workaholics might want to work through their lunch hour without a break, but they can make their hands lock their desks, and they can make their legs walk to the door, and they can make their arms slip into their coats, and they can make their bodies sit behind the steering wheels of their cars and drive to the nearest restaurant.

These two slogans help patients to persevere as they make the necessary changes in their life-style.

The Carmel Community Center: Under New Management During their layover meeting in Dallas, Michael and Virginia Potter gave Dr. Hemfelt a quick progress report on their recovery goals, complete with an appraisal of victories and setbacks. Surprisingly, Michael had had an easier time with his goals than Virginia had had with hers. Friends seemed to understand Michael's need to beg off from his community obligations, his exercise regimen, and even the annual alumni steak fry. They could accept that he had a business to oversee. However, the phone at the C.C.C. had continued to ring with requests for Virginia. In the eyes of the world, she didn't work, so she was fair game for every committee and volunteer assignment in town. She had given in to some pleas, waffled on others, and had stood firm on a few.

Finally an invisible rules list had been posted at the Carmel Community Center. The center was still open to the kids' friends on Saturdays, but not during the week or on Sundays, which was family day. Virginia had taken off her counselor's hat and substituted that of a chaperone, available on this day if needed.

"We can even walk in our own front door on Saturday night, after an evening out, say a quick 'hi' to the kids, and retreat to the seclusion of our upstairs bedroom suite. When we built this room we included the sitting area with the fireplace so we could spend evenings there together. Of course, we never did," Virginia said, with a "what-fools-we-were" expression on her face. "That room was really more of a wish than a reality. Now that's changed!"

"And I haven't seen Ray," Virginia added proudly. "Not

once. He called a couple of times, and I told him that I needed to concentrate on my family right now. I said that his friendship was very special to me, but that it was time for us to break the bond. It had become too strong."

Dr. Hemfelt was pleased with her words, especially since she was comfortable saying them in front of Michael. The couple's communication obviously had improved. The doctor's final questions that day involved their monthly inventory. He had suggested that the Potters take a monthly inventory (or a yearly one after the first couple of years) of their relationships and their recovery goals.

Touchstones for Living a Balanced Life-style

As you look at your own life and begin to identify relationships that need to be built, relationships that need to be nurtured, and relationships that need to be severed, ask yourself ten questions. We call these questions "touchstones." Just as the original touchstones were hard black stones, such as jasper, used to test the quality of gold or silver, these questions will help you to test the relational quality of your life. The answers to these questions will indicate whether you are living a life-style in which the right kinds of relationships will flourish. They also will tell you whether the way you are living your life can fulfill your needs without the false anesthesia provided by an addiction.

1. Do I Adhere to a Strong Set of Moral, Spiritual, and Human Values?

If you have strong values, they will help you to achieve a certain degree of transcendence. Part of our culture asks, "Is that all there is?" It helps us to get back in touch with our set of values and to know what really matters in life, what is important and what isn't. Professor Spock, our college math instructor did that. His spiritual values had been dormant, but they weren't dead, and his life was enriched when he rediscovered them.

"Being passed over for the promotion was an act of God, I believe," he said with a smile one day when Dr. Hemfelt saw him in a local supermarket. "It got my attention and made me realize I was still spiritually bankrupt. I know now that my future stretches a lot farther than my eleven years until retirement. Don't get me wrong, Doctor, I still have every intention of earning that full professorship, but the goal seems very small and unimportant when I compare it to what lies beyond this life."

We weren't surprised by Spock's words. Many driven people become involved in a Twelve Step recovery program as a way to relieve their pain. They understand the value of believing in God, and they view God almost as a means to an end. They're told repeatedly in their group meetings that if they want to achieve permanent healing, they need to accept God as part of the process.

Then a delightful flip-flop occurs. In addition to God's becoming a means of recovering from the addiction, the addiction becomes a means of finding God. In other words, Spock had viewed God as a necessary tool in overcoming his work compulsion, but in the end, he recognized his compulsion as a tool in his finding a personal relationship with Christ.

2. Do I Nurture a Healthy Balance Between Security and Spontaneity?

We all need a certain degree of security, predictability, and consistency in our lives. We need to know that we have a safe place to live, a warm place to sleep, and adequate food to eat. But we also need spontaneity, fun, and unpredictability to provide us with stimulation. If life is too spontaneous or too secure it can limit our ability to achieve transcendence. For example, Virginia Potter's life was so chaotic and cluttered that it prevented her from transcending to a level of peace. Luci Stewart's life was so bland that it tethered her to the routine and mundane.

3. Do I Have Adequate Recreation in My Life?

The word *recreate* means to rebuild and make new. Too many driven people view play as something naughty. They carve out no time for fun. Other driven people approach recreation as another compulsion. They drive themselves to compete against others, and they are only happy if they catch the biggest fish, run the fastest mile, and tally the lowest golf score. If that's your attitude toward your hobby, you may need to abstain from this activity for a while, then resume it with new goals in mind: fun and recreation. Shoot an occasional hole-in-one, but don't make that necessary to your enjoyment of the game.

4. Do I Have a Way of Expressing Myself Artistically?

Patients in our hospital units often tease about their paint-by-number projects or the moccasins they made in class. But it's no joking matter. Each of us needs to find a way to express our creativity. Not all of us may be artists, but we all are uniquely artistic in one way or another. For instance, some persons are amateur gardeners. Their beautiful yards and the multi-colored flowers that border their homes are their artistic expression. Others are photographers. The pictures they take are both memoirs of their lives and expressions of the beauty around them.

5. Do I Have High Quality Love Relationships in My Life?

This includes the relationships that exist between spouses, parents and children, and among a few close friends. We even suggest that God can be a part of those relationships.

During the Potters' last counseling session with Dr. Hemfelt, the doctor had illustrated on paper the ultimate recovery course that was open to them. He placed a dot at the top of one end of the paper and labeled it "God." In each corner at the opposite ends of the paper he drew a dot, marking one with Michael's name and the other with Virginia's. Then he drew a connecting line from Michael to God and from Virginia to God. His point was this: "As you as individuals grow closer to God, you automatically grow closer to each other. How close you move to God, and how close you move to each other, is your decision."

The line from the bottom to the top of the paper may be straight but it isn't smooth, he told them. Among the obstacles along the way are the various compulsions that must either be overcome or brought into balance.

6. Am I An Equal Partner in Several Give-and-Take Relationships?

Emotional nurturance is a lot like maintaining a bank account: We need to make deposits in order to make withdrawals. We need to give if we are to get back, and we need to get back so that we have something to give. Workaholics who never take vacations and don't grant themselves permission to go home without their briefcases full of paperwork eventually burn out. Pastors who minister to troubled flocks but won't allow anyone to minister to them often lose their way, their energy, and their enthusiasm.

7. Am I Part of a Spiritual Body?

Regular church attendance at a Bible-believing church, including regular small group interaction is a given. But beyond that, whether we participate in a Bible study fellowship, a Twelve Step support group, or both, we need encouragement for our ongoing spiritual experience. If we try to do it alone, we are doomed to failure.

Bill Wilson knew that long ago when he established group

meetings as a part of the Alcoholics Anonymous program. Today people suffering from obsessive-compulsive behaviors like workaholism, overeating, and codependency have found that these support groups are a necessary part of their continued recovery.

8. Am I Maintaining an Ongoing Relationship with God?

A dramatic turnaround event is wonderful, but each of us needs to be spiritually replenished every day. The new relationship between the driven person and God continues long after recovery is achieved. The permanent burden of balancing or controlling an addiction is easier for the person who has an ongoing dialogue with God. This includes "listening" daily to what God has to say to us in His love letter, the Bible, and sharing gut-level feelings daily with God in the form of prayer.

"What about your spiritual goals?" Dr. Hemfelt asked the Potters during their pre-Maui visit. "You sound as if you're making great strides in overcoming your addictions, but what are you putting in their place? How are you satisfying the needs that your compulsions used to satisfy?"

Mike looked at Virginia, who indicated with a smile that he should answer for the both of them. That, too, showed the progress they had made.

"You remember that diagram you drew on our last official visit, the one that depicted our relationship with God?" Michael asked.

Dr. Hemfelt nodded. The condition of the relationship on that diagram was a part of the question he was asking.

Michael paused, unsure of how to proceed. "I'm not certain exactly how far we've come in the past three months, but I know we're traveling in the right direction. We're on track, but we have a long way to go."

Learning to Suspend Time Through God The Potters were beginning to discover in practice many of the concepts we had shared in therapy. One was the difference between what the Greeks labelled *chronos* and *chyros*. Both words mean "time," but the first translates into quantity time and the second into quality time.

Driven people recognize only the chronological kind of time, which can be measured. They ask, "How *much* can I get done between 8:00 A.M. and 6:00 P.M.? How *many* items on my to-do list can I complete today? How *far* can I run? How *soon* can I be promoted? They try to suspend time by speeding up the pace. They believe by shoehorning two or three lifetimes into one they somehow can outrun or out-smart time.

In reality, by picking up the stride, they actually forfeit the victory. Only when they make peace with the fact that their time on earth is limited can they begin to enjoy the quality of the brief moments afforded them. Bill Wilson writes about being rocketed into what he calls the fourth dimension. This is the spiritual dimension—eternity—that exists beyond measurable space and time. It's available to all of us after physical death if we have a relationship with God, but it also can be experienced in small pockets during our lifetime. These are the moments that we sometimes describe as instances when "time stands still," the priceless pockets of time when we are totally at peace. They might come when we hold a child in our arms, have an intimate word with someone we love, or watch the sun set.

As the Potters moved toward a closer relationship with God, they also moved toward a better understanding of how to suspend time through that spiritual relationship. By continuing to slow down and keep their lives in balance, they would have more opportunities to catch glimpses of eternity and to enjoy the times of their lives.

Learning to Achieve Perfect Union Through God The only way to break out-of-control addictions is to establish a unity with God. If your God is too remote or impersonal, you will at some time experience insecurity and grab on to your old addictive agent—your pocketbook, your perfectionism, or your need to control the people around you.

The pyramidal drawing Dr. Hemfelt gave to Michael and Virginia Potter illustrates our lifelong journey toward a perfect union with God. Driven people who are about to embark on recovery have to recognize that they may never reach their destination, but they can come close, as long as they aspire to a life-style—that is, as Michael said, "on track."

The only perfect union that exists is the union that we can have with God, but our part of that relationship doesn't have to be perfect. Other key relationships in our lives—with spouses, with children, and with friends—will always be imperfect, incomplete, and inadequate. We have to accept the imperfections and celebrate the fact that no one has to live up to godlike perfectionistic standards.

9. Am I Willing to Admit My Weaknesses?

In Dr. Hemfelt's short pre-Maui visit with Michael and Virginia Potter he noticed that they both finally seemed comfortable in admitting some degree of vulnerability. For example, by halting her friendship with Ray, Virginia had said that she wasn't emotionally strong enough to handle their friendship. This was an area of weakness for her. At the same time, by confiding to friends that he couldn't afford to host the annual steak fry, Michael had laid bare his inability to manage his finances.

Often when we counsel patients we remind them that in the popular TV show "Star Trek" the spaceship Enterprise had a deflector shield that could successfully fend off all alien objects. The only problem was that raising the shield and keeping it in its defensive position required a tremendous amount of energy. If the shield was raised too long, the ship would be drained of its power and would self-destruct.

Driven people often erect an invincible shield similar to that of the Enterprise. They look strong, act strong, and talk strong. They flex their muscles and fend off "aliens" and friends alike. But, like the Enterprise, the driven person has to devote a tremendous amount of energy to keep the shield in position.

When the Potters dropped their defenses and admitted their vulnerability, they freed up a powerhouse of energy. They also tapped into the reserve strength of their support systems. Michael found that his circle of colleagues who knew about his money problems provided good counsel as well as warm friendship. Virginia's "watchdog" who was helping her abstain from seeing Ray was a kind listener who never judged, scolded, or preached to her.

Whereas driven people spend a lifetime perfecting their invincibility, persons in recovery need to practice their vulnerability. We suggest three ways to do this.

First, relax the need to overregulate, overprotect, and overcondition your physical body. We always mention physical conditioning first because for many people this is the most tangible way to take charge and seize control.

Second, relax the need to control other people. Spiritual faith and growth can occur only if you ease your control over the persons around you. Not until Michael Potter gave up his driving need to change his father was he able to concentrate on improving his relationship with God.

Third, relax the need to make yourself financially invincible. In the great Dickens' classic *A Christmas Carol*, Scrooge learned through a sequence of dreams that relationships, not money, are what give people strength. The moment he seized on that spiritual reality he woke up, shared his wealth, and began to enjoy life.

10. Have I Made Peace with the Fact That Life Is Limited?

Everyone has read about people who experience midlife crises and react by getting divorces, quitting jobs, and going to live in communes on mountaintops.

Sooner or later we have to accept the fact that many of our

loftiest dreams won't be realized, our spouses will disappoint us, our children may not want to follow in our footsteps, and we may have inherited Uncle George's bald head and bad gums. Life has its limits. Can we accept this and not beat ourselves down by trying to make right all the wrongs and correct all the imperfections?

When Mike Potter decided to remove his name from all future building projects he took a giant step toward long-term recovery. The decision was his way of stating that he trusted the immortality that comes only through a walk of faith. He accepted the promise of eternal life, and with that acceptance he now could enjoy life without the pressure of having to be his own savior. The heat was off.

As Christians, the doctors of the Minirth-Meier Clinic affirm that our time on earth is less than a blink of an eye when compared to eternity. As Dr. Paul Meier often says, "If I'm driven or uptight, I like to stop and ask myself, 'What difference will this make one hundred years from now? (Or a thousand years from now?) If I could look back on this problem then, how big would it seem?' The answer is obvious. Minuscule." This doesn't mean that we should disregard, ignore, or abuse our earthly life. However, knowing what lies beyond can be an extraordinary source of transcendence.

We're told there is no "Potter Palace" in Maui, so we know that Michael Potter has stayed true to his word. The Potters, the Stewarts, and Barbara Ryan have maintained their recovery. We challenge you to do so too. As Alfred Lord Tennyson said so long ago,

> Our little systems have their day;
>   They have their day and cease to be;
>   They are but broken lights of thee,
> And thou, O Lord, art more than they.[1]

An Afterword
By Dr. Frank Minirth

Dr. Hemfelt, Dr. Meier, and I sincerely hope that this book has been of help to each individual who may have felt driven from time to time. Each of the authors can certainly identify with this feeling.

I wanted to share a final comment in regard to some areas of my own life.

Feelings

As I have learned to deal with internal feelings, my sense of being driven has decreased. If "voices" from the past demand more and more of us, and we never deal with them, we will continue on a destructive path. I have rather enjoyed the process of dealing with these feelings and bringing them into a more healthy perspective and balance. However, the most important feeling these past few years has come from the security of realizing that Jesus Christ loves me just as I am.

Insight

Gaining insight can also be invaluable. Personally, it helped me to realize that the reason I was driven so hard was not the reason that appeared on the surface—my own patterns were rooted in the past. Insight into relationships has also been invaluable to me. Without insight, one is destined to repeat the past. The subconscious mind is one of the most powerful factors within each of us—a vast resource that usually remains untapped. With insight, we can stop being driven and start living productively and creatively. I believe that these insights God has given me have been the major turning point in my life.

Perhaps the most important insight for me was to realize that I do not have to produce anything for God; I do not have to be driven. Jesus Christ died in payment for my sins, and no payment is required in return. To know that I cannot earn God's love and, furthermore, that I cannot lose it because of demerit, is the most wonderful insight of all. Jesus Christ loved me unconditionally and He died on the Cross for my sins. My belief in what He did for me has turned my life around.

Behavior

The common sense of needing to alter my daily driven behavior and thinking has also been a factor in helping me to overcome. Daily behavior can be altered so that one does not literally drive oneself into spiritual, physical, and emotional exhaustion. To discover that, as a Christian, I do not have to be driven to achieve things for God has freed me to enjoy a lifetime with Christ and to choose behavior that is healthy. Certainly the most important step for each of us in becoming less driven can be summarized in three words: knowing Jesus Christ.

Appendix

A Guide to Twelve Step Groups

Listed below are sixteen Twelve Step program offices. Most of them are staffed by volunteers who can direct you to local chapters of the national organizations.

Alcoholics Anonymous
Box 459
Grand Central Station
New York, NY 10163
(212) 686-1100

Adult Children of Alcoholics
   Central Service Board
Box 35623
Los Angeles, CA 90035
(213) 464-4423

Al-Anon/Alateen Family
   Group Headquarters, Inc.
Box 182
Madison Square Station
New York, NY 10159
(1-800) 356-9996

Cocaine Anonymous
Box 1367
Culver City, CA 90232
(213) 839-1141

Co-Dependents Anonymous
Box 33577
Phoenix, AZ 85067
(602) 277-7991

Debtors Anonymous
314 W. 53rd St.
New York, NY 10019
(212) 969-0710

Emotional Health
Anonymous
2420 San Gabriel Boulevard
Rosemead, CA 91770
(818) 573-5482

Emotions Anonymous
Box 4245
St. Paul, MN 55104
(612) 647-9712

Families Anonymous
Box 528
Van Nuys, CA 91408
(818) 989-7841

Gamblers Anonymous
Box 17173
Los Angeles, CA 90017
(212) 386-8789

Incest Survivors Anonymous
Box 5613
Long Beach, CA 90800

Narcotics Anonymous
Box 9999
16155 Wyandotte St.
Van Nuys, CA 91406
(818) 780-3951

National Association for
   Children of Alcoholics
31582 Coast Highway
Suite B
South Laguna, CA 92677
(714) 499-3889

Overcomers Outreach
2290 W. Whittier Blvd.
Suite D
La Habra, CA 90631
(213) 697-3994

Overeaters Anonymous
Box 92870
Los Angeles, CA 90009
(213) 657-6252

Sexaholics Anonymous
Box 300
Simi Valley, CA 93062

For information about other Twelve Step and self-help groups, call or write:

National Self-Help
Clearinghouse City
   University Graduate
   Center
25 W. 43rd St.
Room 620
New York, NY 10036
(212) 642-2944

National Clearinghouse for
   Alcohol Information
Box 1908
Rockville, MD 20850

Notes

1. Are We Really Having Fun?

1. William Glasser, *Positive Addictions* (New York: Harper & Row, 1976).

2. The Many Masks of Compulsions

1. Dr. Frank Minirth, Dr. Paul Meier, Dr. Robert Hemfelt, Dr. Sharon Sneed, *Love Hunger, Recovery from Food Addiction* (Nashville: Thomas Nelson, 1989).
2. Arthur Barsky, *Worried Sick: Our Troubled Quest for Wellness* (Boston: Little, Brown, and Co., 1988).
3. Dr. Frank Minirth, Dr. Paul Meier, Dr. Robert Hemfelt, *Love Is a Choice* (Nashville: Thomas Nelson, 1989).

3. Learning to Say "Ouch!"

1. For more on this subject, see Liz Lufkin, "Slow Down, You Move Too Fast: The Time-Sickness Cure," *Working Woman*, April 1990, 112.

4. Riding a Bike Without a Chain

1. See Earnie Larsen, *Stage II Recovery* (New York: Harper & Row, 1985).
2. Robin Norwood, *Women Who Love Too Much* (New York: Simon and Schuster, 1986).
3. Bill Wilson, The "Big Book" of *Alcoholics Anonymous* (New York: Alcoholics Anonymous World Services, Inc., 1976), p. 25.

5. Events That Set the Cycle in Motion

1. Jeffrey Laign, "Born Famous," *Changes*, July-Aug. 1988, pp. 23, 36–41.
2. Dotson Rader, "At Last, a Safe Place," *Parade*, 20 May 1990, pp. 4–6.

6. Sinister Whispers from the Past

1. Ronnie Milsap, *Almost Like a Song* (New York: McGraw-Hill, 1990), p. 6.
2. Ibid., p. 7.

7. The Shame That Blinds

1. Bob Colacello, "A Star Is Reborn," *Vanity Fair*, June 1987, 117.
2. Carolyn Wesson, *Women Who Shop Too Much* (New York: St. Martin's Press, 1990), p. 141.
3. Ibid., pp. 144–45.
4. Ibid., pp. 136–139.

8. Driven to Be More to Keep from Being Less

1. *People Weekly*, July 9, 1990, p. 30.
2. See *USA Today*, August 16, 1990, B28.
3. *People*, p. 30.
4. Ibid., p. 34.
5. Bruno Gaget, "Still Struggling to Save Her Marriage," pp. 38–40.
6. Wilson, The "Big Book" of *Alcoholics Anonymous*, p. 11.
7. Ibid., p. 12.
8. Ron Rosenbaum, "Riding High: Dennis Hopper Bikes Back," *Vanity Fair*, April 1987, p. 130.

9. The Devastating Boomerang

1. Suzanne Somers, *Keeping Secrets* (New York: Warner Books, 1988), p. xiv.
2. Ibid., p. xv.
3. Jeremiah Abrams, *Reclaiming the Inner Child* (New York: Jeremy P. Tarcher, Inc., 1990), p. 1.
4. Somers, *Keeping Secrets*, p. 346.

10. Our False Gods

1. Rock Brynner, *Yul: The Man Who Would Be King—**A Memoir*** (New York: Simon & Schuster, 1989), p. 217.
2. Ibid., pp. 232–33.

11. The Billion-Dollar Price Tag

1. See Albert Goldman, "Down at the End of Lonely Street," *Life*, June 1990, p. 96–104.
2. Ibid., p. 101.

12. The Split Personality

1. Melvyn Bragg, *Richard Burton, A Life* (New York: Warner Books, Inc., 1988).
2. Wilson, The "Big Book" of *Alcoholics Anonymous,* pp. 60–61.
3. Ibid., p. 64.
4. Ibid., p. 67.
5. Ibid., p. 68.

13. Verdict: Guilty!

1. Anthony Haden-Guest, "The Onassiad," *Vanity Fair,* March 1989, pp. 17–182.
2. The "Big Book" of *Alcoholics Anonymous,* pp. 83–84.
3. Associated Press wire story, 10 August 1990.

14. Touchstones for Living a Balanced Life

1. Alfred Lord Tennyson, *In Memoriam: An Authoritative Text,* ed. by Robert H. Ross (New York: W.W. Norton & Co., 1973), p. 3.

ABOUT THE AUTHORS

Robert Hemfelt, Ed.D., is a psychologist who specializes in the treatment of chemical dependencies, codependency, and compulsivity disorders. Before joining the Minirth-Meier Clinic, he was an addictions specialist with a Fortune 500 corporation and, before that, the supervisor of therapeutic services for the Substance Abuse Study Clinic of the Texas Research Institute of Mental Sciences. He has co-authored several books, including *Love Is a Choice* and *Kids Who Carry Our Pain.*

Frank Minirth, M.D., is a diplomate of the American Board of Psychiatry and Neurology and received an M.D. degree from the University of Arkansas College of Medicine.

Paul Meier, M.D., received an M.S. degree in cardiovascular physiology at Michigan State University and an M.D. degree from the University of Arkansas College of Medicine. He completed his psychiatric residency at Duke University.

Dr. Minirth and Dr. Meier founded the Minirth-Meier Clinic in Dallas, Texas, one of the largest psychiatric clinics in the world, with associated clinics in Chicago; Los Angeles; Little Rock, Arkansas; Longview, Fort Worth, Sherman, and Austin, Texas; and Washington, D.C.

Both Dr. Minirth and Dr. Meier have received degrees from Dallas Theological Seminary. They have also co-authored more than thirty books, including *Happiness Is a Choice, Worry-Free Living, How to Beat Burnout,* and *Beyond Burnout.*